Lanista: Wrath of the Gods

by David Lingard
Edited by Denise Boorman

<u>A note from the author</u>

I just wanted to say here, thank you, whoever you are for however you have arrived at this book and my story. It makes a big difference to authors like me, who like to feel as though their hard work and dedication is appreciated when our work is read.

Your investment of your own time and money is as always, well appreciated. It takes a long time and a lot of effort to write, edit and release a book, so please, I ask that you **rate** and **review** everything that you read – and not just this book, so that lesser-known authors can grow their audience and gain the credibility that they deserve.

Also, I have a website that is usually kept up to date with current works, reviews and a few extra little bits. You'll find it at: www.davidlingard.com

Index.

I - Non Ducor, Duco.	3
II - Panem Et Circenses.	7
III - Igne Natura Renovatur Integra.	19
IV – Perfer Et Obdura, Dolor Hic Tibi Proderit Olim.	29
V – Acta Non Verba.	35
VI – Canis Caninam Non Est.	43
VII – Omnium Rerum Principia Parva Sunt.	53
VIII – Permitte Divis Cetera.	59
IX – Post Tenebras Lux.	67
X - Male Parta Male Dilabuntur.	75
XI - Timendi Causa Est Nescire.	82
XII – Magna Servitus Est Magna Fortuna.	90
XIII – Mens Sana In Corpore Sano.	100
XIV – Semper Paratus.	108
XV – Deos Fortioribus Adesse.	113
XVI – Non Omnis Moriar.	121
XVII – Ars Longa, Vita Brevis.	127
XVIII – Ad Astra Per Aspera.	135
XIX – Cogito Ergo Sum.	141
XX – Damnatio Ad Bestias.	146
XXI – Dors Incit Omnia.	154
XXII – Acta Deos Numquam Mortalia Fallunt	163
XXIII – Audemus Jura Nostra Defendere	170
XXIV – Ad Victorium	176
XXV – Alea Iacta Est	183
XXVI – Veni, Vidi Vici	193
XXVII – Et Tu, Brutus?	199
Epilogue – Mors Vincit Omnia	205
A Thankyou	211

I - Non Ducor, Duco.

"I am not led, I lead."

It was still within the earliest years of the Roman Empire as it had turned from a Republic into an Empire and began to flourish. In the Roman world, the world that I, and everything I had ever known or cared about, it was a prosperous time where the wealthiest enjoyed luxuries that the poorer classes could have only ever dreamt about. My parents had mostly kept me away from the difficulties that befouled the ones who could not afford to live comfortably without having to work hard, manual jobs, or worse: begging in the streets. Rather my upbringing had been somewhat sheltered from the realities of real life and the hardships that came along with it.

I didn't know much about the real world outside our four walls as it had passed me by during the first ten years of my life, living within the safe and comfortable confines of my father's ludus - that's a school for training gladiators to fight in the arena for the lay – but there were some things that you certainly didn't miss whilst being raised in that sort of environment.

For one, you come to realise that no matter the softness, the love and care that a father can show a son, a man will often do what he needs to do to keep his family housed, warm and fed.

My father was a straight and harsh man to everyone else but my mother and I – his queen and his prince. His name was Gaius Brutus, and I looked up to him with all of my being as the greatest man to have ever lived. Of course I knew once I'd grown older, that like many sons, I idolised my father to a Godlike degree without basis, though regardless of that fact, I would eventually become the man I was meant to be because of him.

Although the largest arenas had been built in the centre of the mighty Roman Empire within the capital, Rome, and anybody who was anybody strived to live as close to the wonders as possible, my family and our rather small Ludus sat further south on the outskirts of a small town called Liternum. The gladiator school that also served as our home sat atop of a large hill, and a good twenty-minute walk into the town proper – that way it discouraged the gladiators or slaves from trying to escape – it was just too much of a risk for them to get caught.

Gladiators never tried to escape though, and why would they? They were the superstars of the empire, and it wasn't just slaves, criminals and prisoners of war that found their way onto the golden sands to test their might against their opponents, free men would volunteer to fight in arena battles to gain fame and fortune by competing in wonderful battles in front of the masses.

I had my own room within the main house and the gladiators all had small cells (there were only three of them) out next to the training sands to call their own. They were always well fed to keep them strong, and my father worked them hard every day – even though most of them were twice his size! Never though, did I ever see any of them show him anything less than total respect. They bowed their heads and called him 'Dominus' as a mark of respect.

My mother was wonderful too. She would bring me food and drink, fruits and the like whenever we could get hold of them from the town (or afford them), and always kept me dressed in appropriate robes. It could get hot during the summer, so the thin white robes, held closed with a length of dyed red rope was always appreciated in my eyes. She looked after the household while my father worked and made sure that everything was always kept clean, tidy and functional. Honestly, I never really knew how she did it all.

It was on my ninth birthday that I had received the best present that a young boy could have ever asked for: my very own pet dog. The creature wasn't particularly large and definitely not scary looking like some of the guard dogs I'd seen walking around the town like they owned the place, all pointy and alert, rather my dog was friendly almost to the point that he seemed to be living his best life with every hair on his back… which incidentally formed a short, light brown coat. He also had floppy ears and a curved-up wagging tail that seemed always so pleased about everything.

The dog was clever too; I could get him to do all kinds of tricks but only when he really wanted to do them. I'd named him Dinari.

Dinari and I were immediately inseparable from the moment we had met, like we were the original partners in crime. He would follow me everywhere, around the grounds of the ludus, through the corridors, past the busts of my father's father and his father before him, and even when my mother or father took us into town to shop or watch gladiator fights in the arena. I loved watching the fights, though I didn't particularly enjoy how brutal some of the endings could be. I liked to watch the techniques that different gladiators had perfected over months and years of training – then the loser would be granted mercy and would live to fight another day. That's how all arena fights should've ended in my eyes. I certainly didn't enjoy when the winner of a match would parade around the sands with his opponent's head impaled on the end of his sword, spraying the crowds with the loser's still warm blood. The amphitheatre in Liternum was still young though, and where the spectators in the capital had grown to appreciate the technical prowess of a good match, the crowds in Liternum still seemed to be a little on the 'rowdy mob' side of things. I knew things would change though, my father always said that things were going to be very different in the future.

Our ludus wasn't particularly well known, and the three gladiators that we had the space to train at any one given time were never really the greatest fighters, the strongest or even the quickest, but father tried his best to have them taught in the ways of the arena and generally they put up a good fight when they were out on the sands.

A large part of what our issue was, as my father had said on multiple occasions, was that we didn't have a Doctore - that's a gladiator trainer – at the house. There wasn't room and we really couldn't afford it. Instead, we paid trainers when we could find or afford them to visit our ludus to train our gladiators. It wasn't the best way to train them though, and that's why every few months we'd be off back down to the auctions with a small bag of silver coins to see who we could pick up next to fight our corner. I must admit though, no matter how 'normal' it seemed trading in people, or how many times I had been told that it was the way of the world, I never enjoyed it. Liternum was small too, so when the auctions did come to the town it was more slim pickings than anything else and the Arena Master Galerius – a prominent and wealthy figure - always had the first pick of the day's offerings.

It may have sounded counterintuitive and expensive to replace gladiators on a somewhat regular basis, but when a gladiator won, or at least put on a good show, the recompense would usually far outweigh both this cost and the cost of his training.

My father had always said that one day, the gladiator schools such as ours would be lauded as one of the greatest establishments in all of the Empire... but for now, there were few of them, and the ones that really mattered were within a few hours travel to the renowned arenas of Rome.

Our house had slave workers too, every Roman house did. I tried to treat them all as though they were members of the family and not unpaid staff – though I was told not to become too friendly with them by my parents. It didn't really make a difference to me, people were people and that was that. Besides, the housekeepers all seemed to be relatively happy, they got to live in their own little section of the house, got fed and watered and besides, my father had always said that these people were much better off with us than on the streets of the town, or even perhaps in a less compassionate household that would treat them far less kindly than our own.

II - Panem Et Circenses.

"Bread and circuses."

    It was a warm and sunny day at the start of the summer. The grounds around the ludus that frequently turned colourful in the milder months had began to change already; the green grass that usually flourished and the flowers that bloomed in the mixture of heavy rains and bright sunlight had become scorched in the overbearing heat and unforgiving sun. The view from atop our hill had changed, as it did each year; the beautiful, bright landscape had turned to a barren beige. I knew what this all meant of course: people would be rationing their food and water to ensure that they could make it through to the next time the rains fell, and they'd be saving their fruits and crops. That, in turn, meant that as a household we needed to be careful not to waste anything we had. It was a bit difficult though, because gladiators needed to eat a lot to both grow and maintain the muscle mass that they needed to fight in the arena, and also to keep their energy up for their rigorous training that they went through on a daily basis. Then the heat… it just made them drink so much more water than they did through the milder months. Also as an aside, I'd once picked up one of the spears that a gladiator would use in the arena. It was so heavy that I almost fell over. Our gladiators needed all the food they could get to be able to use those weapons effectively in a fight. I had wondered that day how they even managed to stay upright for so long.

    Dinari was uncharacteristically quiet this day. He still had his trademark smile on his doggy face, though he was laid out flat on the ground, all four legs stretched before and behind him, with his panting head rested on his paws. It seemed as though he'd found a shaded and particularly cold section of the stone floor of the house, and I didn't begrudge him the respite one bit.

"Titus, make sure you have everything you need to accompany me to the arena today. Vettius has his first fight in the arena and I want you to see how he does. Oh, and you can bring the dog if you like, he looks miserable." My father spoke the words from behind me as I watched Dinari relaxing. He didn't look at all miserable but I wouldn't question my father. As my father had mentioned 'the dog', Dinari's tail began to wag and his entire body wriggled animatedly as though he could sense that something good was going to happen.

The gladiator named Vettius was one of the newest intake we'd bought. He was thin but tall, had long scraggly black hair and whenever I'd seen him training from the balcony that overlooked the training sands, preferred to fight as a Retiarius – that's the one who fought with a trident and a net and looked like a fisherman. He didn't wear much armour at all, just a loincloth around his middle and a few leather guards so it meant that equipment for training was cheap and quite easy to come by. Vettius had only cost a few hundred dinari though (the silver coins, not the dog), which was a tell-tale sign that the man would not perform well in the arena.

"Why Vettius father? Why not Polyx? Or Scipio? Vettius has only been training for less than three weeks and you have always said it would take months for a gladiator to be ready for the arena. I have seen Vettius fight father - sometimes I think the training dummy might actually beat him!" I proclaimed loudly.

My father knelt down onto a single knee before me and placed both of his hands on my shoulders. He shuffled us backwards a few feet with a fair amount of purpose and stopped when we were in the square of the house that had no ceiling above – like a kind of courtyard – that was letting the sun shine in. The tiles were warm under my bare feet, though thankfully the heat of the day hadn't yet made the temperature unbearable enough for me to want to move away.

"Listen, Titus. Beneath your feet is something that will someday be yours. I want you to remember this moment for as long as you live. Beneath your feet is everything that you inherit and make your own. Until that day, you must trust me to do as I will. Do you trust me, Titus?" he asked.

I nodded slightly though not confidently. I knew my father was very much a thinker, and he would never take a risk like this on a gladiator unless it was completely necessary. I was worried though. Sending a gladiator into the arena so untrained could mean only one of two things: either our finances were much worse than I had imagined, or my father had been given an offer that was too good to refuse to send our man out there.

"But… father…?" I started to question, although I knew it was the wrong thing to do. Thankfully, he interrupted me before I could say any more.

"I have a new… technique that I think our gladiator will benefit from. You will see once he is upon the sands, OK?" he said.

I nodded again and looked back at Dinari, who angled his head to one side and lopped his tongue out to pant. There was just always something in his eyes that betrayed his intelligence – like right now he was trying to say 'I don't get it either, but let's just wait and see'.

We didn't need to pack much to go to the arena in Liternum. As always, we'd just take a couple of flasks of water, some bread to eat as we watched and perhaps some fruit. We didn't have any fruit on this occasion though, so bread and water was all that we had, and all that we took. We would walk out of the ludus gates with our gladiator or gladiators in tow and down the barren hill towards the town. This time we didn't even take a housekeeper to carry our bags as everything was just so light – I carried the bread and water, and my father led Vettius, who walked without any equipment at all; the arena would provide his arms for him. Although Dinari did sometimes walk calmly by my side, he spent most of his time running about and through all of our legs, trying his best to trip us all as we walked. God forbid if we ever saw a stray cat or a bird on our travels; that could mean a long side-quest to follow the excitable dog to wherever the thing that he wished to make best friends with was trying to escape to. He would never hurt another living creature though - to him everything in the world that moved was something to either play with or love to death.

Thankfully, this trip from the ludus into town was uneventful. I didn't think I could've managed chasing Dinari for too long in the unforgiving heat; my clothes were already damp with sweat and I'd already started sipping regularly on the first flask of water that I carried. I knew we could get more water when we arrived, but my father didn't like mingling with the crowds when I was with him, he didn't always have the time to tend to the gladiators we'd brought and also make sure I was safe with the amount of strangers around. It didn't matter really though, we had plenty of water to hand and once we took our place in the amphitheatre as a lanista (and son), we would have some cover from the sun.

Seeing the large stone construction always filled my stomach with butterflies. It was the first thing I saw every time I came anywhere near to Liternum, my eyes scanning the outline of the town until I saw it, just beckoning for us to come closer and I always wanted to oblige.

The town itself had a wall around its perimeter, wooden in some parts and stone in others. It wasn't a fort though, or even of any particular defensive or strategic note so although there were infrequent guards pacing the walls, there was really almost no military presence within.

We walked through the compressed dirt roads, kicking up sand and dust as we moved. It was still early, so there were groups of people beginning to work their way outside and into the sunshine on their way to the arena, but mostly the roads were still clear. White, stone buildings rose up on either side of us to line the streets and although usually these would afford good protection against the wind when there was any, right now all they did was serve to reflect the sun's glow right onto me and my family. I felt like our party was sitting in a pressure cooker that was just getting hotter and hotter until, abruptly, the buildings finished and we were out in the open. Dinari immediately bounded forward into the open space between the arena and the last building we'd passed and started leaping around as though he was chasing a butterfly that only he could see. It made me laugh, though it was nothing out of the ordinary for the dog.

The Liternum arena was on one edge of the town, set into a large hill that like our own, was usually green and vibrant. The stone steps had been arranged in concentric circles imbedded into the hillside itself so that each row would allow its spectators a clear view of the sands beneath. Either side of the entrance to the arena stood a tall, square wooden tower that were for the lanistas to sit in so that they could properly see their gladiators in battle – and that was exactly where we were headed.

As this arena was small, the gladiator's preparation area was just on the outside of the amphitheatre and allowed entry onto the sands via a single, large iron gate that stood ominously closed at all times until a gladiator was ready to take to the sands. It was all a part of the suspense that the arena masters had managed to cultivate, and I had to say, they did a very good job of it.

We left Vettius in the care of the arena hands as soon as we arrived. The one single gruff word he said to my father was "dominus," before I watched him duck through the side entrance and into his preparation area, off to be equipped for the fight ahead.

The next time I would see him, I knew that he would be carrying his net and trident, emerging from the huge iron gates and walking out into the sands.

Once Dinari, my father and I reached the lanista tower overlooking the sands, I immediately began chewing on the bread and chugging the water from my flask. I knew I shouldn't have taken so much, but the journey had felt so much more difficult in the abusive heat than during milder climes. I pulled a small metal bowl from my small bag, filled it with water and placed it on the floor for Dinari. He lapped at it lazily, but he was happy to have found another cool, covered stone floor that he could flatten himself against. I was grateful that the two towers had roofs atop them, so that at least they provided shade for us. The rest of the crowds were not so lucky though.

As usual, loud horns trumpeted a symphony for the crowds to come to silence, and a single man in white robes walked to the edge of the sands and raised his hands above his head.

"My friends!" he announced loudly, and the sound travelled around the amphitheatre as though it was somehow being magically amplified. I knew it wasn't – this was just one of the clever intricacies of the design of the amphitheatres. "We have a wonderful day of contests for you to behold in our humble arena today!"

The crowd cheered loudly and it made my heart rate quicken with excitement. I loved the spectacle of the arena, and I loved it even more when it was one of our own gladiators in the day's battles.

"A mighty Thracian will face off against the deadly Murmillo!" Another cheer erupted from the crowds. "Hoplomachus facing the ever defensive, stalwart Scutarius!" The crowd seemed even more pleased with this announcement with whistles now heard around the arena. "And the grand finale: Cestus, versus Retiarius!"

My heart skipped a beat at the announcement of our man. Facing off against a Cestus would give him the clear advantage and I turned to look at my father amongst the sound of shouts, whistles, cheers and screams that the crowds simply couldn't contain. My father, though, simply kept his face forward, looking pensive and entirely interested on what was about to happen next. I chose not to annoy him with too many questions.

The huge iron gates opened slowly and the first pair of gladiators took to the sands with confidence. They looked similar in their dress, each wearing a loin cloth, holding a sword and shield and wearing a helmet atop their head that covered their face. Murmillo though, had two long shin guards where Thraex had just one, though I did think that they would do little to protect them against their respective blades. The main difference between the two was that where Murmillo held a straight and very mean looking gladius, Thraex clasped a curved sica sword, which looked very, very deadly. For some reason, curvature in blades always made them look so much sharper.

The arena announcer said a few more words before retreating, leaving the two muscular gladiators to their task. I wasn't listening to what he had to say though, I was ready to see these two skilled fighters test their mettle against each other.

The two gladiators both pounded on their own shields in the usual sign of respect for the crowds, then took a ready stance, facing each other.

Thraex moved in immediately to start the bout, clattering his sword against Murmillo's shield, who in turn deflected the blow, unaffected by the ferocious and sudden start to the battle. The curved sica skimmed off the wooden shield and the straightened gladius of Murmillo drew first blood with a short cut to the Thracian's tricep as his attack followed through. Thraex stepped back and their shields clashed – he looked as though he had been totally unaffected by the attack and the blood that had been drawn.

Murmillo pressed his advantage, keeping posture as he stepped forward whilst stabbing his sword over the top of his shield. Thraex did everything he could to keep ahead of the blows but it was immediately obvious to me that he was being overpowered and that it would simply be a matter of time before he could defend no longer. Then Murmillo suddenly changed the trajectory of his attacks and rounded his shield from the bottom, stooping low to complete the strike. Whether or not the Thracian's shin guard would've been effective was neither here nor there, because the strike had fallen upon the unprotected leg of the gladiator. This time the Thracian screamed out in pain as the strike bit deeply into his flesh and sent red blood spraying out onto the sands, which immediately absorbed it. The crowd's roar was deafening. The Thracian fell to a single knee in agony and I watched, wincing awaiting the final sure to be brutal killing blow.

Murmillo pressed onward again. He bore down over the kneeling gladiator and placed a strong kick to his opponent's face, sending him snapping backwards and onto his back, the curved sword and wooden shield now long forgotten. Murmillo was taking his time to savour his victory, and the crowd were paying him his dues. Every face in the entire arena was eagerly anticipating the Thracian's final moment. Murmillo dropped his shield to the sands and moved to stand over his fallen opponent. I could tell that the Thracian was done for.

Murmillo stood with a leg on either side of the Thracian and drew back his sword to deliver the final blow, then he released his strike towards the gladiator's chest.

The killing blow, though, did not arrive. The Thracian turned his entire body to the side so that the strike simply impacted the sand beneath him with a dusty clang, then rolled his body back onto the weapon, causing Murmillo to relinquish his grip on it. Stunned, Murmillo then forgot that in his current stance he was entirely off-balance and when Thraex grabbed a hold of his helmet and pulled him downwards there was nothing he could do to stop the momentum, falling forward without argument. Thraex then extended a single leg, throwing his opponent high over his head and onto the sands behind them both with a loud clang and an 'oof.' Murmillo scrabbled back to his feet, though now between his shield and the Thracian's sword sitting on the sands, stood Thraex, holding his own gladius.

Murmillo's shout was loud enough to make the hairs on my arms stand on end as he started to run directly at the curved sword on the ground to retrieve it for himself, otherwise he was unarmed and in serious trouble. He passed Thraex in a flurry of activity, then came to a standing halt just feet from his intended weapon. He fell to his knees. The crowds fell silent.

Murmillo looked down at his stomach and almost immediately, a line of red blood spread from one side of his body all the way to the other. This was without a doubt a fatal injury, and before the gladiator could do anything to concede the fight or ask the people for mercy, he was face down on the sands, all life absent his broken body.

The crowds erupted into cheers, whoops, whistles and shouts of 'Thra-ex! Thra-ex!' I, however, could not take my eyes from the limp, lifeless body of the ex-gladiator as two arena hands dragged him from the sands, leaving a thick trail of red blood in their wake.

I turned to look at my father about to ask him what exactly had just happened, how the Thracian had managed to turn a battle that looked like a dead loss in to such a resounding victory, but I could see that he wasn't even looking at the sands where that fight had just played out before us. His eyes were fixed intently on the large iron gates – now closed again – behind which the rest of the gladiators awaited their own battles. Dinari hadn't been bothered with the fight at all, he looked like he was having a hard enough time keeping cool – his head on his paws and his tongue lolloped out onto the cold floor in an attempt to help him cool himself down.

"And for your enjoyment, as though you have not been entertained enough already!" the booming voice of the announcer snapped my attention back into focus, "Hoplomachus versus the mighty Scutarius!"

The iron gates opened again almost immediately and out stepped the two gladiators who were to fight to the death for the enjoyment of the bloodthirsty crowds in the next round. Hoplomachus was a bit of a play on a kind of Greek soldier – he was a heavy brute carrying a long spear, with a short, straight sword and a dagger attached to his belt. He had some armour on his arms and legs, although that paled in comparison to his opponent. Scutarius – meaning 'shield bearer' - was living up to his name well. This gladiator held a huge, wooden curved legionary shield painted bright red with deep yellow lightning bolts painted on it. In his main hand he held a short gladius, though this fighter also had long metal braces on his arms and long metal shin guards. It looked as though it'd be tough for him to move about, though the protection it would afford the gladiator would be impressive and very difficult to overcome. Both fighters wore helmets that covered their entire faces, and both stood to the ready, awaiting the command of the arena announcer.

Again, there was little time for pomp and ceremony for the start of the fight now that everything was ready to go, and the announcer once again made himself scarce after introducing the pair of gladiators.

The contest started immediately with Hoplomachus thrusting his spear into Scutarius' shield, causing a loud thud to echo around the amphitheatre. The dull thud made me wince just thinking about how powerful and deadly that strike must've been. Then the gladiator followed up with another thrust, then another as loud bangs continued to emanate from the weapon's contact with the shield. Hoplomachus then spun the spear about his head, clearly showboating for the crowd before swiping it at his opponent menacingly. I imagined that the strike that inevitably slashed at Scutarius' metal greaves would've been crippling, had the gladiator not had been so well armoured.

For a long time Scutarius did virtually nothing other than defend himself. He really didn't have to, as Hoplomachus tired himself out attacking with vigour over and over but with little effect. Eventually, though, something had to give, and I was surprised that it was the aggressive Hoplomachus, who I'd been attributing match points to as the bout went on. The gladiator, tired at his attacks being shrugged off by his opponent's superior armour, dropped his spear to the ground and drew his short sword from his belt. Scutarius still didn't seem to take any bait, still hiding mostly behind his shield.

Hoplomachus lunged at the wooden shield, throwing his entire body weight at it with no care for his own safety. I cringed as I awaited the killing blow from Scutarius, but it didn't come. His legs buckled as the manic Hoplomachus crunched into him, their combined weight and the weight of his own armour proving too much for him to manage. The pair fell to the ground with a puff of dust and sand, and Hoplomachus saw the bare exposed flesh of his opponent's thigh. He buried his short sword into it with a grunt and the arena erupted with the scream of pain from Scutarius' lungs.

With his armour down and flat on his back, I could now see that the armoured gladiator was not huge and muscular as his armour would suggest, he was small and weak – there was no way he should've been dressed as a shield-bearer – that was unless someone had wanted him to lose this fight.

Hoplomachus regained his posture and regarded his opponent, who like a turtle on his back, had no way to right himself. Plus, he was still writhing in pain, apparently unaware of any impending danger.

After a short moment, the pseudo-Greek warrior collected his spear from the ground and calmly thrust the metallic tip through his opponent's neck, concluding the fight and again staining the arena sands red with free-flowing blood, which the sands thirstily lapped up.

Something really didn't sit well with me after watching this match. The man behind the shield had clearly not been trained well – or perhaps even at all - and it made me worry for our man, Vettius, who I knew had no business being in the arena yet either, with his own lack of training.

"Father?" I asked quietly, though when I turned to face my father again, his gaze was still fixed on the large iron gates that now contained our man. Instead, I simply scratched Dinari behind the ear and he let out a soft growl of appreciation.

"Well, I know we expect a Scutarius to defend himself, but let that be a lesson to all gladiators who wish to fight on these sands! Attack is often the best form of defence!" The announcer seemed a little baffled by the fight too, but chose to style it out for the crowds. It was his job after all and he seemed pretty good at it.

"Your last fight for the day has finally arrived, and has it not been a wild ride?! Hailing from the humble ludus Brutus… we bring you Retiarius!" The crowd cheered loudly, they always liked seeing battles involving skilled Retiarii, those gladiators always seemed to come up with weird and wonderful ways to win – or otherwise provided a bloody spectacle when they lost.

"And to face the fierce fisherman, we are to be graced by way of Cestus!" The announcer punched one fist into his open palm as he spoke, and the crowd cheered even louder than they had for the announcement of our man, the Retiarius.

When the gladiators took to the sands, my eyes were immediately drawn to Cestus, who wore nothing but a loin cloth tied around his middle, and two leather gloves with short metallic spikes attached to the knuckles. The creature must've been seven feet tall and muscled beyond anything I'd ever seen before. I knew what Vettius looked like, and the tale of the tape would certainly not show anything in his favour.

I could tell immediately that this battle had been specifically designed to last longer than the ones before it. Cestus would no doubt look to wear down Vettius, who would have to bide his time, choosing the correct moment to throw his net at his opponent. After all, usually a Retiarius had but one chance to make his throw count because after that, he was left simply clutching his trident and nothing else.

Both gladiators wore metal helmets again, though Cestus' didn't cover his face entirely, allowing a larger and more unimpeded field of view than Vettius. I wondered how our man was feeling beneath that metal, though if it was me, I knew I'd have been scared. I had never had so much as a fight in my whole life.

Vettius also had leather shin guards on, although I didn't see how that was going to help against an opponent who was basically planning on punching him to death.

The contest began abruptly as the others before it had, and I watched as Cestus leapt into action. For a man who was easily over one hundred kilos, I'd honestly never seen anyone move that fast. He whipped and juked side to side before Vettius, who by all accounts looked stunned at the way in which his opponent moved. Then Cestus leapt high into the air and launched into a massive punch aimed directly at Vettius' chest, the deadly spikes on his knuckles outstretched.

My breath caught as everything seemed to go in slow motion. I could practically see the shining points on the tips of Cestus' gloves. Then, at the last second, Vettius turned and the blow aimed at him switched from deadly to glancing. A small puff of red blood faded into the air as the spikes tore into his right shoulder, but I knew that was OK, he would be able to deal with that.

Cestus moved back and regarded Vettius as the Retiarius shook off his new wound with little difficulty.

Vettius then did something that I hadn't been expecting, he hoisted his trident up onto his shoulder and launched it with all his might at Cestus. The large man, having watched the attack unfold before him, ducked and rolled to the side easily. This was not a good development; even the worst trained of all the gladiators knew not to throw your weapon, unless you had a solid backup. A net, I thought, was not much of a backup, let alone a solid one.

Our man was now standing just metres away from his much larger opponent, and I began to worry for him again.

Just then, Cestus sprang back into action and rounded Vettius in a flash. The muscular gladiator kicked out at Vettius' armoured shin and I winced in sympathetic pain as two more kicks to the leg dropped Vettius to his knee. Padding or not, those kicks did look vicious. Cestus then went for the killing punch again, though Vettius again managed to defend himself, bringing a single forearm up between them both. The spikes on Cestus' gloves caused Vettius to cry out in pain as they penetrated his skin, though this time he managed to roll back and away from the offensive gauntlets.

Vettius was panting now and I wondered just how much of this he was going to be able to take. The crowd seemed to be having the time of their lives, watching one gladiator systematically disassemble another right before their very eyes.

Vettius pulled his net from his side and held it between his hands. I sighed; this was not the time to play with the net either and I would've bet that Cestus had thought so too, the lack of training evident in the way our man fought.

The Retiarius then threw his net to cover the distance between them. I knew it was weighted, but beyond that it offered nothing else such as blades or spikes. Then, Cestus grabbed the net that flew toward him and held on, so each gladiator had a hold of one end of it, and I knew which of them was going to win in this makeshift tug-o-war.

Cestus began reeling in Vettius as though he was a fisherman. Vettius tried his best to resist, but the strength of his opponent was just too much to bear. Instead, I watched in amazement as our man changed the angle of his resistance and flew towards Cestus. Before the gauntleted gladiator could do anything about it, Vettius had punched him hard in the face, and had come to a stop on the sands next to him. When Cestus looked down at his hands, he would notice that one of his spiked gloves had been entangled in, then removed by the net, which Vettius still held in his hands.

Cestus practically roared, though Vettius wasn't looking at him, he was staring at the net as though bewildered at what he had just managed to do. Cestus swung a fist at the back of Vettius' head, though the gladiator effortlessly ducked the strike. There was no way he could've known that the attack was coming but somehow he'd avoided it without even looking.

Cestus then shot a kick out towards Vettius' side and again the gladiator dodged the attack. Kick after punch after kick, Vettius just seemed to somehow know where they were coming from, and avoided every last one of them.

The larger Cestus, who had then had apparently enough of this, simply threw his entire body at Vettius, who had absolutely no chance of getting out of the way of his giant opponent. The pair clattered to the ground once again, though this time Cestus did not allow Vettius to roll out of the way, but kept him pinned down beneath him and raised his hands above his head, ready for the final blow. The problem was that when Cestus looked at his hands, he saw that he had now lost both of his gauntlets to the net, leaving him bare-fisted and without any real weapons. He didn't seem to care though, he punched Vettius in the chest hard and I could see the air leave our man. He would've gone for the face of course, but the metal helmet would've provided adequate defence against his bare knuckles. He struck again and again, and I watched Vettius writhe in pain. He had done much better than I had expected, but I could tell that this was going to be his end.

Then something unexpected happened. I was sure that I'd seen something glow a bright blue beneath Vettius' helmet, but there was no way I could tell. I saw my father's leg shift ever so slightly and wondered if he'd seen it too, though he didn't say anything.

Vettius' movement was so quick it was practically a blur. The Retiarius spun his netting around the arms of the large Cestus and pulled it tight against the gladiator's back. Vettius then weaved his legs around Cestus – though that in itself looked difficult as the man was just so wide – and looped his feet into the net. This meant that Vettius had entangled Cestus' arms, pinning them to his side and I could also see the two spiked gloves, still entangled in the netting, moving closer and closer to their owner as Vettius strained with his entire back and legs to tighten his trap.

Cestus roared, though even a beast of his size could do nothing to fight against the power of a back and legs with just his arms. He tried to stand up, but Vettius brought him back down by arching his back and forcing his feet downwards. That was all the movement that was needed though and the gauntlets moved into position atop Cestus' chest. Vettius pulled with all his might, and the spiked gauntlets imbedded themselves into Cestus' chest and throat slowly, producing an ever increasing stream of red blood that cascaded onto Vettius' chest. He did not stop pulling though, he kept on and on until all fight – and life – left his muscular opponent and Cestus fell to the side, dropped by Vettius who apparently had nothing left to give.

I simply couldn't believe it. Vettius had won against all the odds.

I looked at my father and I saw him clenching his fist in victory – though he did not celebrate as wildly as I might've expected.

"Did you see the glow?" I quickly asked the first thing that came to my mind.

My father turned to me and placed a hand on both of my shoulders as he spoke. "Do not worry about that my boy, our man won!" Though I could see the hidden message through his words – keep my mouth shut, 'we'll talk later'.

III - Igne Natura Renovatur Integra.

"Through fire, nature is reborn whole."

The purse that was won for our ludus by Vettius seemed like it was well worth the effort. I didn't know exactly how many coins were in the small bag that my father was given, but I could see that it was bulging.

Vettius had left the sands quickly after his victory so that he could have his wounds seen to by the doctor who worked within the healing room attached to the gladiator prep area. The last thing that anybody wanted was for a victorious gladiator to die later of some infection – that was certainly not a glorious way to die.

I had taken my fill of the water and bread before making any moves to leave my seat. I knew that as soon as the hot sun once again fell upon my skin, I would wish for the bottle again and I didn't want to be left behind. Vettius, however, would not be collected from the town again until the morning. It was normal for a gladiator to spend the little money he had earned from an arena battle in any way he saw fit – and usually that meant wine, women or gambling, and sometimes all three. Besides, Vettius needed to be passed by the arena doctor before he would be allowed to leave, His wounds would be closed, and that meant that he would have to remain still for a considerable amount of time.

I followed my father once he'd begun to move from our covered section of the arena stands and he led the way back through them out of the town, towards our ludus. I wondered if he would be amenable to talking to me yet about what I'd seen in the arena, but after a few attempts to gain his attention failed, I simply stopped trying. My attention was much more appreciated by Dinari anyway, though he also left my side once he'd found a small bird to chase, to try to make best friends with. I was never worried that the dog would kill any other living creature even if he did catch up with one; he was just so in love with everything.

We arrived back at the ludus around twenty minutes later and entered the house through the main front door. Most of the time it stood open, so it wasn't anything particularly out of the ordinary for it to be today. My mother and the house in general would've known we were coming home, so closing the door could've just been an inconvenience all around. What I didn't expect though, was that for the first time ever Dinari's heckles raised. He began to walk very closely to the ground and he growled.

The noise was alien to me, and it took me a moment to figure out where it was coming from. Then it dawned on me that something was wrong. My father sensed it too. He waved me back behind himself with an outstretched arm as we crossed the threshold into the house and I obediently crept behind him, then hid behind a pillar on the inside of the house, close to the door. I shushed Dinari and he followed me into my hiding place without question.

I peered around the pillar once I heard my father's voice, though it did not sound calm.

"What is this? What do you think you are doing?" I heard him almost shout in anger. I could see his back, but I couldn't see who he was talking to.

"We've been sent to pay you a visit after that little stunt you pulled in the arena today," a gruff voice returned. Then I heard a muffled woman's voice that must've been my mother – she had either been gagged, or the man had his hand across her mouth. I froze to the spot, petrified.

Then from behind another of the columns and out of view of my father, a cloaked figure crept out of the shadows and approached him silently. I tried to call out in warning, to yell as loud as my lungs would allow but the loudest they could manage would not even register as a noise. Dinari, who was still following my previous instruction, made no move or sound either as the cloaked man approached my father, then unceremoniously sunk a dagger into his back.

I heard the muffled scream of my mother first, though almost immediately that was extinguished by the sound of a blade against flesh. I pulled myself back into my hiding place as quickly as I could, making myself as small as possible, though not before seeing the lifeless body of my father fall to the ground with blood pouring from his new wound.

"Right, you know what we have to do next," the man who I'd already heard speaking said quietly to his assassin friend.

"Yeah, this whole place has gotta go. Nothing left, right?" the second man replied. I made a mental imprint of the sound of their voices, because I knew that I would have nothing else to remember these men by - these two men that had just killed both my mother and father.

That's when I heard their footsteps coming back towards the entrance of the house, towards me.

I pulled Dinari tightly onto my lap and curled my arms around him and my legs as tightly as I could, tears streaming down my face although I made not a single noise. As the footsteps grew nearer I shimmied as quietly as I could to keep the column as much between us as possible and prayed to whatever God I could that I wouldn't be seen. Then as they passed my hiding place, I prayed to Ultio, the God of revenge, so that one day I would take the very blood from these two men, and learn the reasoning behind their heinous actions.

I waited for a few minutes until I could no longer hear the men walking away and made my way quickly and quietly to where my father lay dead on the hard ground. I almost didn't see my mother on the floor as I kneeled down to check to see if my father was still breathing. It was obvious though that he had died where he stood. My mother's throat had been cut from ear to ear and her deep red blood coated the ground around her. Some of it had even already started to dry.

I could barely catch my breath as the immense pain of losing both of my parents so cruelly began to break my heart in two. I don't know what I would've done if Dinari wasn't there to comfort me.

Suddenly, I heard a noise coming from the back entranceway where I knew the gladiators were housed. I wondered what fate had befallen our men, though had no time to ponder. Instead, I gestured silently for Dinari to follow me, and ran as fast as I could out of the front door without looking back.

Not thirty seconds run away from the house, there was a small rock formation that had created a natural cave that I liked to play in sometimes, and that was exactly where I was headed. I still didn't look back. I willed my legs to carry me as fast and as true as they could, and my feet pounded the ground over and over.

I reached the cave and rounded the stone corner, panting. Dinari had beaten me to it and I was once again thankful for just how obedient and intelligent my four-legged best friend was.

I eventually gathered the confidence to peer around the stone to look back at the house to see if I had been followed, but thankfully it looked as though I had not. After a few moments though, I did see the two men –

presumably there were just the two of them – leave the house via the front door followed by the beginnings of black smoke billowing out of both the doors and windows. I couldn't help but gasp as everything I ever knew as a home began to burn before my very eyes.

I watched and waited for the men to disappear. They'd done what they'd come to do and apparently they didn't have any idea that I hadn't been in the house, or perhaps they were unaware of my existence altogether. Either way they'd missed me, and I ran back toward the house once I was positive nobody else was around to watch the place burn down to the ground.

When I reached the door, orange flames lapped at the entrance and although I made a move to try to enter, Dinari bit into my robes and pulled me back away. The heat was unbearable and when my senses returned, I realised that my friend was warning me not to go inside. He was right of course; I wouldn't have lasted a minute in that heat and fire.

Trying a new tactic, I rounded the house with Dinari in tow towards the back entrance that led directly onto the gladiator training grounds. To my horror, as I entered through the gate, both of our remaining men lay dead on the ground with their throats cut from ear to ear. I didn't know how the assassins had bested our trained gladiators – perhaps they'd surprised them – but they'd killed them regardless. I looked for a way to enter the house, but by now the flames were already lapping out of every window, the doors and the roof. The place was an inferno and I had no hope of ever making it inside. I decided that my best course of action was to move away from the ruined ludus, back to the cave, and gather my thoughts.

When I arrived back at the cave a few moments later, I fell to my knees and sobbed. I cried harder than I ever had before as I watched my house burn from the inside out. Everything my parents had built, their lifeless bodies, our gladiators, just taken away from us for a reason that I couldn't yet comprehend. The only thing I had left was Dinari. Again I didn't know what I would do without him.

Eventually, sadness was overcome by rage and once again if I didn't have Dinari to stop me doing anything stupid I don't know what I would've done. All of the anger ebbed away from my body as I looked into the dog's wide eyes and smiling face. There was just no way anyone could feel rage when in the presence of Dinari.

I spent a long time thinking about my parents and their lifeless bodies. I wondered if it had hurt when they'd been killed, or if the surprise was good enough that they hadn't felt a thing. A part of me envied them, that they didn't have to go on as I had to now, but I understood that it was a selfish thought and shooed it away.

I watched as the flames eventually died down into the darkness of the night and wondered just how long the fire would last. Eventually, I had no choice but to curl up with Dinari and fall soundly asleep from my exhaustion.

The next morning when I awoke, the first thing I did was to make sure that Dinari was still curled up with me – which he was - still snoring quietly with his eyes tightly shut. I smiled before I remembered where I was and why, and peered out of my cave and across the hill to my house. I wished it had all been some wicked dream, but there it was, right before me. The still smoking, smouldering wreck of my former home.

 The morning sun was already warm, though the smoke still coming from the house made me think that the place was probably still hot, even if it wasn't on fire anymore. Nevertheless, I knew I had to go and investigate, so I made my way back to the front door and stepped inside.

As predicted, it was still hot inside, even though most of the ceiling had collapsed and the walls had been damaged beyond recognition. Thick black soot covered practically everything and I noticed that Dinari simply refused to enter the place. I looked to the place where my parents' bodies lay, but all that remained were two charred skeletons in their place.

I made the effort not to touch anything as I moved deeper into the house. I wanted to see if there was anything that I could salvage. I knew that I would need money to buy food and water; I was already getting both hungry and thirsty, but remembering that my father had had the winnings from the battle on his person – and that there was no sign of the small leather pouch now – I assumed that the coins hadn't made it either, and neither would any of the others that he usually had in his study. I had to make sure though, so I made my way to the room at the back of the house in search of coin.

The hallways were black and dark, just like the entrance foyer had been, and the heat was still offensive. Every time I heard a creak or the sound of falling or crumbling sections of wall or ceiling, I cringed as though the whole place was going to bury me alive. I picked up my pace so that I could get out of there as quickly as possible.

My father's office stood as though it was undisturbed structurally. Everything was charred and sooted, though I could still see where everything was supposed to be: the large wooden table that had stood with a bust of my grandfather atop it was now gone apart from a few charred remains; the bust itself had fallen to the ground and smashed. My father had apparently been trying to decide which floor tiles to use to upgrade our entranceway, because there were a few stacks of the brittle, yet fireproof objects stacked against the walls. One stack, though, was propped right up against a bookcase in the corner of the room, and behind it I could see some books that the fire had passed right by.

I went to move the tiles, but they were still hot to the touch. Balling my tunic in my hands, I fashioned a kind of glove and hefted the stack away from the bookcase to reveal the books. Only four had made it, the ones with the thickest leather bindings. I picked them all up one by one although the first two immediately fell to ash in my hands. The last two were badly burnt, though they held together well when I scooped them up delicately, so I took them. These books would have to be what would remind me of my parents and my house. There was nothing else that I could take. I tucked them into my tunic below my belt. It wasn't the most comfortable thing in the world, but I had nowhere else to put them.

When I left the house, sure that there was nothing else useful or salvageable inside, I was greeted by Dinari, sitting and panting in the outside sun. He did not look concerned that I'd entered the house this time, rather he looked intrigued to see if I had brought him anything from inside and I had to show him my hands to prove that I wasn't hiding anything from him. He looked disappointed. I knew the feeling.

My stomach was rumbling. It'd been a couple of days now since I'd had a good meal and I knew that Dinari probably felt the same but the only thing I could think of doing was going into Liternum to see if anyone would take pity on me. I didn't know anybody anyway – I had nowhere to go and no one to ask, save for perhaps Vettius, who I knew my family still technically owned, but I didn't know how well that was going to wash with our newest gladiator now. It didn't matter. If I could find Vettius and take some of his coin then that would make things so much easier. If not, well I'd cross that bridge when I arrived at it.

Dinari and I made our way back into the town, it was already becoming uncomfortably hot underneath the sun again and I longed for a drink of water. The further away from the ruined ludus I got, the more my mind wandered, wondering if I'd missed anything, a flask of water or some food, although I knew I hadn't been that stupid. There was nothing left for me in that house and pondering on that would do me no good. I imagined Dinari would be hungry too, though he bounded around my feet, and on occasion through my legs as I walked, apparently unconcerned about his own hunger or thirst.

At the town walls, I was surprised at just how much bigger it seemed now that I was here alone. With no clear direction to go in either, I felt like the tiniest spec of sand on the largest beach.

I'd heard before that children would sometimes be left in the centre square of the towns, awaiting adoption by wealthier families, though I also knew that Liternum wasn't famed for its wealthy populace. It was more likely that any children awaiting aid in the centre square would be turned into Delicia – children taken as playthings for, in the best case, the children of the scarce wealthy families, and in the worst, for individuals with more perverse intentions. I was young, but my parents had raised me with awareness of the dangers that existed around us at all times, and it had always come down to one thing: the less you had, the more danger you were in, and right now, I had nothing. Well, nothing other than Dinari of course, who had found some sort of small lizard and was practically bowing to the thing, his front paws and nose touching the ground and his bottom high in the air, tail wagging so hard his body was moving. The lizard simply didn't seem to care at all and just sat there, blinking nonchalantly.

My plan had changed to simply deal with what I knew. I would go to the Liternum amphitheatre and try to find Vettius to see if he would let me have any of his winnings. Then, I would either use that to buy some food and drink, or if not, I would seek shelter in the shadow of the construction. I knew there was always food and drink near to an arena so that the gladiators could keep their strength up, but I was somewhat unaware of the intricacies of that particular procedure.

The route to the arena was the same that I'd walked the previous day, though as no arena battles were scheduled, there were more people on the streets going about their business rather than sitting inside the amphitheatre cheering for their favourite gladiators. I noticed a few glances in our direction as we walked and wondered if I was being recognised, though eventually it dawned on me that my once white robes had been covered tip to toe in black soot, and my face similarly was most probably covered. I didn't know how many times I'd rubbed my hands on myself or where, so I assumed I looked quite the sight walking on my own through the streets of Liternum with my small pet dog.

The arena was quiet from the outside when we arrived. There didn't seem to be much of anything going on in there. The gates were open and I could see the sands beyond, though any sign of the previous day's battles had all but disappeared, cleaned up or had otherwise been raked over by the arena hands. I still knew better than to walk out onto those sands though.

I turned and moved towards the gladiator prep rooms to the left of the arena entrance. The door opened with a creak as I pushed it, and I walked inside as though it was the most natural thing in the world to do.

There was no one in the first room, which I knew was the intake area for new arrivals, so that was to be expected today. I walked straight forward and into a corridor lined with rooms with stone benches, pots filled with oils and some cloth wrappings, presumably to make the gladiators skin shine in the sun as they stepped out onto the sands. Room after room was empty, until I passed the walkway up to the golden sands. I peered at the path leading to the large, closed iron gate and spared it a moment of thought before entering into a much larger room equipped with a stone table stained with blood, buckets of water, sponges and cloths littered around the place. In one corner of the room sat a very old, very thin gentleman with a long white beard wearing an old, tattered grey robe that had been stained with blood and dirt.

"What the bloody hell are you doing back here, boy?" The man said abruptly, raising himself to his feet before I could say anything. Clearly I'd just interrupted his rest. Dinari came and sat by my side.

"I... uh..." I started to speak.

"Well? Uh... what?" The man quickly replied before I could form my words properly. "This is where the gladiators come to have their wounds tended to, are you a gladiator hmm? Do you have a dire wound that needs dressing? I don't think so... why don't you run along now before I am forced to call the guards?"

"No!" I cried before I could stop myself. I realised immediately that it made me look very guilty. "I'm looking for someone... a gladiator."

"You need to come when the games are on to see a gladiator, boy," the man replied with a sneer. "Tomorrow would be better, but you need to go stand outside like everyone else, OK?" His words sounded sarcastic and I didn't like it, though he had clearly missed my meaning.

"No, a gladiator from yesterday," I said. "His name is Vettius, he was the Retiarius who won the third match against the Cestus. He would have had some injuries from the spiked gloves when his opponent had hit him."

The man stroked his beard thoughtfully. His eyes told me that he knew exactly who I was talking about, though it looked as though he was deciding just how much he was going to tell me.

"As I said, if you want to see a gladiator fight, you will have to come back when they are actually blessing the sands with their presence..." he began, though I interrupted him.

"No, Vettius is owned by my family, and if you do not tell me where he is, then I shall be forced to tell my father..." I knew it was an empty threat and I knew that the man probably wouldn't care, but I felt like I was approaching the end of our conversation and I just needed the information.

"By the looks of you boy, you have not seen your father in a long time..."

the man replied slowly, though I could tell that he was slightly less sure of himself. Then he sighed. "Listen, the Retiarius that fought… and won in the arena yesterday was not too badly injured. I patched him up and sent him on his way, but I do not know where he went. Knowing gladiators, he probably went into the town looking for women of the night. Retiarius are renowned for that you know… I think it could be the net… or maybe the trident…" he trailed off apparently in thought, though I heard the underlying message in his statement – Vettius had gone and I didn't know when or even if he was going to come back.

"Ok, thanks…" I replied slowly, then as I turned to leave, I added as an afterthought, "Do you have any water?"

The man practically spluttered at the question, though when he managed to calm himself, he passed me a small flask from by his feet with a shrug. "Do not go telling anybody I gave you anything mind. The last thing I want is people thinking I am offering free shelter down here else I would be inundated with 'em."

I nodded in response as the cool water filled my mouth and quenched my thirst. Once I'd had my fill, I offered some to Dinari who threw his head back, mouth open for me to slowly pour some in. When he finished drinking, he simply shut his mouth and I poured a little water onto his nose for luck. He didn't seem to care. I passed the flask back to the man and muttered a 'thank you'.

I left the gladiator pen without another word, though I did hear the old man call out 'and don't come back!' As I left – presumably it was so that anyone else in the vicinity would think that he'd thrown me out of the place, I didn't begrudge him that. I knew he must've worked hard and had also seen more death and injuries than most other people had seen in their lives. He deserved his privacy, I was sure.

The next thing I needed was food for Dinari and I wondered if I could sell either of the two books that I still carried just to get a loaf of bread or something, though judging by their state, I wouldn't have been surprised if they weren't worth a bean. I had also noted that they were also empty when I had tried to read them, and I didn't know if that meant that they would be worth more, or less.

I tried to rack my brain as we walked into the town proper again. 'What did people do for food? I kept asking myself, though without money, there was only one answer left. People begged.

I wondered if I would have any advantage in being a young boy begging for food, though I knew that the main thing that would do would be to make me a target. I needed to be careful and not make silly mistakes that could get me into serious trouble.

I followed my nose to a stone building near the centre of town. The buildings had been getting closer together and it was clear that the people were getting poorer and poorer as I moved toward the inner town. The building I'd eventually arrived at was a kind of bakery, I could smell the bread and other lower-tier foods cooking and people were approaching bare-handed and leaving with small bowls of what looked like porridge, or with small, flat loaves of bread in their hands. I knew immediately that this was 'puls' and the aroma combined with my hunger made my mouth positively water.

I may have been brought up in a household that was pretty well-off, comparatively speaking, but in my current situation I knew that there would be no turning my nose up at anything. Beggars couldn't be choosers and all that.

I milled around the entrance to the bakery for a while in the hope that someone might take pity on me, and I was surprised at just how effective that tactic was. As people left the bakery, they would see me, then tear off a corner of their bread and hand it to me with a caring look in their eyes. Immediately, I felt as though I was amongst my people – they didn't judge me, they didn't horde what little they had – they were kind and charitable, and it made me feel warm inside.

By the time a few hours had passed, I was positively bloated, and so was Dinari. It was actually the first time I'd ever seen him turning down food - he'd eaten so much and I shared that feeling. What had happened here today was remarkable, and the whole situation had seriously opened my eyes to what the world was really like outside the gates of my privileged upbringing.

The time had finally come though for me to find a place to sleep for the night. Being the summer, I knew it would be warm through the night and I didn't have a problem with sleeping outside. I knew that in the winter though, if things didn't change, I was probably going to get wet, and have to deal with temperatures plummeting to somewhere just above freezing.

I made my way back to the arena. I knew it was nothing different to what the town proper would offer me, but a part of me just felt like it was at home there.

I spent a short while looking for the best place to park up for the night, and eventually I found a small stone alcove cut into the perimeter of the amphitheatre. I pulled Dinari tightly into my arms and fell straight asleep with my only friend in the world nestled in my arms. It had been a very, very long day.

IV – Perfer Et Obdura, Dolor Hic Tibi Proderit Olim.

"Be patient and tough; someday this pain will be useful to you."

I was awoken the next morning by the feeling of the warm sunlight on my skin again. It felt nice, though it reminded me that I was still outside and although I'd found myself a quiet little nook the night before, now there were people moving back and forth before me, either coming to or going from the arena – there must have been an event scheduled for today and the arena hands were preparing for it. It made me think about how much work actually went into creating a show for the people, and how the people in turn repaid that effort with their bloodlust. It did show, though, that the people *loved* the arena and everything about it. I wasn't very far detached from that feeling myself actually.

I knew that on a day like this, where the arena was going to spring into life, that there would surely be work to be found, and where there was work, there would be money and that was something I sorely needed if I wanted to start to *really* survive.

Being a young boy who had never had to work a day in his life in the real world though, I had no idea where even to begin looking for work. I presumed that you'd simply find the man who was highest up at the place you wanted to work and tell him you're ready to do whatever it took. The arena, though, was not the kind of place where the highest-up-guy would be simply walking about and I knew that. Instead, I did the next best thing, well in my eyes anyway.

The thing was, I'd been brought up to respect soldiers and also the military in general, so I might be forgiven when I say that I simply walked with Dinari slightly behind me, and approached the nearest legionary I could find, who was standing guard at the front of the arena.

The legionary wore a shimmering metal breastplate, a helmet with a neat plumage of red bristles, and a long red cape, and attached to his side was a short gladius.

"E... excuse me?" I asked. The man didn't even acknowledge my presence. It annoyed me.

I breathed in deeply. "Hey!" I called up to the soldier, who finally looked at me, then away, still not saying a word.

"Can you hear me? Are you deaf?" I asked, now genuinely unsure of the answer to that question.

"Piss off will you, you little shit. Can you not see that I am busy?" The man said under his breath. "Get back to the fucking gutter with the rest of the homeless cretins."

That was an unexpected response for me; I'd never been spoken to like that in my entire life. I felt as though it was a little harsh, though before I could form some sort of retaliation, Dinari decided he would have a go at garnering some proper attention from the legionary. The smiling dog sauntered past me slowly, stood right next to the man's feet, cocked his left leg and pissed on the uniform's metal shin guards, making what I was sure was smiling eye contact with me the entire time, as though this was the funniest thing in the world.

It took a few good seconds before the legionary realised what was happening, but as soon as he looked down and discovered why his leg was becoming both warm and wet, his face turned practically purple and utter rage filled his entire being.

The legionary made a move to kick Dinari, but the wily dog was far too quick to allow that to happen. He skipped back and to by my side and I knew immediately that we only had one option here: we needed to run.

"You just made a big fucking mistake," the legionary growled as he took a step forward and swiped out an arm to grab me. I ducked under his hand and turned on my heels. Before the man knew it or had the chance to try to grab me again, my feet were pounding the ground beneath me. Dinari thought this was absolutely hilarious, and being much faster than I, he basically ran in circles around me as I moved.

I could hear the legionary giving chase and shouting for people to stop me, though nobody attempted it – I did make sure to give everyone a wide berth though as I ran along the perimeter of the amphitheatre just in case. I kept the building on my left, which meant that after a few moments I'd be going uphill, which would probably be difficult for the legionary in full armour, although I was under no illusions that his training would've easily included running up and down hills, so he was probably used to it.

I had passed a few other soldiers though, who by the sounds of it had joined in the chase as the legionary beckoned them to his cause in passing. The situation was getting way out of hand very quickly and I knew that I wouldn't be able to run in circles around the amphitheatre forever.

Still keeping to the walls of the amphitheatre, we ran down the hill and back towards the front of the construction. I knew that I would be better off trying to hide rather than keep running out in the open, so as we rounded on the door to the gladiator preparation area, Dinari and I slipped inside and kept moving all the way towards the doctor's room and the back. I knew there hadn't been any games yet this day, so the room should've been empty and the perfect place to hide.

The prep area had no less than ten gladiators in and they paid me no mind as I passed. I glanced about to see if I recognised any of them or if Vettius had appeared, though sadly it was futile.

The men were all wearing either cloths around their waist or otherwise nothing at all. Some arena hands were pouring oil onto their gladiator bodies so that they would look bigger or more defined out in the sunlight and by all accounts it seemed that everyone in the room was enjoying it. The room had no weapons or armour, though I presumed that these would either become available after their preparation or would be picked up from another room. It wasn't that I would've picked something up to try to defend myself with should the need arise, but I was always on the lookout for decent weapons, especially when gladiators were around. It must've just been a part of my upbringing.

We passed the other doorways through the main hallway as we moved without stopping and I still didn't take the time to investigate any further. Outside I could hear the heavy footsteps of the soldiers as they ran past the prep area and the sound gave me new cause to quickly dive into the doctor's room, fall to my ass and prop my back against the cold hard wall. I shut my eyes and hoped that everything would be OK. I felt Dinari wriggle himself into the gap between my chest and my knees and I took his full weight on my lap. It was comforting.

Then I heard the slow, purposeful footsteps entering the prep area. The soldiers had somehow figured out where I was hiding and had entered the area to finally catch up with me. There was more than one pair of footsteps too, I could hear at least three people approaching menacingly through the hallways and I wondered if the gladiators or the arena hands were pointing them in my direction. I kept my eyes tightly closed and I could feel Dinari's warm little body shaking with anticipation, or perhaps even fear.

The ominous footsteps entered the doctor's room and stopped right before me. I felt a single hand grab the scruff of my robes and I was lifted off the ground and into the air. Dinari scampered off around the stone table to hide from the soldiers. I could do nothing other than let out a yelp as I was raised from the ground by large hands under my armpits.

Looking into the eyes of the legionary, he didn't look as though the chase had been taxing for him at all, although he looked furious beyond all belief. Knowing that I'd been caught and that I had no other options, I simply let my body hang limply at the mercy of the huge soldier.

"What the fuck is all this?" An older man's voice came from a corner of the room. It startled everyone as we'd presumed that we had been alone, but I recognised the voice as belonging to the doctor who I'd met previously; he must've been asleep in the room and nobody had noticed him – my yelp rousing him to consciousness.

"Get back to your dreams, old man, this is official business," the guard spoke without turning to face the doctor.

I peered past my captor and saw that the doctor was standing now and stroking his long white beard thoughtfully.

After a moment, the doctor spoke again. "I am afraid though, that your official business is interfering with my official business," he said levelly. "You see, the boy that you hold in your hand is my assistant and being so old and as frail as I am," he was clearly making a show of seeming old and decrepit, "I am unable to carry out my tasks effectively without the help of this young boy."

The legionary turned to face the doctor fully now with a hard expression on his face, still holding me out to his side.

"And why should I give two shits about your work?" He sneered.

"Because, legionary, I am the arena doctor. I am tasked with ensuring that all gladiators are fit to fight another day. My role may not be as glorious as those of the soldiers in the army, or of the gladiators in the arena, though without my art gladiators would find it much more difficult to survive even the slightest of wounds. Plus, if I do say so myself, I am the only skilled physical doctor in all of Liternum." It sounded as though the doctor had won the argument with his statement, which was punctuated by the legionary dropping me to the ground. I heard Dinari growl softly at my abuse, though he was doing the very clever thing of staying out of the spotlight for the moment.

The legionary thought for a moment. "OK, though punishment must be given for the insult to my person and by extension the glorious armies of Rome," he said more officially than angrily. "A fine then," he punctuated.

To my absolute surprise, the doctor unfastened a small purse that hung around his waist and handed it over to the soldier without a word, who didn't even inspect it, though he immediately placed it inside his breastplate with a cocky grin on his face. Then he swiftly turned on his heels, and left the room accompanied by the two other soldiers either side.

I honestly didn't know how to react or what to say. A part of me was thankful that the doctor had saved me from the soldiers, but a slightly bigger part was worried about the motives that the man had had in doing so. In the end, all I could manage to say was "thank you."

The doctor didn't reply directly to me, though muttered "fucking soldiers," before retaking his seat in what was apparently his sleeping chair in a corner of the room.

After a long moment, and after the doctor had closed his eyes again, I decided to ask the burning question: "why did you do that?"

The doctor opened his eyes and they focussed on me. Then they flickered to Dinari who had taken his position, by my feet. He was wagging his tail and it looked like he was smiling.

"There is… something wrong with your dog," the doctor said. I looked down at Dinari, who wagged his tail even harder at my attention and his entire body began to move from side to side.

"No… he is just… like that" I said slowly. "But you did not have to pay that fine for me… I have no way to pay you back or anything, though I promise that I will try…"

The doctor's gaze fell back to me as I spoke. He sighed. "The soldiers may not have noticed it, but underneath all that dirt and soot that you seem so keen of, I can see that you are wearing the robes of a lanista, or at least of a ludus. Your clothes are not torn and tattered, so I am guessing that you have not been out by yourself for very long, right?"

I was shocked by the correct and astute observations, but managed to nod slightly.

The doctor continued. "You have a pet that seems quite well and intelligent, you are entirely unaware of social etiquette – especially how not to run into somewhere you are not supposed to be, waking up the old man… and you seem to keep coming back to me. The Goddess of misery and pain is prevalent enough around here, and I am nothing if not one to defy the Gods of their plans."

That last statement confused me. "So you want to defy the Gods?" I asked with a furrowed brow.

"By the Gods, no boy!" The doctor stroked his beard thoughtfully. "Just the bad ones!" He chuckled at his own words. "I took an oath to help anyone in need, and today, you have been the lucky recipient of my good nature."

The man was definitely odd, though I could tell that he did seem particularly caring. I guessed that you had to be to become an arena doctor – all you would ever see were people in dire need of your help. I also assumed that this man had seen more death than anyone else that I could think of – and what was more, that he had probably had more men die in his arms than even the mightiest of gladiators.

"Can I repay you?" I asked slowly. "I could help around here, fetch water, or sponges or something?" I recounted the things my mother had done for me when I'd fallen sick on the odd occasion. I didn't want to confess that I'd never actually seen anyone have their actual wounds tended to though.

The doctor regarded me for a long moment before he spoke.

"This place is not a good place for you, boy. There is death, misery and suffering almost every day. More blood than would fill a bath house and the risk of disease and decay. You would be far better gaining the favour of a rich family who needs a plaything for their little prince…" I could see the words pained the doctor, and I moved to press that advantage.

"I do not want to be some plaything for some little shit who thinks he is better than everyone else," I said sternly. "I know that I was put here – no *sent* here to help people. I can help you, and in turn repay you the kindness you showed me. I do not need you to pay me, I can get my own food and water, all I ask is that in the winter I might be afforded a roof if things get particularly cold. Dinari is no bother either. He stays by my side and never makes a sound…"

"Alright alright," the doctor placed a hand on his forehead. "Just… stop talking… you can help me here for today and see if your stomach hasn't turned so much that you do not *want* to come back tomorrow…" he closed his eyes again but continued speaking. "You sit in the corner. When the first battle is over, you shall see why nobody enters this room unless they are either brought here, or are bringing someone else here."

V – Acta Non Verba.

"Deeds, not words."

I knew what an arena fight looked like in Liternum, though if I thought that things got bloody and gory while watching the events, that was nothing compared to what happened away from the watching eyes and the roars of the crowds.

I didn't get to watch the first arena battle that I was the 'doctor's assistant' for, although I certainly heard it. By the way the crowds were cheering with delight, I wondered exactly how many pieces the gladiators were going to be in when it was all over and they arrived in the small room that I now worked in.

The first gladiator arrived at the doctor's table and by all accounts he was in a bad way. He wasn't alive by any stretch of the imagination; the man who had fought as Murmillo had managed to have one of his arms severed at the elbow – the bottom half was missing - there were multiple puncture wounds to his stomach, a long slash across his chest and beneath his helmet I was sure that I could see blood covering his face from some additional grave wound.

"Pass me that knife over there," the doctor ordered as two arena hands hoisted the gladiator, still in his armour, onto the hard stone table in the centre of the room. The hands waited as though they were after payment or something, but I realised what they were waiting for once I picked up a short, sharp knife from a small pile of tools and handed it to the doctor. He then mercilessly cut the fallen gladiator's neck from ear to ear. After that grim deed was done, he began to remove all of the armour from the man, including his helmet and that is where I saw that the killing blow to the gladiator must've been the 'sword in the mouth' style execution.

"Get that bucket underneath that cut," the doctor ordered, "quickly now."

I dutifully obliged, though the sound of the blood dripping from the table and into the bucket made me retch. It was certainly not something that I thought I'd ever get used to.

The doctor then picked up a sponge from a bucket of water and began to clean the blood from all of the wounds that the gladiator had sustained. I had no idea what any of this was for. The doctor then wrung out the sponge into the blood-bucket and continued his work until the gladiator was practically clean, despite still being very much deceased.

I then discovered the real reason that the arena hands had been waiting. They had piled the used armour into the next room along, then returned to carry the gladiator's still body away from the room. I followed them curiously with Dinari in tow, who really didn't seem to be enjoying the spectacle either, with his tail between his legs and his mouth clamped closed. Even animals understood and disliked death.

The arena hands bundled the body onto a small cart at the back of the arena and began to walk away with it towards where I knew the river passed by the town. I didn't want to follow any further, but assumed that they were going to bury the body nearby. I returned to my new place of work quietly and re-entered the doctor's room to find him pouring the bucket of blood into drinking flasks and corking them as they were filled.

"Um... what are you doing?" I asked quickly, though the doctor didn't look away from his task. The sight made me feel sick and I had to look away a few times as I watched the thick liquid entering the flasks.

"Do you know what this is, boy? he asked, then answered his own question before I had the chance to reply. "This is warm, fresh gladiator blood. It has two main uses in today's world and these are as follows: one, it is a cure for the epileptic; drink a flask once a day and your disease is all but cured!"

"And the second?" I asked curiously – though the thought of anyone actually drinking the stuff made me want to empty the contents of my own stomach.

"Secondly, ah... it makes men feel... more like men when they're in the company of a good woman..." he said carefully. I understood a little about men and women, though this one stumped me. I didn't ask any more questions, but tried to wonder why men would ever need to feel more like men.

Instead, I asked the questions that I'd amassed whilst watching the arena hands do their job.

"Why did you cut the gladiator's throat? And where did the arena hands take the body?" I asked. There were so many questions that I wanted to ask, but these two stood out as the two I could get my head the least around.

The doctor visibly sighed at the fact that he was literally going to have to teach me about *everything*.

"First," he said, "every time you see a gladiator who has lost their fight and is on the brink of death – actually, even sometimes the winners – it is better to make sure that they are dead rather than let them suffer. Also, sometimes they are not exactly sure what is happening to them and they try to grab you – you do not want that to happen. Even close to death these men are both strong and dangerous and you will not want one of them to take you with them. You may have noticed that this Murmillo had been dragged off the sands to this room; that meant that he had lost, and pretty badly. If they get carried in on a stretcher, then they fought well, but still lost. In Rome, losing is not so much of a death sentence as it is here… these small-town crowds are always begging for blood…"

I knew that much at least, and let the doctor continue his explanation.

"If the gladiator is dragged from the arena, we remove their armour and drain some of their blood to sell, then the body is taken away to the river and thrown in to be taken away by the spirits therein. If a gladiator arrives to us on a stretcher, he is buried on the banks, the body being covered by dirt allowing his spirit to be freed to the afterlife."

This was all new information to me. I never really thought about what happened to gladiators after they'd died.

As I was thinking this though, a gladiator in full Murmillo gear walked into the room and started unbuckling his own armour and dropping it to the ground for the arena hands to ferry away. Eventually the muscular gladiator – who was clearly the victor in the last fight - stood before us in a simple loin cloth and nothing else.

I could see a few bruises on the gladiator's knuckles and a slash atop his left shoulder, though none of his injuries seemed all that bad. The doctor moved in to clean the wounds silently and cover them in a thick, mud like paste and placed the gladiator's hands into a bucket of clean water to soothe their bruising. After a few moments, the doctor ushered the gladiator from the room as there was nothing more to be done for him.

"I've seen that one a few times, never really been hurt but his opponents are always slaughtered like dogs…" the doctor stopped and looked at Dinari, who was looking back up at him and smiling. "Uh… no offence," the doctor added in the dog's direction. Dinari wagged his tail.

It occurred to me that the doctor may have had a pretty good insight into the fighting styles of the gladiators on the sands, even if he didn't actually watch any of the fights. Just by his last explanation, I could see that he knew how this particular gladiator fought, and to some that would've been valuable information.

I cleaned the whole room before the next gladiator arrived. I wasn't exactly sure how illnesses and disease spread, but I knew that clean places tended to be better than dirty places when it came to the sick. Plus, I thought that anything I could do to make the room a nicer place to carry out our work in, was a good thing.

The next gladiator that was brought in followed a much shorter fight and again he was dragged through the door and dropped unceremoniously onto the stone table. The crowds hadn't sounded as enthralled with this match and it made me wonder who the Retiarius had faced off against for the bout to have been so one-sided and over so quickly. This gladiator looked as though he had been speared through the heart and it made me think that he had been quickly dispatched by a more agile or able Hoplomachus.

Again the doctor carried out his work efficiently, cutting the man's throat, stripping him of the little armour he wore, and taking as much blood as he could from the gladiator before the hands took him away again and off to the river.

Without protest I cleaned the room of the blood in silence, though this time the victor did not grace us with his presence. I assumed that it meant that the gladiator had suffered no injuries at all and had simply disappeared, back to wherever he had come from.

When I was done with my cleaning, I began to eagerly await the next gladiator to the room, although I quickly berated myself at just how morbid that thought had sounded. The doctor seemed as though he had sensed it too and decided to give me a new task.

"Think you and that dog could do with a little fresh air?" he asked. Dinari practically bounced on the spot at the doctor's mention of him, though somewhat more levelly I enquired as to what he needed of us.

"I need you to take these flasks into town and see about selling them. There are a few physicians in town that require these for their patients and will pay good coin for their delivery. I can tell you where they will be at this hour, though if you choose to do so, it may be more beneficial for you to try to sell some of the flasks to the general populous for their... uh... other needs." The doctor seemed to think it through for a moment before he spoke again. "You know what, there are five flasks here. If you come back with anything more than five dinari for the lot, then I will be impressed. How about you go see what you can do to impress me?"

I liked the sound of the challenge and hoisting the flasks onto my shoulders with their long straps, Dinari and I made our way out of the holding area and back towards the town. Of course, most people would still be in the arena watching the matches as they happened, but I was sure that there would still be plenty in the centre of town going about their usual business.

I really had no concept of the value of money though. I'd once heard my father say that a soldier would get about one dinarius per day, but I didn't know if that made five dinari for all of the blood very expensive, or otherwise very cheap. I did think though that if it truly was a cure for a disease, then a day's wages was probably worth it for a flask.

I made my way back to the bakery where the people had been so charitable on the off chance that they were charitable in more ways than just handing out bread. I also thought that perhaps I could pick up some food for my rumbling stomach while I was there and I was sure that Dinari would've been hungry by now too. That fact was confirmed when my furry friend realised where we were going and began to wag his entire body as he ran ahead following his nose to the bakery.

When I arrived, there was a queue of people awaiting their food, and rather than join them I stood to the side and looked for anyone that I recognised, or that had a friendly looking face. Most people, though, looked both tired and hungry and I immediately concluded that this was not the place to sell my flasks of (probably) expensive gladiator blood.

Inevitably, I couldn't muster up the courage to announce what I was carrying to the crowds, I simply didn't have it in me, so I kept my mouth shut and my head down.

Eventually, a man in the queue called out to me.

"That's a nice dog you have there," he said loudly, "and what do you have in the flasks there? Wine perhaps?"

I looked up at the man who'd spoken and could tell immediately that he was not a rich man. However, his words had attracted a few gazes from the line of people, each of them presumably wanting to get in on the action, if of course there was any wine involved.

"It is… uh…" I stuttered. "It is gladiator blood, fresh from the arena today," I managed. My voice hadn't been loud, but the statement had drawn even more attention to me and my wares.

"Fuck off is it," the man said loudly. "You really expect us to believe that you are just carrying around armfuls of the magic ingredient? Come on boy,

I have heard more believable tales from singers in the night!"

"But it is!" I protested. "I work with the arena doctor and I myself watched all of this gladiator blood being collected earlier today!" I uncorked one of the flasks and let a tiny drop out into the palm of my hand. The blood was deep red and it still felt warm to the touch – there was no mistaking it for what it was and once again it made me feel queasy.

The man left his place in the line and came up to speak to me a little more conspiratorially after seeing that I had indeed been telling the truth.

"Listen boy," he said quietly. The man smelt like onions and he was very clearly in need of a good bath. "You should not just go around announcing something like that, you know – some people might want to take what you have…"

"I know," I said, "I came here to sell it, actually. The doctor said…"

"The doctor told you to come here to sell that magic potion?" the man practically guffawed. "There ain't nobody around here who is going to pay you what those flasks are worth, I can tell you that for free!"

My heart sunk at that a little. I'd clearly been mistaken in coming here where I should've just looked out for the physicians and been done with it.

"Tell you what though boy, I have…" the man reached into his robes and his hand returned full of small copper coins. "Listen, I got four asses right here; you can have 'em if I can take a swig from the flask."

Honestly, I had no idea what these 'asses' were worth, though it sounded as though it was going to work out OK. The blood hadn't cost the doctor or me anything anyway, so what did it really matter if I returned with a little less than he'd expected.

What I didn't expect though, was that after the man had struck his own deal, everyone in the line then offered me *something* for a swig from the flask. It turned out by the end of a long session, that each flask contained about five 'swigs', and by the time each flask was totally empty, I had been given over a hundred of the small copper coins. Handily, someone had also given me a small pouch to keep them all in.

The baker was one of the people who had taken a swig from one of my flasks, so he had been kind enough to also give Dinari and me some of his delicious bread. I wondered what this kind of diet was going to do for the ever-ecstatic creature, though he seemed more than happy to hold the small loaf between his paws as he tore at it. Once it was too small for him to hold any more, he then placed it in the end of his mouth and carried it around with him proudly as though to show everyone what he had, though it was his own choice when he would decide to eat it.

We returned to the doctor once I was out and as I entered into the room,

I could tell that he'd been busy in my absence. The walls of the room we worked in were spattered with blood, along with the table, the floor and the doctor himself. Immediately I placed the flasks down onto the floor to fetch a bucket of water and a sponge to begin my cleaning.

"You made no sale then?" the doctor said as he watched me place the empty flasks down, and when I looked at them again in confusion, I could see that it was hard to tell that they weren't still full.

"What? No these are all empty," I explained quickly and the doctor walked over and picked them up one by one as though to test whether I had been lying.

"You… brought back the empty flasks? What did the physicians do with it all?" The doctor toyed with his beard as he spoke, as though he was deep in thought. "It does not matter, pass over the coins then," he ordered with an open palm.

I pulled the pouch out from inside my robes and handed it to the doctor. It was full and heavy and I saw the bemused look on the man's face as he opened it. He tipped the copper coins from hand to hand a few times before looking up at me with a smile.

"There are over one hundred asses here!" he announced looking even more confused. "That is more than six dinari. How did you get them to pay more than the value of the flasks?" He eyed me suspiciously although I could tell that he was happy about it.

"I… I did not sell it to the physicians… I sold it in the town centre, near the bakery," I replied honestly.

The doctor didn't say anything for a long while, all the time stroking his long white beard whilst looking down at the coins.

"And they had all that money?" he asked thoughtfully.

"Well, they are actually pretty poor people, so rather than sell them the whole flasks at a time, they gave me what they could for a 'swig'. It was not a lot, but I made everything that was in that pouch from them."

The doctor peered at me for a long moment before he spoke again. It seemed like this might actually have been the first time that he was looking for something about me, and then eventually he asked the thing I'd somehow been dreading:

"What is your name, boy?" he asked.

"Titus," I replied automatically without hesitation. Then added "Titus Cicero."

The doctor again peered at me for a long moment without saying a word. Both of us knew that it wasn't my real last name, though I'd said it and I was going to stick with it. It wasn't lost on either of us too, that when we'd first met I'd told the doctor that my family had owned Vettius – and I'd threatened the healer with the wrath of 'my father'. He didn't seem to want to bring up that little piece of incriminating evidence.

The doctor opened his mouth to speak, but at that moment, and possibly sensing the tension in the room, Dinari barked and wagged his entire body happily.

"And this is Dinari," I said with a grin, very happy for the diversion that the dog provided.

The doctor closed his mouth and sat back heavily into his chair in the corner of the room.

"You can call me Ovidius," he announced. "And you have done well on two counts today – first with your acumen in selling all of the blood in the flasks, and secondly because even though you received more money than I had asked for, you did not try to keep any of it. Honesty is the thing I cherish the most, so it is a good thing for you to remember, OK, Titus?"

I nodded and smiled. I knew I'd done well today and whilst I was on a roll, I began to clean the room from top to bottom once again.

VI – Canis Caninam Non Est.

"Dog does not eat dog."

I initially thought that with an income of a good five or six dinari every single day - when a soldier would receive just a fraction of that amount - Ovidius would've been a wealthy man. The thing was though, I didn't take into account the fact that battles in the arena only happened at most once per week, and sometimes even less than that. It made sense; in the capital, gladiators would be allowed to live after a battle well fought, but out here in Liternum, the naïveté of the crowds had led to a somewhat shortage of skilled fighters, as every time someone lost in the arena, they were generally killed in cold blood. In my entire time watching fights in the arena as the son of a Lanista, together with my few weeks working with the good doctor, I was yet to see a losing gladiator let live. Of course we tried to save the losers where we could, but generally as soon as the gladiator was laid onto our stone table, it was already too late.

This of course, was all going to change and I was going to make sure of it.

I listened to the roar of the crowds as the battle on the sands came to its conclusion. It'd gone on for so long that I wondered exactly how bad this next patient's injuries were going to be. I'd started to be able to anticipate the state of the gladiators based solely upon the length of the fights and the reactions of the crowds - and this one sounded as though it was going to be a bloody affair.

Sure enough, the arena hands dragged our next losing gladiator in and hoisted him up onto the table before us. The man was a Retiarius, though after the doctor had stripped him of his very light armour, he would've been no different to any other gladiator that we'd had on our table.

I was about to pick up the sponge to pass it to Ovidius, but as I stooped down to retrieve it, something caught my eye. The gladiator was bloodied and injured with bruises, cuts and stabs all over his body, but the blood didn't seem to be as free-flowing as I was used to seeing from our patients.

The man was thinner than the gladiators I was used to dealing with too – though that might've been the reason that he lost of course – but as I peered at his body in wonder, I could see that his chest was slowly and slightly rising and falling. The man was still alive.

"Wait!" I announced before Ovidius reached for the knife that I knew he was going to use to cut the man's neck. "Maybe we can save him?"

Ovidius spoke quickly without stopping, retrieving his knife still. "Listen boy, this man is going to die and he can either do it quickly, or slowly and painfully, I know which I would prefer".

I looked again at the man lying still on the table. There was definitely something different about him. He was covered in sand, dirt and dry blood, but when I looked closely, underneath all of the foreign detritus I could see the outline of something unusual. I leaned over the man and wiped his skin to reveal whatever it was under there, then eventually I made it out; there was a small caduceus painted onto the gladiator's skin in some sort of ink. The more I looked at it, the clearer it became. The winged symbol for Mercury had been very intently placed upon this gladiator and as I inspected it, the symbol shone bright blue before fading back to its previous grey-brown.

The gladiator coughed and spluttered and Ovidius raised his knife to the man's throat.

"Wait!" I called again. "I really think we can help him... can we try, just this once? If it doesn't work I will take his body out myself..." There was just something about this gladiator that intrigued me. I had the distinct feeling that I was *supposed* to help him, as if I had been placed in this very room at this very moment to ensure the survival of the mysterious gladiator.

Ovidius sighed and placed the knife back down on a table behind him. I noted that he purposefully kept it out of reach of the fallen gladiator, just in case he became disoriented and frenzied. I didn't blame him for it.

"Pass me the sponge then, quickly," Ovidius ordered. "I need to clean all of these wounds so that we know what we are to deal with."

I passed my mentor the sponge and he began to clean the wounds and cover them with a thick paste to keep them from opening back up and bleeding out. As I watched though, I could see that it was unnecessary – the wounds had already begun to close on their own and not a single one of them was still bleeding. Ovidius didn't say a word, but I could see in his furrowed brow that this was unexpected. To his credit though, he narrated his actions as he went, teaching me how and why he was doing the things he was doing, and I was grateful for that.

The gladiator was eventually cleaned and treated. He had no less than twenty wounds all over his body and most were deep. It was clear to both Ovidius and me, that this gladiator should've perished, though he seemed to have the fight in him to struggle on and that in itself gave me hope and a kind of warmth that was apparently borne from helping another human being in need. I wondered if this was the feeling that Ovidius had experienced when he'd saved me from the hands of the legionary when we'd first met. The one thing I knew, though, was that I wanted to feel this feeling again and again.

The gladiator slept on the table and Ovidius sat in his chair with an air of mild disinterest about him. I could tell that he wasn't used to helping a losing gladiator back to life, though there was something else too. The way that the man's wounds had started to heal already, and the way that he clung onto life I knew was something very different to what Ovidius was used to, and it made me think about the glowing symbol that I'd seen adorning the man's skin. Then something hit me.

Sitting on the floor with Dinari by my side, who was panting heavily, I began to scratch the back of the dog's neck, moving his fur about. I knew I'd seen the symbol on here somewhere before but I wasn't entirely sure when, or where. I had been so positive that I knew every inch of the dog, that it had entirely slipped my mind – and there it was. Just behind Dinari's right ear was the very same symbol, only much smaller, though the winged figure was clear. I could only think of one thing; this had been drawn onto the dog somehow when he was younger – there was absolutely no way that this was a natural phenomenon.

Dinari looked up at me once I ruffled his fur back into position. The look in his eyes was somehow knowing and he kind of frowned at me as though this was all a huge conspiracy that nobody needed to know anything about. The dog was just so expressive and usually I didn't think very much of it, but this time I saw something a little more. The situation was just too specific and coincidental for all this to mean nothing and inside I knew that I needed to speak to this gladiator, to ask him exactly what any of this meant. What I didn't need though, was for Ovidius to listen in to our conversation - there were still some secrets that I needed to keep to myself.

Thankfully, Ovidius didn't sleep in the cold, dark and bloodstained room. I didn't know why that fact surprised me, though it did make sense on reflection. The doctor eventually left the place as the sun started to set, and he made a point of telling me to sleep in one of the other rooms within the pen this night, closing the iron doors as I moved about so that there was no way that this gladiator might've caused me any harm if he saw fit to. I didn't object, it sounded like a very good idea to me.

I took Dinari into the next room and pulled the iron gate closed, locking it behind me. Thankfully, this room was lined on its perimeter with stone and wooden benches, so it had a more comfortable feel to it than the stone floors I'd slept on, on more than one occasion.

I'd been sleeping inside the holding area for weeks with the permission of Ovidius, though he never stayed with me, leaving me alone each night to cuddle up with Dinari to share our warmth. Ovidius did, however, find us a pair of blankets to sleep underneath in case it became too cold, though thus far in the summer I'd simply been using them as pillows and Dinari had slept atop my legs.

I liked sleeping on the floor actually, and once I'd become used to it after a few days I felt as though I would have trouble sleeping anywhere else. My posture remained straight, and my body heat that warmed the stone floor remained beneath me at a constant temperature for a long while. It took just a few days before I realised that any pains and aches that the floor had caused me were simply distant memories.

I stayed awake for as long as I could once I'd positioned myself on a wooden bench that overlooked the doctor's room and the resting gladiator on the centre table. He didn't seem to be moving at all, although I knew that he could've been faking sleep, waiting for me to drift off. Inevitably though, slumber took me.

I was awoken a short while later by the sound of the iron gates to my makeshift bedroom being rattled lightly and I was shocked to see the gladiator up on his feet and looking well, trying to figure out why he had been imprisoned in such a way. A cursory glance of him showed no signs of the cuts, bruises or the other injuries that I knew he'd sustained in his arena battle. It was still dark outside though, so I supposed that the faint torchlight that illuminated his body could've been masking some of them.

"Are you here to make sure I don't escape?" the gladiator asked in a heavily accented and deep voice, which made me jump.

"Uh... no, I live here," I replied curtly. I wasn't expecting to have a conversation with the man, though I could see how he would've been disoriented.

"Your wounds, from the arena... what happened?" I asked.

"They were not that bad," the gladiator replied a little too nonchalantly for my liking. "More like scratches than actual wounds I should say. Looks like your doctor did a good job at patching me up anyway…" the gladiator appraised himself and his lack of wounds. I knew better than to fall for that though.

"You… you were going to die… they were so bad…" I said slowly. Then, remembering what I'd seen on the man, I pointed to where the glowing symbol had been. "And I saw the thing there on your chest, the symbol? It was glowing and…"

The gladiator interrupted me before I could finish my sentence. "You did not see anything little one; now I suggest you let me out of here so I can be on my way."

The statement and how forcefully it'd been delivered made me stutter for a moment. I hadn't been expecting our conversation to be over so abruptly, but it did reaffirm to me what I'd seen – there was certainly *something* about that symbol and the way that it had glowed and it was something that this man wanted to conceal from me.

"I… sorry, I did not mean to offend you," I said quietly. "The doctor said you need to get some rest to heal properly…" I tried to change the subject to put the gladiator at ease, but he was having none of it.

"Listen," he said with a sigh. "I really need to get something to eat, so if you would just open the gate I can get going, OK?"

I thought about it for a moment, but really I couldn't be sure if this man was going to cause me any harm or not. Internally I decided to try to steer the conversation back around to the symbol that was upon his skin, but when I looked for it now, it was nowhere to be seen.

I called Dinari to my side with a tap on my thigh before I said anything else to the gladiator and the dog dutifully bounded over to me and rested his chin on my leg. Reaching down I began to ruffle Dinari's fur behind his ear where I knew the symbol lay upon his own skin.

"Listen boy…" the gladiator began speaking again when he was certain that I wasn't going to let him out, but he abruptly stopped when he saw what I had revealed on Dinari's exposed skin. The very same symbol that the gladiator had had on his own skin was present and clear on my best friend.

"What is this…?" The gladiator asked quietly and with a sense of wonderment. "It… cannot be, can it?"

"So you know something about this?" I asked. "It is the same as yours, is it not?"

"Did you draw this, boy? The detail, I must say is very good, though I fear that it will have no use without the skills provided by those of a magical Sigilarius," The gladiator asked, though I had no idea what he was talking about.

"The… A Sigilarius? And no… I did not draw this symbol, I think he was born with it or something," I replied. I had no other explanation for the mark, though by the gladiator's expression I could tell that he thought that it was unlikely.

The gladiator then did something that made me jump back in surprise. He pushed his hands through the iron bars of the gate and took a hold of Dinari's fur. I was worried at first, though the dog didn't seem at all flustered, and the man's touch was gentle, not forceful. He stroked Dinari's fur, who in turn purred like a cat and moved his entire body so that he was pressed against the gate, allowing the gladiator to rub him and pat him all over.

"How old is this dog?" The man asked eventually.

"Uh… he is one year old, I think," I replied. I couldn't see why that would make any difference, though the gladiator offered nothing further on the subject.

The gladiator then spoke nonchalantly, "The symbol that I wore upon my body… is one of protection. It is there to ensure a longer life to any who bear it. I suspect that your friend here was given it for the very same reason, though I am sure that where my marking was temporary, his has been permanently tattooed onto him, meaning that it will never wash off."

I looked at my four-legged friend a little more intently than I had been used to. When I had been given the dog as my birthday present I had just been so overwhelmed with joy that I hadn't even thought about where he had come from. I couldn't remember the first time I'd seen the marking on his skin, though it made me wonder if this was something that my father knew about – possibly even making the mark himself – or if the animal had arrived with it already on him.

"What is a Sigilarius?" I asked eventually, circling back around to the unfamiliar word that the gladiator had used when I had run dry on ideas of Dinari's past.

The gladiator didn't answer my question though. Instead, he indicated to the iron gate and said: "If you let me out of here, I will tell you everything that you need to know about Sigilarii, sigils and the one on your dog… uh, what is his name?" he asked.

"Dinari," I replied curtly.

"Dinarius," the gladiator replied. "You have many dinari and one denarius."

"No, that is just his name," I objected. "I do not really know too much about money and stuff, I just liked it. Besides, it suits him, does it not?"

The gladiator looked down at the dog's smiling face and as he made eye contact with Dinari, the ever-pleased animal began to wag his tail so hard again that his entire body wagged from side to side. It always made me smile when he was happy.

"So…" the gladiator asked, gesturing to the gate once more. "Do not worry, I'm not going to kill you or anything."

Some things just didn't need to be said though, and when they were, it just made the entire situation uncomfortable.

I thought about it for a long moment, then slid the bolt back and out of its housing in the wall that kept the gate locked in place. It clanged loudly and my heart skipped a beat as the man slowly walked through the opening that the gate now afforded, then stooped down and began to rub Dinari all over. Dinari fell over and onto his back so that his new best friend could get to his undercarriage for those all-too-important tummy rubs, and he wriggled his body back and forth. After a moment, the dog let out a half moan, half growl to signify the fact that he was having the time of his life.

The gladiator looked up at me from his crouched stance. "My name is Ludo, and I am a gladiator… By the way, what have you been feeding him?" he gestured to Dinari with an inquisitive look on his face.

"Uhh… bread," I answered honestly, though when I said the words aloud, I somehow knew that I should've been embarrassed at the fact.

Ludo looked up at me and laughed. "You cannot just feed a growing dog bread! He needs meat! Tell you what, once the sun comes up I shall take you down to the river and show you how to fish. I think he would like that."

Dinari jumped up onto Ludo's bent knees and licked the gladiator's face. It seemed like this was a very acceptable idea to the dog.

"So… the sigils… and the Sigilarii?" I asked the leading question.

"Right," Ludo replied and stood to his full height. He was much, much taller than me and without the dirt, sand and blood covering his body, I could see that I had been correct in my first assessment; he was rather slight for a gladiator.

"So a sigil is a magical symbol that contains a great amount of power. They are a direct link to the Gods that created them, and the sigil themselves share in the power of that deity. A Sigilarius is someone skilled in the art of creating these sigils."

I scoffed audibly. I knew that magic and Gods and the like were all make-believe and I wondered why exactly the gladiator would try to insult me so obviously.

"You do not believe me?" Ludo said with a knowing smirk. Come and have a look at this. He moved back toward the stone table in the healer's room and sat on the edge so that there was space next to him for me to sit. I didn't take the implied offer though. Eventually, he patted the stone table and somehow the gesture made me automatically move to sit next to him. Then, Ludo pulled a short wooden stick from his loin cloth. I could see that it had been sharpened to a dull point, and he dipped the end into a small pool of blood that was yet to dry on the table and began to draw on his exposed thigh.

The movements he made as he drew were expert, as though he'd drawn the symbol a thousand times before. Almost immediately I could tell that it was the same caduceus that I'd seen upon his skin before, but I kept quiet as he worked. He dipped the makeshift pen into the wet blood a few more times before he was finished, and when the drawing was complete, it looked as perfect as I could've ever imagined.

"This is a sigil," Ludo explained. "The power within this very symbol is linked to Mercury himself and affords whoever wears it the ability to heal from their wounds at an accelerated rate. From what I understand, there are other sigils that borrow of the power of Mercury, though I am afraid I am unaware of their forms."

I looked closely at the sigil as Ludo spoke, still not entirely on board, then I saw it: the sigil glowed a shimmering bright blue for just a moment, then faded back to its previous red-brown bloody hue.

"So… this is the symbol for Mercury then?" I asked still not entirely sure if I was being conned or not.

"No, as I said, this is one of the sigils that link to the power of Mercury. There are others that link to his power in differing ways, but this is the one that is most important to us right now. The caduceus sigil affords long life and advanced healing to its wearer – you must understand how important that can be to a gladiator?" Ludo explained. "It is said that if you do ever find sigils that link to other Gods, it is important not to utilise them all at the same time, as the results can be somewhat deadly."

"Do you know all of them?" I asked, now very interested in the conversation.

Ludo looked at me sternly before he spoke again, though when he did, I could tell that he was a little more upset with himself than he was by the question. "I have been searching for a long time… yet I am still unable to discover any additional sigils than that of the caduceus of Mercury. I fight in the arena in the hope that one day I will find the tell-tale glow of the magic of the Gods, though that trial has been fruitless to this day."

"So the one on Dinari here, that is the first time you've seen one of these sigils on anyone else?" I asked. Dinari raised his head from his paws and wagged his tail at my mention of his name. I smiled at him and he lay back down.

"Well yes, other than the person who taught me how to draw the sigil that is. The secrets of channelling the power of the Gods are very well guarded of course, though I had the feeling that if I was going to find any traces of it anywhere, it would be upon the skin of gladiators."

"I have seen one before," I said hopefully in an attempt to raise Ludo's spirits, then realised what I had just said. The gladiator's head snapped about to face me and his eyes looked as though they were trying to see directly into my soul.

"What did you see boy?" he asked almost urgently. "And what effect did the sigil have?"

I was shocked at Ludo's new gait, though after a moment the intensity left him and he allowed me to speak freely.

"It was… it was on a gladiator a short while ago. I never saw what it was, I just think I saw the glow underneath his armour… he survived blows that I didn't think was possible and he moved so quickly that he could defend himself where I did not think it would be possible…" I explained slowly, trying to remember all of the details of Vettius' fight in the arena.

Ludo visibly relaxed, though I couldn't tell if it was because he'd been worried, or if it was because this was not the information that he'd been searching for.

"Mercury is," he began to explain, "well known as the messenger to the Gods. His speed and agility are what makes him so powerful, so I would guess that what you saw in the arena were also the effects of Mercury, and not those of another God's powers."

"So one of the Gods can give a gladiator more than one power? And what about the other ones?" I asked intently.

"There are many things that I myself do not know," Ludo admitted. "Though what I do know is that the Gods do not always play so nice with each other, so generally speaking I have been told that it is not wise to mix the powers of the Gods on one body."

"Can you teach me?" I asked slowly after a moment of pondering.

Ludo simply laughed. "I just know the one sigil – and yes I can teach you how to make it, though it is not very easy and it will take you some time to master. First though, I think we will have to go get your animal some fish, he looks like he sorely needs it!"

Dinari barked loudly and jumped up at my legs. I guessed there was no arguing with that.

VII – Omnium Rerum Principia Parva Sunt.

"The beginnings of all things are small."

Ludo had kept his promises to me on both fronts by the time the next day was over. I hadn't seen Ovidius at all, though I thought that perhaps it was a good thing as Ludo had taken me away from the gladiator holding pen and out to the river, where he was to teach me how to catch fish effectively with a net. I was actually pretty good at it after a while and a few castings, and when we returned to my makeshift home adjoining the arena, we had caught a handful of the fish in the river.

Dinari was particularly excited about what we had achieved in the morning: he practically bounced the short distance back home, leaping just behind the fish that I carried as though he knew it was good to want them but definitely a bad idea to try to eat them before they were cooked. Having never cooked anything for myself before, I was once again at the mercy of the gladiator who seemed to know, well, pretty much everything I wanted to know about everything.

Ludo, the font of knowledge that he was, then taught me how to light a fire with a small knife and a piece of flint. He'd arranged some dry kindling and logs inside a small stone circle on the floor in the room that I'd used as my bedroom the previous night – presumably he didn't want to actually cook in the room that was generally covered in blood – and had a blazing fire going in no time. Then he skewered a few of the fish and propped them up over the fire, turning them occasionally so that they would cook evenly. Dinari made growling and whining noises as the fish cooked, and I was half expecting him to just steal them from atop the fire by the amount of fuss he was making, though he remained in place, his anticipation palpable.

The fish was delicious. It was the first hot meal that I'd had in a long while and I could tell that Dinari was thankful for it too. By the time it was all gone, it was obvious that not one of the three of us could've eaten another bite.

"You said you would show me how to make the sigil?" I half asked – half pointed out once we had finished our meal and I still had a little fish in my mouth. I knew I was asking a lot of the man but, well, he'd offered so I wasn't really doing anything wrong.

Ludo looked at me with a fair amount of wonder in his eyes. It made me think that he was just going to tell me 'no', or that I was too young for all of this, but to my surprise he retrieved the pointed stick that he had used as a pencil previously and ushered me to follow him back to the healer's room. I knew he was after some blood to use as ink, and this time he was going to have to find what he could from the few remaining nooks and crannies that had collected small pools, all the rest having dried by now.

Ludo then proceeded to draw on the ground the symbol that I already knew. Again, his motion was faultless as though he'd carried out the action a thousand times. Each stroke he made was filled with both purpose and confidence and a big part of me thought that I would never be able to be that accurate. Once Ludo had finished, the symbol did not glow as it had done before - rather it did absolutely nothing. Then, he handed me his makeshift pencil and announced that it was my turn to try.

Admittedly, I did a pretty poor job. A combination of the fact that I'd seldom actually held a writing or drawing utensil, my obvious unfamiliarity with the symbol itself, and my lack of confidence led to my drawing of the sigil being lop-sided, completely out of proportion, and in some cases even broken where I'd failed to recharge the pencil with fresh blood as it had dried. All in all, my sigil next to Ludo's, was not even a comparison.

Ludo looked down at the drawing that I'd made and I could see that he wanted to laugh, though he managed to hold it in.

"That... is not what we are drawing," he said eventually. "And in this case, I would not be surprised if this drawing would draw the anger of the Gods, being a little bit insulting I would say."

I quickly rubbed at the floor to remove the drawing lest Ludo was actually being serious. I'd already had enough bad fortune in my life, I didn't need any more.

"You must practise this art over and over. Only when the sigil is perfect can it channel the full might of the Gods." Ludo explained.

I heard something in that: "So, if the sigil is a little bit wrong, it can channel a smaller amount of power?" I asked.

"Yes," the gladiator confirmed. "A perfect sigil is best to gain as much power from the Gods as possible, but an imperfect sigil will gain an imperfect amount of power. Be warned though, there is a line of quality that when crossed, can result in negative effects."

That certainly sounded like something I didn't want to experience. It sounded though that all I needed to do was to practise, and to the point that I was damn sure I was going to get it right every single time.

Practise was going to be difficult though. I couldn't just go and buy a book to fill with my scribbling. I didn't have the money to just waste on such frivolous activities. In the back of my mind though I knew that I still had the two books that I'd rescued from my burning home, although they were not something that I wanted to deface, and were half-burned to ash as it was. I could buy singular unbound sheets of papyrus, but again, the thought of spending money on anything other than food and drink for myself and Dinari didn't seem the smartest thing to do, especially when I had a perfectly good canvas and ink right here in my new home. It was going to be morbid, but at least it was free.

"I am going to be leaving you today," Ludo said abruptly to interrupt my pondering. "I am to fight in the arenas to the north, before making my way to the arenas of the capital so that people may learn of my name and strength."

This made me think about the circumstances in which we'd met – the gladiator had lost his fight and was close to death. I certainly didn't think he'd have much of a chance against any really skilled opponents in the capital. Keeping my silence though, I simply nodded.

"I expect you to practise this sigil until you can draw it perfectly every single time. When we meet again, you can show me just how much of an expert you are."

Ludo left shortly after that. He bade both me and Dinari a fond farewell, though he paid the dog a lot more attention than he had me. He held the dog's face in his hands and told him to 'look after the boy', though judging by the fact that Dinari rolled onto his back to expose his tummy, I wasn't sure if he had actually received the message or not.

I was alone again for the rest of the day. Again there were no arena fights planned, so Ovidius was nowhere to be seen. It was quiet in the holding pen, and it gave me the time that I needed to start the practise of my new art.

The first ten times I drew the sigil on the ground with Ludo's stylus he had left for me resulted in similar atrocities that I had created with my first attempt. It was almost unrecognisable actually and I knew that I needed to do better. I knew that practise would make perfect, but each time I drew the sigil, I just couldn't see any improvement in it.

Changing my approach somewhat, I decided to concentrate on small parts of the sigil rather than trying to draw it all in one go. It actually made things a little easier and after a few attempts at just one small portion of the drawing, I could tell that it was becoming easier to draw. I didn't know if this was the normal way in which artists learned their craft, but it didn't really matter to me; if I could do this for all of the parts of the sigil, then eventually I knew that I'd be able to combine them.

When Ovidius returned the next day, he was surprised to note that Ludo had disappeared from the table.

"Die did he?" Ovidius asked as he walked into the room that I had been using as my bedroom in his absence.

The statement confused me a little at first, though I then realised what he was asking.

"N... no," I replied. "He just got better, and left."

Ovidius eyed me for a moment as though I was telling him a lie. "The wounds on that gladiator, boy, would have taken weeks to fully heal. He should have been on that table for days, unable to move... and you are telling me that he just got up and walked out of here?"

I nodded, then raised myself off of the bench I was sitting on to my feet. "He looked fine actually, maybe the wounds were not as bad as you thought they were?"

The doctor's face went slightly red at my question. "Do you not think that I have seen enough injuries and wounds in my days? Do you not think that I would know how long wounds such as those on that gladiator take to heal?"

I could hear the anger in his voice and I wanted more than anything to make it stop.

"No of course not!" I protested, "I am just telling you what happened – he just got up and left!"

"Did you not lock the gate?" Ovidius asked incredulously. Was it by some divine intervention that a locked gate opened itself to let through this unfathomable gladiator with the power to heal mortal wounds in a matter of days?"

I knew I had to tell the truth to the man who'd shown me many kindnesses, so that is exactly what I did – well, to an extent of course.

"I let him out," I said in a very small voice, hanging my head in shame. "He said he was fine and needed to go, so I opened the gate for him..."

Ovidius seemed to go even redder at that statement and I could see that he was ready to shout at me. Then, he inhaled and let out his breath very slowly before taking a knee to reduce himself to my own height.

"Do you know how dangerous that could have been for you boy? He could have killed you, or even worse he may have chosen to take you with him as a slave. Not everybody in this world is as they seem, and it only takes one wrong decision on your part to illuminate that fact. You must promise me Titus… that you will never be so reckless again, and when I tell you to do something, you do it, OK?"

I nodded silently again, feeling not a small amount of shame at my actions, though truth be told, if I hadn't done what I had done, I would never have learnt about the sigils, their meaning or their power.

Over the next month, I kept my practise secret and away from Ovidius. I had a suspicion that he knew more than he let on about the whole sigil thing, but I figured that if he did, and didn't want to impart that knowledge to me, then he must've had a good reason not to. I certainly didn't want to push it.

It had taken an entire month of drawing each section of Mercury's caduceus over and over until I thought that I had finally nailed it. I was ready to connect the five parts of the sigil that I'd broken it down into to see if I was indeed correct in my assumptions.

Over the month, I had been working with Ovidius and learning more and more about his trade and by all accounts, things were beginning to sink in. When a gladiator arrived with wounds covering his body, regardless of whether he'd won or lost, I looked them over and tried to determine if Ovidius was going to reach for the knife, or the healing paste. On some occasions, I'd even been so sure of the result that I'd passed the doctor either of the implements before he'd even asked for them.

Thankfully too, the doctor had a tendency to narrate to me what he was doing as he was doing it and it was a very helpful experience for me. He described the wounds as he treated them and told me how deep they were, what had caused them, how he was treating them and how long they would take to heal. I learned about infections, fevers, cuts, bruises, breaks and everything else that gladiators had to endure as a part of their trade, and I learned eagerly.

What I never saw though, was another glowing sigil on any of the gladiators that entered our healing room. It made me wonder just how rare these Sigilarii could've been.

I was ready to become one though. I knew that if I could simply join all of these parts of the sigil, I would be able to recreate it over and over, and I wondered at the possibilities that the healing symbol could provide to our injured gladiators. There were so many occasions when I'd wished we could've done more for a defeated gladiator, but every single time when it looked as though things were going to end badly, Ovidius had drawn his knife and taken the man's life. Thankfully, that was not something that he'd ever tasked me with.

The blood that the fallen gladiators provided though, kept us in enough coin to eat, drink and live. Of course, Ovidius took the lion's share of the money, though he had been giving me a small amount of the copper coins that I kept receiving by selling the gladiator blood in small batches to the poorer citizens of Liternum. He said that as it was my idea it was only fair. I didn't object.

My mind was set on my latest task though - the sigil that I'd drawn on the floor with blood and a stick in secret once Ovidius had left for the day. I drew each part individually as I'd practised, though as I'd finished each section I moved onto the next. I could see that it was working, everything was coming together and my sigil was looking as though it was *exactly* the same as the one that Ludo had drawn, and the one that sat upon Dinari's neck. Then finally it was finished and I let out a sigh of relief.

The sigil burned with bright blue energy as it was completed, much, much brighter than anything I'd ever seen before. It was so bright in fact, that I was momentarily blinded by it and instinctually, I closed my eyes tightly so that the offensive light didn't render me blind.

Then, I sensed that the light was gone, and slowly I opened my eyes again. My mouth hung agape at the sight that hit me once I'd returned to my senses. I was outside, in a long apple orchard that seemed to go on as far as the eye could see in all directions. It was warm and sunny, and when I looked to my side, Dinari was looking up at me inquisitively as though he had no idea what had just happened either.

"Hello, Titus," a booming voice filled my entire being, though I had no idea where it was coming from.

"H… hello?" I stammered.

VIII – Permitte Divis Cetera.

"Leave all else to the Gods."

Eventually, I felt a presence behind me, and turning quickly I was greeted by the sight of something I'd never expected to see, even in my wildest dreams. The man standing before me was unlike anything that I'd ever seen before and had possibly even expected of a God. I knew that Gods were powerful beings, though personifying or visualising them was not something that I could claim I had ever really done. Growing up, my family had respected the Gods, even worshipped them to some extents, but as they were not an actual physical, or even tangible presence, I believed that they were most probably not real. This man though, was very real indeed.

The being that stood before me was no shorter than ten feet tall, wearing a flowing, bright white toga and a rimmed, metal hat. On his feet I could see that his sandals were flanked by solid golden wings. There was no mistaking it - this man was indeed the God Mercury.

"Greetings, Titus. I am Mercury, messenger to the Gods and guide of all lost souls to the underworld." The God's voice was loud, confident and clear and it gave me goosebumps as he spoke. I really hadn't needed the introduction, and I believed each and every word that he spoke.

"I have been watching you, Titus," Mercury continued after I said nothing in return. I was awestruck and no matter how hard I tried, no words would leave my lips.

"Do you not have anything to say to your revered God, Titus?" Mercury asked after a short moment of silence.

I stuttered for a moment, then said the only thing that came to my mind when speaking with an omnipotent, all-powerful being. "Do you know what happened to my parents? Do you know who did it?"

Mercury was silent for a second as though he hadn't been expecting the question.

"I did indeed see what happened to your parents, Titus," the God eventually replied. "Though I do not know why this happened, or who it was that made the command. Do you understand my words, Titus?"

I did think that it was a strange question to ask, though I nodded silently. I looked up at the God's face and stared into his bright blue eyes as I asked my next questions:

"Where am I? And how did I get here? Am I dead? Are my parents here...?"

"Slow yourself down, Titus," Mercury commanded and held out a flat palm to stop me in my spiralling. "You are not dead but I can see how you might think that, given that I am responsible for taking souls to the afterlife. On this occasion though our meeting is more pleasure than business."

"I… don't understand," I said, scrunching my nose up. "Do you want to play with Dinari?"

The dog leapt up and bounced over with a huge grin plastered onto his face at the idea of play time. Mercury simply held out his hand for the dog to inspect, then Dinari obediently sat back down at my side.

"You have finally been able to open a pathway to my power. I must say that I am impressed with the effort and respect that you have placed into your art. It has been a long time since anyone endeavoured to draw my sigil of healing with such care and precision, and I thank you for that."

If I didn't know any better, I would've said that Mercury seemed a little upset at that statement.

"So… what happens now?" I asked. "Do I have to pray to you to give my sigil its power or something?"

Mercury laughed heartily. The sound was so loud though that I had to cover my ears with my hands to save my eardrums from perforating.

"No my son! I do not meet with every human who learns to draw my sigil. As I have said, I have been watching you for some time. Both of you," he gestured to Dinari, who wagged his tail.

There was still something that I was missing in all of this.

"Why me?" I asked.

"Why you?" Mercury repeated. "Because, Titus, I believe that you are the first person to ever want to use the skill that you have learnt to help others, rather than to seek glory for yourself in the arena. That is, of course, except for your father, who similarly did not want this power for himself, but for others.

"My… father?" I asked slowly. Then I looked down at Dinari and saw that the sigil that lay upon his skin was glowing.

"Your father," the God confirmed, "is the one who gave your dog his mark. He wanted you to be free of the pain of losing a beloved companion, although that would seem somewhat tame compared to how the events of the recent past have occurred."

I nodded again. At the mention of my father, I seemed unable to speak again, a large lump forming in my throat.

"Now that you have the ability to open my power to others, I must ask you to be very careful who you impart this blessing upon. It is also important that my power is not abused, or the consequences, I assure you, will be quite deadly."

It sounded to me as though Mercury already knew what I was planning to do with this sigil, but in truth I had no idea. It was one thing to gain the ability to draw it properly, it was another entirely knowing how I was actually going to use that knowledge.

The God seemed to know what I was thinking and spoke to reassure me. "You do not plan to use this sigil of power on yourself, do you?" he asked.

I shook my head. There was no way I thought I'd ever be fighting in the arena.

"Then it stands to reason that, unlike the others, it is your intent to draw this sigil upon others so that they may gain both power and protection as they battle?"

I thought about that, then nodded slowly. If I truly did want to dedicate my life to helping people, then this was going to be a great way to achieve that.

"In that case, I must tell you more about these sigils, and how they will aid you on your journey. There are twelve Gods that all have their own sigils: some only have one or two, but others have up to four. These sigils will impart different powers onto the ones upon whom they are drawn, for instance, my caduceus as you know imparts health to the bearer."

"You have more sigils?" I asked quickly, though I felt somewhat embarrassed at the sound of my urgency.

"I have three, actually," Mercury replied with a smile. Though I will not share with you what they are just yet. You must prove yourself worthy, and they will become known to you in the fullness of time."

"But what do they do?" I asked, almost pleading for more information.

"I see no harm in telling you this information. As you know, my caduceus sigil will impart the bearer with divine healing."

I nodded.

"The other two sigils that represent my power, give the bearer access to divine perception, and divine speed respectively, for these are the powers that I possess."

I thought about that information for a long while. Had Vettius had access to these powers? It certainly seemed as though his speed and perception were above that of a normal being.

My pondering was cut short though, as Mercury spoke again. "I must warn you though, that once a man has been adorned with the power of the Gods, he will be unable to call upon the power of any of the other Gods in his sigils. This means that if you were to draw my sigil upon yourself, your blood will be marked, and if you were ever to learn of any of the sigils of the other Gods, you would be unable to use them to aid others. It is only one with pure blood who can call upon the power of *all* the Gods."

I scrunched my nose at that statement. "What does that mean?" I asked, not quite grasping the concept.

"Titus, my boy. All you need to know, is that you are to never draw a sigil upon yourself for all the time you wish to aid others. Is that clearer?" Mercury asked.

"Not really," I said. "But I will not draw on myself, if that solves anything – besides I do not wish to fight in the arena anyway."

"That is all I ask, for now," the God replied. "Though a warning: the Gods will not always have your best interests to heart. Some may try to deceive you, others may attempt to weaken you. You must trust your instincts in all things, and above all, try your best to do good at all times."

I was about to agree with Mercury and tell him that I would do as he asked, but as I blinked, the world around me disappeared and I was suddenly back in the gladiator holding pen, looking down at the sigil which had now stopped glowing, with Dinari by my side who I was sure was blinking over and over as though he didn't believe what he was seeing either.

I inspected the sigil for a long while before I concluded that what I had seen was indeed real and had actually happened.

"Well Dinari," I said as I looked down at the dog, who in turn opened his mouth and breathed at me loudly. His breath smelled strongly of fish and it made me scrunch my nose. "I think we are going to have a lot of work to do the next time the arena has a fight on. And then I went to bed. It had been a long day and I simply needed to take the time to arrange all of my thoughts into neat lines so that I could tackle each issue one by one. The largest issue though, was just how I was going to discover the rest of the sigils, which by all accounts could be anything between twenty and about fifty, if I had understood what Mercury had told me correctly.

"Wake up, boy!" I never got tired of hearing Ovidius' voice first thing in the morning. I knew what it meant: that today was a day for the arena to be filled with crowds and the spectacle of gladiators fighting to the death upon its sands. I had already cleaned the entirety of the healing room, although if we wanted to make any coin for the day, the cleanliness of the room was going to have to be tested.

I eagerly anticipated the arrival of the gladiators into the preparation rooms that adjoined the healing room and my makeshift bedroom, but as I thought about the sigil and its power, I wondered how exactly I was going to convince any of the gladiators therein to let me draw on them. Plus, how could I be sure which ones deserved the help? And besides, who was I really, to be able to decide who should live or die; was that something that a mere mortal such as I should be able to deliberate upon?

The answer that I arrived at, was 'no'. I should not be able to decide these things. My job was to help one and all and to not pass judgement as to who deserved that help and who didn't.

I resigned myself to the fact that the gladiators that were preparing for their fights would almost definitely not allow me to interrupt their preparations. Instead, I decided that a way to impart the power that Mercury himself had bestowed upon me, was to wait until I saw some dire injury received in the arena, that I would be able to heal with the sigil – well, try to at least. That way I would not affect the outcome of a fight, just one gladiator's fight for survival.

It was the first time that I'd ever built up the courage to do so, but as the first pair of gladiators walked along the tunnel and up to the iron gates of the arena, I followed them at a short distance behind, and when they walked out onto the burning summer sands, I clasped my hands around the hot iron of the closed gates, ready to watch the fight in real-time.

The arena announcer did his thing and his voice carried for all to hear.

"For our first showing on this sweltering day, to cool you down and provide entertainment worthy of the Gods, I offer to you, Deus! The mighty Retiarius!"

As always, the crowd cheered for the gladiator who held net and trident above his head, basking in their applause.

"And facing him on the sands today, the bane of every Retiarius in the land, a Secutor who needs no introduction - the bringer of destruction, the breaker of tridents: Renatus!"

The name sounded familiar to me, and the crowd around the arena erupted into a cacophony of noise that I never thought possible of human beings. I watched the gladiator, with his heavy armour, large wooden shield and short gladius, bask in the crowds adoration. He was clearly the crowd's favourite and it sounded, by his titles and introduction, as though he enjoyed some level of fame.

The fight began quickly, with the Retiarius backing away as quickly as he could from his opponent. I knew that Secutors had been trained specifically in defeating Retiarii, and combined with the fact that this particular Secutor knew what he was doing, I held little hope for the Retiarius in this battle.

Essentially, the Secutor moved to close the distance between the gladiators as quickly as possible. I was well aware that in this type of fight, the standard was for the Retiarius to keep away from the Secutor for as long as possible, so the heavy armour combined with a helmet that made breathing a little more difficult than usual for the Secutor would eventually tilt the scales of fortune into the Retiarius' favour. This was exactly what the Retiarius was trying to achieve.

However, the Secutor, named Renatus, was apparently familiar with this basic technique. Moving in quickly and chasing his opponent until the edge of the sands grew near, Renatus was unyielding in his attacks, and with no choice but to fight back, the Retiarius dug his heels in and began to strike with his spear at the exposed helmet and shins of his opponent, the large wooden shield between them unable to cover everything.

Again, Renatus knew how to deal with the attacks and moved his shield quickly and expertly to deflect the trident as it came at him. I knew though that unless one of them saw an opening soon fatigue would endanger them both.

The Retiarius, was the unfortunate gladiator to blink first. He hefted his trident at the face of Renatus, who in turn raised his shield with such force that the trident flew out of the attacker's hand and fell to the ground with a loud clang. The cheer from the crowd at the parry was deafening.

The Retiarius then drew a short dagger from his side and held it as though it was a sword. This weapon, along with his net as his only means of attack, would pale in comparison to the gladius and shield that Renatus held in each of his hands.

The Retiarius then did something that nobody had been expecting: he leapt high into the air and directly *towards* his opponent. His feet impacted the Secutor's shield and the gladiator both leapt and was thrust high into the air as Renatus deflected his wild attack. To my absolute surprise as well as that of the crowd's, the Retiarius landed next to his own trident, picking up the weapon as he rolled next to it on the ground. My mouth hung agape at the skill that was on display.

As the fights in the arena were just so more *intense* when viewed from ground level, combined with the unexpected skill of this gladiator, I found myself lost in the event.

The Secutor then turned just in time to see the trident thrust at him again and again though each time he managed to parry the weapon that he'd previously thought was done with. The strikes were strong and straight at Renatus' covered face, though I suspected that the attacks would've been killing blows if even one of them had made it through his guard.

Renatus then let out a terrible roar and dropped his gladius to the ground with a metallic clatter. I tried to see if he had been hurt, but it was immediately apparent that he had dropped the weapon on purpose as when the Retiarius attacked next, the Secutor grabbed a hold of the trident and pulled his opponent into a hard, straight kick to the stomach. The Retiarius doubled over, clearly winded by the blow. I waited for Renatus to deliver the killing blow.

It didn't come.

It made me wonder how a gladiator could toy with his opponent for the enjoyment of the crowds, and this man certainly knew how to work the citizens of Liternum. They cheered his name over and over, and each time a blow struck his opponent, they cheered even louder no matter the damage it caused. I came to realise very quickly that this match was much more of a pantomime than a simple fight to the death.

The Retiarius regained his footing, though again he was without his trident. Somehow he'd managed to hold onto his net, and at that moment he seemed to realise that fact too. He swung the net around his head as though it were a lasso and feinted menacingly at the Secutor, who didn't seem to care in the slightest. If anything, the armoured gladiator looked as though he *wanted* his opponent to give up his last weapon, trident and dagger already lost to the sands.

Then the Retiarius threw his net. it sailed through the air, bridging the distance between the two men in an instant and Renatus didn't look as though he was going to move. The net struck the Secutor's shield and the crowd held their collective breath. Renatus then *dropped* his shield along with the net and the noise from the crowd was deafening as they realised that the fight was now all but over.

I'd never seen anything like it - the way this gladiator baited his opponent; the way that he used both his own and his opponent's equipment to his own advantage. This man was simply on another level to anything I'd seen before.

The Retiarius had apparently sensed that fact too, because now unarmed and looking into the eyes of an opponent with superior armour, holding a short and very sharp gladius, he lost his nerve, turned and ran for his life.

The crowd booed loudly at this show of cowardice and I felt for the man with all of my being. I wanted him to run and keep running until his opponent could chase no longer, and then I realised - , the gladiator was running *towards* my gate.

He reached me in an instant and I could see the fear in his eyes as he met my own on the far side of the iron bars. I took a large step back towards the shadows so that the crowds couldn't see me but it was too late to hide myself from the unarmed gladiator.

"Please, boy, open the gate…" the Retiarius begged and I realised that he was talking to me. He had pushed his face against the bars and gripped them with his empty hands as though they were his only lifeline.

I took another step back. I wanted to help, I truly did but it would have been more than my life was worth to interfere with an arena battle.

"Please…" the gladiator begged and I could see the tears in his eyes. "I do not wish to die…"

Then suddenly and with a sickening squelch, the tip of the centre spire of his own trident appeared in his open mouth. He could no longer speak, though a loud, gurgling sound reached my ears as his final breath was released along with a waterfall of thick, red blood. The trident and defeated gladiator stayed in place even as Renatus moved away, his arms raised in triumph and the crowd showering him with their adoration.

IX – Post Tenebras Lux.

"Light after the dark."

The sight of the gladiator being torn down right before my eyes was enough to make my legs shake. I willed them to move, to take me back and away from this place, but they simply wouldn't comply and I was forced to watch as two arena hands arrived behind the fallen gladiator. They removed the trident from the back of his head and pulled his lifeless body from the iron grating. The sound it made was sickening, but still I couldn't move.

Then a third hand appeared to pass me in the tunnel, and opened the gate. The three of them dragged the gladiator along the rough floor, past me and along to where I knew Ovidius awaited to carry out his final task.

"Poor fucker, ain't no one stood toe to toe with that Renatus," I heard one of the hands say in passing.

"Still, did not have to run like a little girl though, did he?" Another replied.

For whatever reason, their words snapped me out of my stupor and I found that I was able to move once again. I quickly followed the fallen gladiator along the tunnel and into the healing room. I needed to be quick before Ovidius caused any more damage to the man. If there was any chance that I could save the Retiarius I needed to work before it was too late.

I arrived in the healing room as the gladiator's body was flopped onto the stone table and I grimaced as his head made a sickening crack as it impacted on the solid surface. I waited a moment for the hands to leave, then moved closer to Ovidius so that our conversation could not be overheard.

"I want to try something," I said in a whisper. "I want to see if I can help him."

Ovidius looked at the body of the gladiator, which was clearly lifeless on the stone table. He already held the dagger in his hand that he used to ensure that gladiators did not suffer in their defeat. Then he looked back at me and cocked an eyebrow.

"He is surely dead boy. There will be no helping him now." Then he moved as though ready to continue his work.

"Please? It will do no harm and just take a moment..." I begged.

Ovidius looked into my eyes as though searching for something there before he let out a sigh. "Why must I always have to cave in to people in need." Then he began to mutter under his breath, though I could still hear what he was saying: "why must I always give aid to those in need? Not once has my life ever been made easier..."

I didn't care what he was saying, I simply retrieved my stylus-stick from within my robe and coated its end in the blood of the gladiator that sat atop his body in a thin layer. Then I moved to my task.

I found the sigil easy to form this time. I couldn't tell if it was because of all the practise I'd been through, or if it was because this time it would actually mean something. It didn't matter which, or even if it was a combination of the two, but within just a moment I had drawn the perfect caduceus onto the centre of the gladiator's chest.

Ovidius leant over to look closely at the symbol that I had drawn, and we watched and waited for something, anything, to happen but the whole endeavour had apparently been futile. The sigil did not glow, the gladiator did not awaken and a life had not been saved by the power of the Gods.

"Well boy, what did you think was going to happen?" Ovidius asked me as we both stepped away from the gladiator's still body. Then the doctor retook his previous position with the knife, slit the gladiator's throat without ceremony and moved on to collecting the blood and cleaning the body.

"I... I thought that..." I started to speak though I was having trouble finding the words.

"Do not take me for a fool, boy. I know what that symbol is and I have seen it on more than one occasion... but did you really think that it would be able to bring a fallen gladiator back to life?" he asked as he worked.

"You... you have seen it before?" I asked, casting my mind back to when I had asked the doctor about my man Vettius.

"Yes I have seen it. I have seen that it can be a powerful symbol that imbues its wearer with the capacity to withstand heavy blows in the arena but nothing more. From what I have seen, and the few gladiators that I have seen dead on my table with the symbol on their bodies, it is not much more than a boost to their confidence and a plea to the Gods."

"So... you do not believe that it holds any power?" I asked.

"That is not what I said," Ovidius grumbled. "The symbol holds power there is to be no doubt about that, though whatever pleading the gladiators carry out towards the Gods by making the symbol, from what I have seen it has done little to make them invincible."

What he was saying actually did make a lot of sense to me. Ludo had lost his fight, and without my intervention Ovidius would've made sure that he couldn't have been healed. The caduceus sigil did not turn him into an unbeatable warrior, and like so many before him, he had ended up at the mercy of man.

"I think this one is done with," Ovidius announced once he'd collected all the blood he could and cleaned all of the wounds on the gladiator's body – including my expertly-drawn sigil. Then the arena hands reappeared and took the gladiator away to where his soul could rest. I wondered if Mercury would be kind to him, having been adorned with his sigil of power for at least a small time in his life.

"These flasks are full boy, lots of blood in that one," Ovidius announced to interrupt my pondering. "Why not get yourself some fresh air and see about bringing back some coin, eh?"

I could tell that he was giving me a reason to get out for a while so that I wouldn't ruminate on my failure. I had just been so sure though.

I beckoned Dinari to my side with a whistle and hoisted the three flasks that we'd amassed onto my shoulder. The dog was so excited that his wagging tail pounded into my shin so many times that it began to hurt. After a moment he realised where we were going though, and Dinari led the way out of the prep area and out towards the bright sunlight.

I exited the construction and immediately the warmth and brightness of the sun offended my face. I looked around nonchalantly for Dinari, who must've run off somewhere - possibly chasing a butterfly - though once my vision was no longer impaired by the bright sunlight, I was horrified to find that Dinari was at chest height, in the arms of a fully uniformed legionary.

My breath caught in my lungs and my heart immediately began to beat out of my chest as I watched the legionary who had once chased me around this very arena, softly stroke the fur on Dinari's back. The man was smiling and Dinari didn't seem to be in any distress, but I knew this couldn't have been anything good.

"I have seen you boy. Coming and going with those flasks, off into town. Tell me, what do they contain?" the legionary asked.

I took a step back, though knew that I couldn't run and escape from the man this time. I would never leave Dinari behind, even if it meant that I myself would be in mortal trouble.

"I... uh... it is..." I stammered my words as I tried to decide if I should tell the truth, or try to lie. "It is... water," I lied. There was going to be no good to come by telling this legionary about the blood in the flasks, so I tried my luck. "For the gladiators... they get thirsty from all the fighting."

The legionary eyed me suspiciously and I could already tell that he didn't believe me. It didn't help that my clothes were still covered in blood from dealing with the last gladiator, and I attempted to wipe the drying blood off of myself with my bare hands. It didn't work.

"Give one here," the soldier ordered. "Quickly now."

I stepped back away from the legionary again, though still I could see no way out of this. The legionary took a large step forward and closed the distance between us in an instant. Dinari wagged his tail at my proximity; he didn't seem to realise the danger we were both in.

The legionary, now within reach, pulled one of the flasks from my shoulder and I let it slip down my arm and off of my hand. I wondered if the man would put Dinari down so that he could inspect the flask properly, but to my dismay he managed to cradle the dog in one arm, leaving both his hands free for the task.

Uncorking the flask, he then poured a tiny amount of the thick red blood into his hand. I knew it would still be warm and saw him smirk as he realised just what the liquid was.

"Selling blood without a license, are we?" the legionary looked at me with a huge shit-eating grin on his face. "This is a very dire offence boy, very dire indeed."

I felt the bottom of my stomach sinking as the subtext to his words reached me. Was I about to be arrested? Thrown into jail, or perhaps even be forced to fight in the arena?

"Well, boy. I think you had better come with me then, eh?" I noticed that the legionary had recorked the flask and attached the container of blood to his waist, hiding it under his flowing uniform. It was odd, it looked as though he was planning on keeping the blood for himself and it made me think that there may have been an opportunity for a way out of all of this.

"Are you keeping that for yourself?" I asked as the legionary half turned away from me with Dinari still in his arms.

"Perhaps you didn't hear me boy," he said, turning back to face me. "What you have done here is a crime. Do you know what they do to young boys and their pet dogs in prison around here?" He placed a hand open wide atop Dinari's head. "They squeeze them until there's nothing left."

The legionary squeezed Dinari's head as he spoke. At first I was worried, but if I was being honest about the situation, the dog looked like he was actually enjoying it. It certainly didn't look like he was being hurt by the action.

I was taken aback by the threat to my person, though I knew that I had a thread to tug on here.

"What if I can get you some more of that?" I asked, gesturing to where he'd attached the flask.

"What are you trying to say, boy?" the legionary snapped back at me, though I could tell that he was making an effort to keep his voice down.

"Uh… nothing…" I said honestly. I still didn't really know why people wanted the stuff so badly. "It is just…" I lowered my voice to a whisper. "I can get more, and all the time too, if you want it?"

The man straightened his back and finally placed Dinari onto the ground gently, which made me exhale the breath I hadn't known I had been holding. Flattening his robe out, the soldier's expression changed from slight anger, to official and straight.

"Well… I should say a flask a week, if it truly is what you say it is. And a tax," he added thoughtfully. "You are probably making what, three dinari off of all this … let us say half to you, half to me, paid weekly, shall we?"

One and a half Dinari seemed like it was a steep price to pay to keep the soldier's nose out of my business but I knew I had little choice. I was just thankful that today it was a light load, only a single battle having been completed in the arena, otherwise he might've asked for more.

I nodded silently. I thought about haggling to see if I could get the man to come down a bit, but it looked as though it was fifty-fifty between him taking the deal and simply taking us away as it was. We could afford to lose a little coin though, and a little blood. As long as things kept going the way they'd started.

I took what I had left of the blood into town and sold them to the people that I was becoming very used to. They called me 'Sanguis', which literally meant 'blood', but I didn't mind, it was kind of nice to be both recognised and welcomed by the people. The coin that they gave me, although little in value individually, added up to a respectable amount.

It was pretty much the same every time I visited the bakery with my wares: the same people in line taking the same amount of the magical liquid – well, in their eyes anyway – and paying me the same amount of coin. It had become somewhat of an unspoken rule that this was the way things had to happen and I liked that. I didn't need to argue or barter, I simply took what was owed and went off on my way. I guessed that the only losers in all of this were the physicians that now had to get hold of their gladiator blood elsewhere, at presumably a higher price.

I was thankful that after Dinari and I had had our fill of bread and water from the bakery and made our way back to the arena, the legionary was nowhere to be seen. Dinari didn't look as happy though, visibly searching for the soldier that had given him the best head rubs. I shook my head as we entered into the prep room.

"Fucking legionaries, eh boy." A gruff voice came from my right and I turned to see where it had come from. It sounded as though there was an accent to it, but I couldn't place it. It was definitely familiar somehow though.

Sat on a wooden bench, was a gladiator wearing nothing but a loin cloth, with long greasy black hair and a long black beard. He had already been prepared to fight, his skin shimmering in the flickering torches where he'd been covered in oil. He was the only person in the room so I knew he was surely the one who'd spoke.

The gladiator stood up. I could see his ribs through his skin where he had clearly been malnourished, and on his wrist he had been branded with a deep and very painful looking letter 'F'. I didn't know what that meant, though it certainly didn't look like this man had been prepared for the arena at all.

"Are you a gladiator?" I asked the first thing that came into my head.

The man let out a long laugh, though I could see no humour in his eyes.

"Do I look like a fucking gladiator to you, boy? I was a farmer... but a legionary came and asked for a tax, just like what happened to you when you left... now I am here because I could not pay." He spat on the floor as though to punctuate his statement. "That is all it takes you know, they keep asking for more and more and one day that will be it, you are fighting for your life where before you'd never so much as lifted a trident."

"They *forced* you into becoming a gladiator?" I asked. "I thought people wanted to fight in the arena?"

"Seriously boy, look at me. What chance do you think I would have against a trained man out there? I am no fighter, but perhaps I shall fill some flasks for you, eh?" The gladiator tried to sound nonchalant, though I could hear the fear in his voice. It made me want to help him. And then suddenly it hit me. I *could* help him, if he wanted me to.

"I... uh, I think I can help," I said slowly, "if you would trust me?"

The gladiator looked at me for a long moment as though he was trying to decide if I was being serious or not, then finally he spoke. "You have some secret daggers or armour or something back there?"

"Not exactly, I can do, uh… a thing," I replied.

The gladiator looked down at Dinari, who was rubbing his face on my shin, covering it with his dog slobber. The dog looked up at me and smiled. "It is better if I just show you I think," I said.

It didn't take too much convincing in the end, but I understood that this man had nothing to lose. He had quite obviously been placed into a situation that he had never been prepared for, and the small mercy that I could do him, was at least try to help by drawing my sigil onto his skin.

I chose a small area on his left forearm for the sigil as he had told me that he would be fighting with a spear and that meant that it would be covered by cloth wrapping or a leather bracer. There was no need for anyone else to be aware of the mark of the God, though if it was going to glow bright blue like the ones I'd seen before, I thought that doing my best to hide it would be a good idea.

The gladiator didn't seem to bat an eyelid when I retrieved my makeshift pencil and a small pot of blood that I had made for convenience. I'd also gotten into the habit of watering down the liquid as it didn't seem to make any difference what the mark had been made from.

"You are a Sigilarius?" He asked in somewhat shock and a whisper once I'd marked the first couple of lines of Mercury's caduceus.

"You know what that is?" I asked without looking up from my work. Again I was shocked at what people did or didn't know about this mystical art.

"Yes I know what a sigil is. This one seems to be for Mercury and I would guess for health, or healing?" the gladiator replied.

I didn't reply. I simply carried out my work in silence and before long I had completed the sigil just like all those times I'd practised it before. When I finished, it glowed brightly, illuminating our corner of the room and I noticed the gladiator take a heavy inhale as though he could breathe properly for the first time ever.

"I feel good, boy…" the gladiator said and abruptly stood up. "I just hope this makes the difference out there," he gestured to where I knew the arena sands were and I pitied him again. His position was not somewhere I'd liked to have been either.

"My name is Crassus," the man said gruffly. "I hope to see you again soon…"

"Titus," I offered in return. I saw something in the man's eyes as I spoke my name, though he didn't vocalise whatever it was.

Crassus moved away from me and into the next room where he would collect his weapons and armour for his upcoming fight. I could see from what had been made available to him that he wasn't to dress as a normal Retiarius style gladiator as I had assumed, he was to carry a spear and absolutely nothing else. This seemed very unfair to me, though who was I to question the arena master or the lay of the games.

I followed the gladiator onward in silence until an arena hand opened the iron gate for him to exit onto the golden sands, and I watched from inside the gate as no other gladiator seemed to announce his presence. It was the first time I'd seen a gladiator go to the sands alone and it gave me a very bad feeling.

The arena announcer took to the sands as the crowds muttered quietly amongst themselves and Crassus looked about himself as though unsure of what to expect.

"People of Liternum!" The announcer bawled, to which the crowd fell silent. "The man who stands before you is a convicted criminal!" The crowds booed loudly at the statement and I inwardly berated them for it. "This man has stolen and killed at the behest of masters he yet refuses to disclose! He puts you and all of your families at risk, do you think he should be allowed to live?"

There were whistles, boos and shouts of 'no way!' returned to the announcer, but I feared something much, much worse. With the announcement of this gladiator's criminal activity, I remembered who he was. More specifically, I remembered that gruff voice and the promise I'd made to never forget it.

This gladiator, this criminal named Crassus, was the man who killed my mother. And I had just *helped* his chances of survival in the arena.

X - Male Parta Male Dilabuntur.

"What has been wrongly gained is wrongly lost."

I felt my eyes beginning to well up at my internal conflict. How could I have been so stupid that the first man that I would be to ever bless with the power of the Gods, would be the very man that killed my mother? Was this some kind of cruel joke?

I almost didn't hear what the arena announcer had followed up with.

The boos from the crowd were deafening and they pounded their feet onto the stone floor around the amphitheatre causing a rumble akin to thunder to roll out from the stands. Then from my right and the main arena entrance, the gates opened slowly as though to build the suspense. Bright sunlight silhouetted the three legionaries that stepped forwards and onto the sands. They all wore matching red cloaks covering full leather armour, had silver helmets with upright red plumage in their centres and each carried a rectangular red wooden shield and a straight, sharp gladius.

I thought that this was going to be a just end to Crassus, though once the legionaries stepped out of the sunlight and their faces became apparent, I could see that they were the men who'd chased me before, and their leader was the very man who'd inserted himself into my business. I thought in passing that if there was any justice to be had from the Gods, these four men would all kill each other and the world would be a better place because of it. Or at least Crassus and the legionary leader would kill each other – I'd settle for that too as the others mostly had just seemed to be following orders.

"If the Gods see fit for this man to be absolved of his crimes, he will do so through arena contest!" the arena announcer shouted. "If this criminal can best three trained and well equipped legionaries in straight combat, then we will be obliged to set him free, as the Gods will have made their ruling. Otherwise if he falls, he falls as a criminal at the hands of justice!"

The crowd cheered at that notion, though all I'd heard was the part about the favour of the Gods. I knew that in my poor decision-making, I had given him such a favour, and I could only hope that my efforts weren't going to be enough to spare this man's life and absolve him of his crimes.

As the fight began a moment later, I tried to see if the sigil that I had made upon Crassus' skin was glowing though I'd done a very good job at making sure it'd been hidden before he took to the sands, so I really had no idea. The best that I could hope for, was that I had made a mistake somewhere in the symbol and that it would be rendered useless, or that Mercury would've seen my mistake and nullify his divine powers.

The three soldiers moved to surround Crassus, and as they did I let out a sigh of relief that they were taking things seriously with this criminal. They moved in time and closed their triangle around their enemy as he stood to the ready, holding his spear in both hands.

The legionary to Crassus' front held his shield to the ready and when the group were in range, this one stabbed his gladius at his target around the side of his shield. Crassus dodged the blade quickly, but as he did, a heavily booted foot planted itself on his back and he fell forward, his body hitting a shield as he fell to the ground. The soldiers all moved away then encircled the criminal again.

I could tell right away that Crassus had no chance against these three. The legionaries were simply too methodical and took their time with their attacks, leaving no opening to be exploited. Crassus, though, to his credit, did not simply give up. He stood his ground and prepared to be weighed.

The legionaries all moved in as one again, though this time Crassus had already become used to the tactic and as the legionary before him struck out around his shield, Crassus moved his own body *into* it, impacting the wooden shield heavily but still managing to dodge the blade. The attack that had come from behind this time though was the stab of a gladius and because the soldier hadn't been expecting to miss with his attack or even defend himself, he had neglected to hold his shield up and to the ready. Crassus' spear swung around and sliced the soldier's arm to draw first blood. The crowd went silent.

Of course spears weren't particularly designed to be swung; they were of most use at range as a stabbing weapon so the attack had done little damage, but the line of blood on the soldier was clear as day for all to see.

The third legionary then took the place of the injured one, his shield held high and between the two soldiers, they sandwiched Crassus between their shields. As though in retaliation for their injured brother, both legionaries lashed out with their gladii, puncturing both Crassus' sides with identical wounds where his kidneys sat and the criminal let out a wail of pain.

This time Crassus fell to a knee and again the soldiers moved back and away from their enemy. They didn't seem to have any trouble regrouping as a three now, the injured soldier apparently happy that his affliction was simply a flesh wound.

When the crowd saw the wounds and trickles of blood upon Crassus, they let out a loud 'whoop' in appreciation, their favourites for this battle made clear.

"Kill the fucking traitor!" I heard a voice carry above the rest of the noise from the crowd. "Cut his fucking head off!" another followed. This then seemed to spur the legionaries on, though in the lull of battle I could see that the wounds on Crassus had already begun to heal. My sigil was working as it should, and that was surely bad news.

Crassus stayed on his knees, though he didn't make any move to right himself. He looked both injured and tired, but something inside of me just seemed to know what his game was. Without thinking, I shouted across the sands to the legionaries as they moved back in, somewhat less concerned with their shields now.

"He is faking it! Get your shields up!" I shouted.

It was too late.

When the legionaries were close enough to be within range of his spear, Crassus shifted his weight to his back foot and raised the spear to the attacker to his front. A short thrust followed by a sickening squelch and eruption of blood, the spear tip entered into the legionary's throat at the front, and protruded from his neck at the back. As much as I wanted to see my unwanted business partner taken down, unfortunately he still stood with the remaining soldier against Crassus. The man who'd been killed, honestly I'd had no issues with.

Crassus let go of his spear and rolled forward to take the shield and gladius from the hands of the dead legionary before he even coughed out his last breath. I wondered if the killer would be more skilled armed with these over his spear, though something told me by the way he fought that he was practised with many weapons, and he had been spinning a web of deceit with me.

Crassus roared and pounded the hilt of his gladius on his large wooden shield in defiance of his sentence, the crowd and his enemy.

My breath caught in my chest again. Was there a chance that Crassus would win this fight?

The two soldiers stood before Crassus though they looked decidedly more worried than they had previously when the battle had been three against one. Thankfully though, with all three men holding equal weapons, any advantage afforded by the reach of the spear had been removed and that meant that two against one was still likely to end in death for Crassus.

The soldiers now did not attempt to stand either side of their enemy, now they fought as though they were a unit facing an enemy force, standing shoulder to shoulder with their shields held stalwart. This was how they had been trained I was sure – not to surround a single man but to attack and defend as one.

Crassus moved towards the soldiers with his sword held poised to strike by his face. The stance was unlike anything I had ever seen before – he both looked and moved as though he was a viper and the soldiers were apparently dumbfounded by the tactic too. In their minds, this man should've been backing away into a defensive stance when confronted with a larger force. As it was, Crassus was stealing the advance from them.

The soldiers linked their shields to form an impenetrable wall, although I could still see openings at the top and bottom of their defence. It was inevitable, no shield would cover the entirety of a person, that would both impair vision and restrict movement way too much. I could tell though, that with two swords and twin shields, the two fighting together would make for one single, mighty opponent.

Crassus struck out quickly and swiftly with his cocked arm. His strikes were straight and true and each time one impacted one of the wooden shields, it did not deflect off and away, rather the tip of his weapon dug into them, causing them to chip and splinter and I wondered if eventually the attacks would be able to break down the shields entirely.

Perhaps I should've given a little more credit to the two soldiers though. Their unwavering determination in the face of unrelenting attacks was something that I was sure that I wouldn't be able to muster. They kept their shields held strong and chose not to attack until the absolute right moment. That moment came when Crassus took a single step back from his attacks to catch his breath. I imagined that it must've been tiring for the man.

The legionaries shifted their formation to separate and as they did, *both* men swiped out with their swords as they stepped back into range of their opponent. Red blood again puffed into existence as their attacks landed on the upper arms of Crassus, one on either side. It was a marvel really, both times the soldiers had attacked, both times the wounds that had been caused were both identical and symmetrical. Crassus didn't seem to care though as his attention returned to the battle; he was now faced with an enemy in front, and an enemy behind once more. The soldiers raised their shields to the ready again.

Crassus took the lead once again and moved into range of the legionary before him. I could tell that his form had started to fail though he kept going, swiping and stabbing and the soldier blocked and parried with his shield. The noise that filled the arena was deafening as the wooden shield sounded hollow when struck by the solid, sharp gladius.

The second legionary closed in with his shield up, though Crassus turned and leapt at him. His leading foot impacted the shield and as he pushed back and away from his opponent, he used the motion to spring into an attack on the other soldier.

The legionary whose shield Crassus had used as a springboard fell back and to the ground and the killer used the momentum he'd gained to throw himself at the other man, sword outstretched and his body flattened as he flew as though he was some sort of glider.

I could tell that this was an all or nothing attack and I could only watch in fear as the soldier was unable to take the full weight of the flying man. Even though slight, Crassus' attack was successful. His gladius hit the wooden shield first, and although it did no damage the thud that echoed around the silent arena was deafening. Both men fell to the ground and the soldier was trapped beneath the killer and his shield, unable to move anything at all to defend himself. Crassus brought himself to his knees atop the shield and stabbed around it and into his enemy's side over and over. Then he switched hands and I heard the moans and groans as the legionary was systematically removed from the battle, torn from this world.

I couldn't believe what was happening. The three on one was now a one on one and I could see no further than Crassus for the victor. The soldier that was left though, was the man that I had already had dealings with, and disregarding the rest I internally wished that these two would kill each other and be done with it.

As the second fallen soldier lay bleeding out onto the sands, I watched in surprise as patches of the crowd began to cheer for Crassus whilst he was closing in on victory. I did not share their enthusiasm and internally willed them to leave the battle to play out as it would. Of course, they only liked Crassus because he had spilled the most blood in the battle so far, something that I really hoped would change very soon.

The last remaining soldier moved in before Crassus had the chance to right himself from the shield and ignoring all form and forethought, he lunged with the tip of his gladius at Crassus. To my relief and delight, the sword pierced the killer's stomach as he turned to face his attacker and I saw the tip of the cold steel blade protrude from his back.

Crassus took a hold of the blade with both hands as the legionary still held onto it. The pair's eyes met and in that moment I saw the determination plastered across Crassus' face and the fear in the legionary's.

The soldier let go of the blade and moved away in shock. Crassus *pulled the sword* from his own body, forcing a curtain of blood to flow from his stomach and onto his loin cloth, but still he did not fall. The wound bled for a moment and then stopped and again I cursed my own naïveté at helping the man. He was clearly skilled in subterfuge though so I reminded myself not to get too upset about it.

I could actually see the killer smiling and the sight made my blood boil. How dare this man smile after all the things that he'd done – assuming that killing my mother (and having a part in my father's death too) was not the crime he'd been placed on trial for here, as I presumed either nobody knew or cared about it other than myself.

The sight of the killer smiling seemed to return the legionary to the battle and he raised his shield without showing any further emotion. There would be no tricks, no diversions and no advantages any more – the battle sat at a one-on-one and any hope that I had for my parents' killer to be brought to justice was all but gone.

Crassus raised his sword once again as though he was a coiled serpent and took two steps forward towards the legionary, who in turn did his best to brace himself behind his shield for the incoming attack. As Crassus came into range though, the legionary caught him off guard by slamming his wooden shield into Crassus' chest and face, lifting him off of the ground and his back contacted the hot sands with an 'oof'. I was glad that the only sigil that I knew how to draw was Mercury's caduceus, as although the man's wounds were obviously healing quickly, there was nothing that would make him fight any better, or remove the pain from the attacks that struck him.

The legionary moved in and pressed his newfound advantage. It was clear that using his shield had surprised his enemy, so before Crassus could get up and off of his back, the legionary placed the bottom of his shield against his opponent's chest, then slid it up to his neck. It was clear that the battle was over now, Crassus had no way to escape the shield or the attack that was to follow.

Unceremoniously, the legionary slid his gladius down the length of his shield and into the neck of the struggling Crassus. The thick red blood that spilled out onto the sands was a waste for sure, and I knew that there was no way that the killer would be recovering from that injury, no matter what sigils had been drawn upon his body.

Eventually once the cheers of the crowds had abated and it was clear that the battle was truly over, the arena hands dragged all of the fallen men from the sands, except for the legionary who stood to his full height, turned and abruptly left the arena via the main gates without a single look back.

Once the sands were clear, the arena announcer returned to the sands. "Our victor and one of your very protectors here in Liternum: Callistus!" The response from the crowd wasn't as loud or as wild as it had been for other bouts that I'd witnessed, but justice had been done, and by all accounts everyone was happy about it.

I retook my position, tailed by Dinari who had been uncharacteristically quiet back in the healer's room and awaited the bodies of the fallen. If of no other use, we could still collect their blood to sell in the town.

XI - Timendi Causa Est Nescire.

"The cause of fear is ignorance."

It had been ten years since the fall of Crassus in the arena and ten years since the last time I'd drawn a sigil on another person. I had been so expertly tricked by the killer that I simply couldn't trust myself to make the right choices any more. The last thing I wanted to do was to impart the power of the Gods onto another individual, only to find that he was the worst kind of person. It was just easier to remove myself from the situation entirely.

Of course, that didn't mean that I hadn't been practising the art for all that time; I'd practised drawing sigils as well as other forms that had no magical backing almost every single day for as long as I could remember, and by all accounts I had become an expert at wielding a stylus and ink.

I had continued to work with Ovidius and living within the gladiator prep area for the entire time had made me highly skilled at determining when wounds were a death sentence and when they could be healed to save the gladiator in question. What it had also conveniently done, was to turn me into a highly skilled healer. I wasn't at the level of a physician where I could prescribe medicines for longer term or mental ailments, but when it came to wounds borne of fighting in the arena with sword or spear, I couldn't think of anyone else in the empire that could rival my skill; I had just had too much experience.

Handily, as the crowds in Liternum had become more seasoned, there had been a shift toward technique and tactics rather than simple bloodshed, so as gladiators lost and begged for mercy, it was more often granted. That meant more patients that could be saved, as well as alleviating a shortage of gladiators after a particularly busy schedule.

Nobody knew of my skill as a healer, however. Word of a skilled arena doctor who brought gladiators back from the brink of death was seldom passed; what made for a better story to save face for all, was that the gladiators had the fortune of the Gods, or were simply too strong to perish from such skin-deep wounds.

The legionary that had inserted himself into our blood business had all but disappeared too. If I was honest about the situation, I would've said that he had either decided to simply leave the service after the things he'd watched happen to his comrades in the arena, or perhaps the fact that he and his men had almost lost a battle that should have meant certain victory, had led to him being transferred by his superiors to somewhere a little less public. I didn't care which it was, all that it meant was that our business remained booming and by all accounts, unmolested.

Life had been surprisingly good over the past decade. I'd worked, cleaned, learned to heal and cook, and the most important person in my life was still by my side for every moment of it.

Dinari looked as though he hadn't aged a day in the last ten years and a part of me wondered if that was due to Mercury's caduceus that had been tattooed onto his skin when he'd been just a pup. His demeanour and attitude towards life hadn't changed either; by all accounts he loved everyone and everything around him and even when the dark setting of death descended upon the healing room, his smiling face was often the thing that kept me going where all else seemed so gloomy.

I'd been fairly frugal with the small amount of money that I'd been gaining from the blood business, but that was mainly because the money didn't actually go very far. It had kept me in fresh clothes as my body had grown into that of a man and I could eat and drink when I pleased. I knew it was never going to be enough to afford to live anywhere other than where I had been staying next to the arena, but I didn't care. By all accounts life was pretty good - I had what I needed and I felt as if I'd made a difference whenever I'd managed to pull a gladiator back from the brink of death.

"You want to get that table washed and ready for the next patient, boy?" Ovidius asked. It was the middle of the day and we had already healed two gladiators with mild injuries.

I knew that the schedule for the day was for five arena battles, so we needed to make sure we kept on top of the cleaning otherwise the risk of infection would rise exponentially.

"You know I do not remember the last time you picked up a bucket and sponge, old man," I replied.

Ovidius still liked to call me boy, even though I was now larger than him and my body had grown into a man's. My hair had turned dark and thick and I liked to keep it as short as the soldiers did. I liked to call Ovidius old man, though it was more of a mark of respect than an insult.

I picked up the bucket of water and sponge to carry out my work. It was the most normal thing in the world to do now and I had the perfect method for cleaning the room from top to bottom.

It took no time at all and when I was finished, the room was clean and if anyone had taken a magnifying glass to the stone, they wouldn't have found a single spec of blood. That was of course until the next gladiator graced our table.

The man who was dragged in and onto our table was quite obviously gravely injured, though I could see that he was still breathing, his chest rising and falling rhythmically. The arena hands left us to our task, and in what was becoming more of a normal situation now, I moved to argue with Ovidius for saving the man over making his death quick and painless.

More often than not, my argument won. I thought that Ovidius really did want to help people, though if he made a big deal about not wanting to help, I would have to offer up something like taking the body out or cleaning up afterwards. I didn't mind, I cleaned up after every patient as it was anyway.

This patient inevitably would be no different to any other. I fought for his right to live, and Ovidius relented once I said that I would pay for his lunch if the man died. It was a morbid gamble, but I was confident in our abilities.

Ovidius placed down the knife that he had been holding to the man's throat to end his life, and picked up a wet sponge to begin cleaning the wounds.

It all happened so fast. I don't know why on this occasion Ovidius hadn't moved the knife away from the table, but it was a mistake that my mentor and friend would pay dearly for.

The gladiator's eyes snapped open and he leant forward off the stone table.

"Do not take me, I'm not ready to go… please…" he moaned.

I presumed that he was talking to Mercury as the guide of lost souls, and in this unfamiliar room he must've been disoriented and scared. Then he saw the knife.

He picked it up and pulled the closest thing to him toward him. Before I could do anything to intervene, the gladiator had cut Ovidius' throat and blood had begun to coat them both. I did the only thing I could, I slammed a balled fist into the biggest wound I could see on the man's chest and he howled in pain, dropping the knife. I picked it up and cut the gladiator's throat without another thought; I needed to help Ovidius and I couldn't do that with this threat looming over me.

Every part of my being screamed at me for the act of complete violence that I had committed but I pushed the voices away and into a part of my mind that I seldom ventured into.

I rolled the fallen gladiator off the table and caught Ovidius before he fell. He was holding his throat in an attempt the keep the blood from spilling out and I laid him gently on the table that the gladiator had previously vacated.

Ovidius didn't say a word as I worked though I could see the fear in his eyes. I pulled a cloth bandage from the pile by the table and wrapped it around his neck but there was just so much blood when he removed his hands from his neck and I knew that this wound wasn't going to be something that I could cure.

I just needed to stop the blood though, and then I could gather my thoughts and decide upon the best course of action.

I didn't know what else to do. I ripped the old man's robes open, coated my right index finger in Ovidius' wet blood and began to draw on his exposed chest. I drew the sigil quickly and larger than I'd ever drawn one before – of course I didn't know if the size made any difference but I wanted to give my friend the best chance I possibly could.

When I finished, the sigil illuminated itself in the bright blue glow as I had been expecting and I breathed a sigh of relief at the fact that it had taken. Ovidius, though, still did not look well although he did look much calmer, his breathing was somewhat more stable and his eyes were now closed. There was nothing more I could do right now other than wait.

I watched Ovidius for a long time before I was certain that he was peaceful and resting, but I knew that his wound was going to be touch and go, even with the fortune of Mercury shining down upon him. It had been so long since I'd drawn the sigil on another person, and I hadn't even seen one in a decade now so the intricacies of what they could achieve were somewhat lost to me. A part of me wondered if my trauma damaged brain had made up the whole thing – the meeting with Mercury, the glowing symbols, the magic that they provided… then as I was about to go deeper down that rabbit hole, Ovidius opened his eyes.

"T… Titus," he feebly croaked out without turning his head.

"I am here," I assured the old man, moving to the side of the stone table. "Do not try to talk, it could open your wound again and it is trying to mend."

"No… it is OK," he replied. He didn't make eye contact with me, instead choosing to stare directly upwards at the stone ceiling.

"What do you mean?"

"I… saw Mercury…" Ovidius said, still making no attempt to move any part of himself. "Listen boy… I need you to know…"

I tried to shush Ovidius to get him to keep his strength, but I could tell that he needed to tell me something and I wouldn't be able to stand in the way of that.

"Boy… Mercury has granted me this opportunity to speak to you… this last… opportunity." I could tell that he was weak, though he didn't seem to be faltering in his desire to speak to me.

I tried to say something but I didn't know what to say past either 'go on' or 'try not to speak'. Either way the result would be the same.

"You have been like a son to me for these past years," Ovidius said. "You are a far better person than you know… and I have done something for you that will show you who you are."

Tears began to well in my eyes as he spoke. It was as though these were his dying words and my heart bled for him and all of my being internally begged for the Gods to show him mercy.

"You must go to my room in the town and look in the wooden chest below the window. Take everything you find there and you will understand what I have done. My son… boy… I am old and there is nothing more that the Gods can do for me…"

I wanted to ask him what he was talking about, what he had done and why me, but nothing could come out save for a single teardrop that fell from my eye as Ovidius closed his own for the very last time. I didn't spare a moment to thank Mercury for his mercy in allowing us to say our goodbyes, but as soon as I was sure that he was gone, I bawled. I loved the man, and I told him so as his soul passed from this world to the next. I just hoped that Mercury was kind enough to show Ovidius my final words to him.

I did not send Ovidius out on a cart and off down the river for his soul to never reach peace in the afterlife. Instead I went with his body and the arena hands to bury him on the banks so that he would find clear passage now that he was not of this world. As I placed the first handful of dirt over his lifeless body, I prayed to Mercury to look after my friend forever more.

It made me feel better knowing that the Gods were going to look after Ovidius as he left the mortal realm and I consoled myself with the fact that Mercury had taken the time to allow Ovidius to talk to me before he died. It did occur to me that even the power of the Gods couldn't save my mentor in that moment, but as he had said, he was old and frail and had little time left as it was.

Once I had said goodbye to the kindest man that I had ever known, the person who'd taken me in from the streets, given me work and shelter, I needed to follow his instruction. I knew where his room was in the town and it was a tiny affair, even smaller than the room in which I slept by the arena, the only difference being that it wasn't inside the place where he worked. As it was still light and warm, I made my way to his room without delay.

I'd seen the place a few times and knew exactly how to get to it. It was in the poorest part of the town where the streets were routinely lined with beggars and by all accounts it was dangerous. I assumed people just left Ovidius alone because he was old and frail, and had nothing of particular worth to offer anyone. I had wondered on occasion what he had been spending the dinari on that he received when I'd been selling the blood for him though.

Ovidius' door was never locked, though he had once told me that there was little crime in the town because most people were in the same boat. There was no sense in the poor stealing from the poor after all and because most of the time in this area there were people outside, there were eyes on everything, so the risk of being burgled was extraordinarily low.

I entered the place with Dinari by my side, who seemed as morose as I felt and it made me worry for the dog; there was only the very odd occasion that he wasn't smiling and bouncy, and in general living his best life. I looked for the wooden box that Ovidius had told me about and sure enough there it sat, right under the window.

I opened the box slowly, my hands shaking, and was immediately hit by the stench of rotten vegetables. The box looked as though they were full of the things and I was about to close the lid, thinking that this was Ovidius' last laugh, when I saw the spine of a book propped up against one of the walls of the chest.

I immediately recognised it – it was something that I hadn't seen in over ten years: it was one of the books that I had rescued from my family home, the ludus just outside of Liternum.

I let out an audible 'huh' as I let the book fall open to the first page within my hands, revealing a single piece of parchment therein. I read the scratchy text that'd been written on the paper. Immediately after reading the first few words, I could tell that they had been written by Ovidius.

"Boy, you came into my life when I was a lost soul. I have never been a wealthy man, or a man of any particular note, but the day you came through my door I saw a purpose. I cannot say if it was the Gods that sent you to me, or if I was sent to help, you but the reason does not matter. This book that you arrived with, I am sure is important to you, though you do not seem to appreciate it yet and I have kept it for you so that one day you may do with it what you are supposed to.

Also, I believe in fair pay for hard work. Without your ingenuity, selling the gladiator blood would never have been so profitable, so I will be saving a little over half to give to you when you need it most, I will try to save what I can for you as I have little need for wealth, I just hope that when the time comes there will be enough for you to live your life the way you are supposed to, without the restrictions of affordability.

I look forward to seeing how you grow into a man Titus; I have the feeling that your story will be one of greatness.

See you again soon,

Ovidius."

The words on the page turned my stomach and caused a sharp pain in my chest. Ovidius had been keeping this secret from me for all these years? And what had he meant about saving coins for me?

I looked back into the wooden chest and then I saw it, the glint of shining metal just beneath the rotting vegetables that the old man had used to obscure them from anyone but himself.

I scooped the rubbish out of the way, disturbing the smell that wafted up to my nostrils. It almost made me gag though I paid it no mind. Dinari practically fell backwards and put his back against the far wall of the room with a very upset look upon his face. I guessed that as dogs had a superior sense of smell, this must've been torture for him.

Beneath the top layer of spoilt food stuffs, the wooden chest was half-filled with shining silver dinari, and copper asses.

I didn't want to count them, but I knew that what was in the box was akin to a fortune. It certainly would've been more than enough for Ovidius to have moved out of his rather lacklustre accommodation and into a nicer part of Liternum, but for whatever reason, be it love, affection or a sense of owing, he had been saving the coin for me. I didn't know what to do with myself.

Dinari appeared by my side and against his better nature and sense of smell, he craned his head into the box to see what had left me so dumbfounded. He looked at the coins and then back at me as though he was saying 'well take them, then,' and then he picked up a single coin in his mouth and walked about the small room triumphantly before dropping it into my hand. The gesture was clear and it brought me back to myself; this, all of this, was now mine, and I owed it to Ovidius to do something useful with it all.

The thought of the late Ovidius did something to me as I held the coin in my hand. It was a little wet from being in Dinari's mouth, but more than that it was warm and heavy and as I thought about my mentor and unintentional father, I thought once more about my real parents, the house that I had been brought up and the way that they had been taken from me so cruelly and so prematurely.

Then the thought occurred to me. I hadn't been to visit the home that I had been brought up in in over ten years, not since the day it was taken from me and it made me feel a profound sense of shame.

XII – Magna Servitus Est Magna Fortuna.

"A great fortune is a great slavery."

Dinari and I made our way back out of Liternum and to the hill where my parents' ludus had once stood – after of course replacing the rotten veg that was doing such a good job at keeping the fortune well hidden. I had tried to lift the box, but it was a task that was beyond the strength of one man and a part of me thought that if it had remained unfounded and untouched so far, it was probably in an adequate hiding place.

The town itself had grown substantially over the last decade with the outer walls now not strictly on the 'outer edges' of the town. Buildings had been growing taller in the centre and more numerous on the outskirts and I wondered what my previous home would look like as we approached.

Dinari knew where we were going. He leaped and bounded around my feet for the whole twenty minute walk, though he didn't stray too far away from me. I half thought that he looked as though he was trying to act natural and that he knew what our intended destination was, but as usual I could do nothing to prove my assumptions.

The ludus atop the hill looked very much as though it had not been disturbed for the decade in which I had kept away from it. In the most literal sense of the word, the building was a ruin. The roof was all but gone, the walls had crumbled through years of abandonment and decay and the once shining white paint of the exterior walls had faded and was stained. The signs of the fire that had initially ruined the construct were still evident, black soot coated the walls all around the windows and doors.

Once the house had come into our sight, Dinari's gait changed immediately to obvious sadness. His tail lowered to between his legs, his passion for leaping and bounding apparently having left him. I couldn't say that I felt any differently to my dog, though my own pace remained constant.

We entered the house where the front door used to be and immediately I could see the sky through the missing roof and most of the walls. The contents of the house had all but disappeared and eventually I let my eyes fall to the place where my parents had lain dead on the floor. I could see it all so clearly once again, their lifeless bodies, the flames that engulfed them… even their killers. It was not a memory that would ever fade, though over the last decade I had done a very good job at not thinking about the scene for even a moment.

Dinari and I investigated the ruin for a good amount of time before we concluded, as we had ten years ago, that there was nothing to be salvaged. In addition, if there had been anything worth taking, it had been looted a long time ago for sure.

I sat on the floor by the front door with my back to the very column that I'd hidden behind as my parents had been killed, and after a short moment, Dinari placed himself on my lap between my knees and my chest. The dog still fitted perfectly, not having grown, although I had put on a great amount of size and height since the last time we'd sat in this very spot. I hugged the dog and radiated toward him all of the love that my body contained. He was the only thing that had ever been constant in this world, and I didn't know what I would do if anything ever happened to him.

We sat in silence for a while as I remembered my life before those dark times. This very ludus had been the crowning jewel in my parents' existence, my father having put all of his blood, sweat and tears into the building.

Then as I reflected upon my train of thought, Dinari turned and looked up at me. His doggy face was always so expressive and this look was no exception; I could see what he wanted without him even moving a muscle. Dinari wanted to stay here, the place where he too had grown up and formed so many happy memories as well.

There was no way that I would be able to take on the place myself; I had no background in construction, labouring or engineering, but now I had a fair amount of money to spend, and I knew exactly where I could find people in need of some work.

We went back to Liternum and made a beeline for the centre of town, to the bakery where so many people had come to know me and I them. Of course to them I was simply the peddler of magical gladiator blood, the 'Sanguis' that brought the liquid down to the affordable for them. I didn't care if it worked for what they wanted it for really, all that mattered was that they wanted it, and if it wasn't me selling it then it would be someone else. At least I knew that my gladiator blood was the genuine article and was affordable.

"Sanguis!" One of the men waiting in line for the bakery announced happily as he saw Dinari and me approaching. "But where is the blood that you carry for us today?"

The man was larger than average, which was odd for the poorer people in the town though I was never really one to pass judgement.

"Apologies Janus, I have not come to sell gladiator blood today," I said. "I have come to offer some work to those who need it and I know many amongst you here are labourers."

"We are always in need of good work, Sanguis, though what is it that you are in need of?" Janus asked.

"There is a house outside of Liternum, atop a hill… there was a fire ten years ago that reduced it to ruin, I would like to rebuild what is there so that I may have a home to call my own." I explained.

"A home of your own? The Gods must be smiling on you and your business to be able to afford such luxury!" The man laughed, though I could tell that there was no malintent in his words. "I know the house that you speak of well, and I can tell you that it was indeed fucked by the fires of Vulcan himself. It was the ludus Brutus, if I am not mistaken?"

I had already thought about what it was that I was going to say if and when I was to be confronted with this question, though even knowing the answer, hearing my true family name brought a lump to my throat.

"That… is the ludus…" I replied slowly, trying my best not to betray my discomfort. "What are your thoughts on the matter?"

"It is a doable task," Janus replied. "I am a simple labourer though, and a more skilled engineer would need to assess the work. The cost would be mostly in the labour I would think, each man costing no more than a half a dinari per day. The engineer would cost more but would not be needed for any length of time. If you wish, I know of a team of at least twelve that would take on the work including myself. We would take but a fair wage from you, Sanguis, as you have been fair to us for many years."

"Thank you, my friend," I announced with a warm smile as I took a hold of Janus' forearm to signify our friendship and our deal. "I will return in the morning to speak further on this. Please arrange for an engineer to be present and we will go and see what needs to be done."

Growing up in Liternum and serving the people without greed or prejudice had been something that I never thought would afford me anything more than the favour of the Gods when the time would come for me to finally meet them in the afterlife. As it happened, however, these people had become grateful, helpful and willing to do things for me that I would never have expected of anyone. The next day, Janus had rounded up a team of labourers, along with an engineer, carpenter and painter who would all accompany Dinari and me back up to the ludus to assess the damage, and see what would need to be done to give me my family home back.

The labourers were cheap at just six dinari per day all told, however the carpenter would cost fifty and the painter seventy-five. Thankfully the engineer would take a single payment of one hundred dinari – though what this all meant, was that for *each day* of construction, my ludus was going to cost me one hundred and thirty-one dinari before any materials had been bought or transported to the construction site. It was an amount of coin that I was uncomfortable in parting with, though I did realise that the painter would only actually be needed for a couple of days at the end of the project, and the carpenter similarly wouldn't be at the house for the duration.

"The place is a shit-hole," the engineer said once he returned to meet me at the front door to the ludus, "but her structure is sound. The roof needs replacing and a lot of the internals… the walls too… though she was built of stone and lime, so the work is possible and not too overbearing. Are you looking to have any amendments made to the structure or layout?"

"No," I replied simply. "I want it to look exactly as it had before it was burnt down."

The engineer looked at me curiously but didn't say a word. I wondered if he suspected that I had some link to the ludus, though if he did he didn't say.

I decided that whilst construction was ongoing at the ludus, Dinari and I would stay in Ovidius' room back in the town. I knew I could simply go back to the arena and live in the prep room as I had become accustomed to, but something inside me was telling me that that part of my life was over. I knew that helping people was still a big part of who I was, and who I was going to be, but I needed something different now and that place simply wasn't for me. Besides, the arena could find someone else to be the doctor now that Ovidius had passed; I certainly didn't want to take on that mantle.

I stayed in the room with the chest for the best part of a month following the initial discussions with the workers that were going to rebuild the ludus. I refrained from eyeing it too often or even counting the coins inside, though I knew that there would be more than enough to pay the workers with at least something left over. The last thing I wanted was for someone to see how interested I was in the chest, and to have a look at the contents for themselves, so generally I did my best to ignore it.

With the end of construction in sight, I visited the ludus as I had done on many occasions over the month. In the summer, although the climate was hot, the days were also long, so the work had been carried out rather quickly and it was obvious to me that there was little time left before the project would be completed.

I was amazed at the skill and ingenuity of the workers that brought my home back to where it had once stood. The flat white walls, the beautiful textured columns, and the orange profiled tiles reminded me of my childhood, and seeing them standing in position almost brought a tear to my eye.

"I am to travel into Neapolis tomorrow to see about staffing my new home," I told Janus once he'd come to stand next to me to admire the work that'd been carried out.

"That shall be a costly trip I have no doubt," the labourer replied. "Probably for the best though; this house of yours won't be easy to run without help, and the best help you can get in the Empire is bought in Neapolis."

I'd been with my father to Neapolis before and although I couldn't say that I knew the journey like the back of my hand, I remembered how things worked there. As prisoners of war, deserters, children of slaves and criminals, and criminals themselves became 'available' for sale – essentially as they were brought into the city and taken to market – people looking to purchase such individuals would bid for them.

It was not something that I was looking forward to doing however, no matter the circumstances in which I'd been brought up, I simply didn't think it was right to own other human beings. What it did do though, was to give me the opportunity to liberate some of these people in the hope that they would take up my offer of shelter and pitch in with the workings of my household whenever it was required. I understood of course that I was essentially looking for slave labour, but I wanted to remove the sense of ownership from these people; if they wanted to leave then they could do so at any time.

I had been given a cost for the work by Janus before I left the ludus to return back to my current abode. It was a costly affair that ran into the thousands of Dinari, though I was still sure that the wooden chest would have been able to foot the bill. I asked him to meet me along with all of the rest of the workers at my home later that evening so that I could pay all of the individuals that needed it.

The queue that formed outside my door that evening was a little longer than I had expected, but at least it meant that I could pay all of them without having to actually carry any of the coins anywhere.

Each time a man came to the door, he told me what he had done for the project, how long it had taken and the salary that he had been expecting. Janus stayed with me in the house to ensure that nobody was trying to pull a fast one, though more often than not, the labourers asking for coin actually asked for less than their usual salary. It seemed that being one of the 'people' of Liternum, and having a generally positive rapport with these people had once again created a benefit to me that was previously unknown and certainly not expected.

When the last man had left the small room, the chest that had been so full and heavy of silver and copper coins had been reduced to having a small covering at the bottom. I paid Janus what he was owed, plus an additional handful of coins as he had done so much for me without expecting anything extra. He thanked me and left me alone with Dinari, who was lying on the bed, looking decidedly bored at having to watch all of the payments being made. He loved life and everything about it, but once he'd realised that the workers had come to the room to get paid, rather than play with him, the game quickly became old. At least most of the workers had petted him after they'd been paid before they left, though even Dinari had his limits on how much petting he could take.

I slept better than I had for a week that night. I didn't know if it was because I had paid the workers and the task had been removed from my thoughts, or if it was because the house that I'd grown up in had been reborn from the ashes, and I knew that the very next day, I would be able to move back in.

The journey to Neapolis was more difficult than travelling into Rome, or even between the two cities. Long straight roads had been built between the two opulent settlements, as many of the wealthier citizens of Rome had bought villas in Neapolis as it was by all accounts a beautiful city adorned with bath houses, temples, and arenas. A grand aqueduct also provided fresh water to the city, which was a marvel to behold for most who visited for the first time.

I had of course seen all of this before, but I had been very young so the engineering genius that had been required to build the aqueduct alone had been lost on me. What I also noticed this time around, was actually how well managed the city was. There was no homelessness, no begging, the buildings and roads were well maintained, there were busy markets, banks, temples and everything that a budding and wealthy population could have ever wanted. In Neapolis I felt very much the outsider in my rather basic attire.

I had bought a new set of white robes for the journey, though, and with the little extra coins I had, I had paid for a golden rope to tie them with at my front, along with a sash to cover my shoulder and hang down to my side. It was what I'd seen the slightly wealthier people wear in Liternum, though the fashion hadn't quite reached the town en masse yet. What I noticed that people did have a lot of though, were dogs.

The canines of the citizens of Neapolis were very much the higher class of dog though. These animals were quite obviously meant to intimidate, and possibly deter criminals. Pointed ears, short coats and an alert demeanour made me wonder how friendly any of these animals would be, though when I watched Dinari regard some of them as we passed, save from wagging his tail at his kin, he did not approach them. Apparently he knew better.

I walked through the streets of Neapolis with the sense of wonder. It had changed vastly since my last visit and it was very obvious that I didn't belong in the place to all who saw me with my mouth practically hanging agape the whole time. This was a fact that was punctuated by merchants of all kinds calling me to their stalls to peruse their wares.

"Come my friend! You will see no superior clothing in all of the empire!" one merchant called.

"If you would like to know what real luxury is, then come and sample the silks from lands to the Far East! You could truly not be closer to the Gods, than sleeping on this mysterious, magical material," came the loud reply of another.

I had to admit, that one made me smile as I had already conversed with one of the Gods, and by all accounts it really had been nothing special.

"What is it you seek, friend?" A voice came from my side as I walked and it surprised me. This was the first person to actually *ask* what it was that I was in the city for, and not simply tell me what I could buy from them.

The middle-aged man was short, wore a white robe with a red sash and had a pleasant smile upon his face. I smiled back.

"I am here for the auctions," I said confidently. "I am moving into my new home and I am afraid I have nobody to run the place."

"Nobody to…" the man started speaking with a very bemused look on his face.

"I… had to leave them all behind," I said quickly, grasping the man's confusion.

"Ah, I see… well the auctions are held along the docks at the moment, the next is to begin within the hour. Though tell me, are you looking for men, women or… something younger?" The man asked and that was the moment I saw it. He had a look in his eye that betrayed malice and I understood that these people, no matter how friendly that they seemed to be, were not my kind of people.

"Just men and women," I replied acting as nonchalant as possible and increasing my stride somewhat. "If I need anything else I will find you again, friend."

I moved away from the man as quickly as possible and made my way to the docks and from that moment on I did my best to avoid eye contact or conversations with anyone at all, unless it was absolutely necessary.

The slave auctions were much larger than I thought would be the case. There were no less than forty men and women of all sizes and a handful of children mostly lined up and chained together, though a few of the larger looking men were inside wooden cages. I wondered if they had been placed in there to artificially inflate their value; if people thought that they were particularly strong or aggressive perhaps they might have paid more for them.

The auctions began not long after Dinari and I arrived and the format was simple: a single person would be brought onto the wooden stage and an auctioneer would take bids from the crowd of how much they would pay for them. After the first couple of people had sold, I became acutely aware that these individuals were far more expensive than I could've ever imagined.

With just five hundred dinari to my name and the first few people having being auctioned off for two to four *thousand*, I knew that I was probably out of my depth and I let out a short sigh of defeat. Of course, I didn't really care about getting the best, the strongest or someone who had already fought in the arena; one man who had won five arena battles already had actually sold for twenty *thousand* Dinari. I just wanted to save a person from that kind of existence, and maybe get some help around the house in return.

What I hadn't thought of though, was that this had all happened because some of the best and most expensive people had been brought out to keep the crowds interested. After these came a slew of lower-tier slaves, the ones that were decidedly more average than the rest, though the cheapest amongst these still went for just over a thousand dinari.

As I was about to give up on the whole situation, not expecting a single one of the people to sit within my own price range, I looked down at Dinari sitting next to me, who as usual somehow had sensed both my feeling and my intent.

Abruptly, the dog rose to his feet and moved closer to the holding area to the side of the auction stage. I watched as he walked up and down in front of the faces within, some forlorn, some angry and others sobbing into their hands. As I watched these people have their lives dictated to them right before their very eyes, the desire that I had to help as many of these slaves as possible redoubled in both my heart and my mind.

Dinari came to stop face to face with a man who I wouldn't have put much older than myself. He had clearly been beaten, malnourished and mistreated and it had left him practically fighting for his life. He lay on the floor, curled up into a ball as though he was waiting for the next kick or lash.

The dog pushed his head through the wooden bars of the holding area and licked the man's cheek. The man opened his eyes and when he saw Dinari, he slowly extended a shaking hand and patted my friend on the head, giving him a weak smile. I could see the pain in his eyes and I immediately understood that this was the man that I was supposed to help.

The auctions lasted for hours. Every single slave was sold to the highest bidder and not a single one was sold for less than eight hundred dinari. Apparently children in general were more expensive than the adults, though trained and successful gladiators demanded the highest prices.

The man who I'd already decided was the one that I was there for was last onto the stage, this was mainly because he couldn't actually stand on his own and had to be carried by two hands onto the platform, where he lay feebly on his side, struggling to breathe.

The crowds had all but dissipated once the 'good' stock had been sold and at the sight of this last man, most of the remaining patrons followed suit. However, this gave me the opportunity to play the game that I knew I needed to play.

"One hundred dinari!" I announced as the opening bid. I knew I wasn't alone in wanting this man, though the other people here must've been almost as desperate as I.

"One hundred and ten!" A woman called out to my side. The small increment that she had added onto my bid betrayed the fact that she had been near her limit with that bid as it was.

"One hundred and fifty!" another man offered.

"Are you insane? Look at the state of him, he is practically dead!" the woman objected loudly.

"Two hundred dinari!" I called out to interrupt the pair. I knew it was a big jump, but I didn't care.

"Two hundred!? That is some price to pay for a corpse!" the man joined the woman in her annoyance in being outbid. As though on queue to interrupt our one-way conversation, the man on the platform currently the object of the bids being received, coughed and spluttered loudly. When all of the remaining bidders turned to look at the man, they would all see that he had been coughing up blood, and his teeth were now stained red as he struggled with whatever it was that afflicted him.

"Well that is me out for the day!" the woman announced, and clutching her robes, she turned and disappeared. I watched as almost all of the remaining crowd, little as it had become, followed suit.

Inevitably, there were few people that wanted to pay for a dying man and my last bid held as the winner. I could tell from the look that the auctioneer gave me as I handed over the coin, that he felt as though he was robbing me and a part of me couldn't help but agree with him.

XIII – Mens Sana In Corpore Sano.

"A healthy mind in a healthy body."

The auctioneer and the hands that had helped bring the man onto the platform were less than helpful now that their wares had all been sold, and it left me to deal with the man I'd just purchased with just Dinari to help (who other than being able to kill the man with saliva, I presumed would do little else). The man seemed almost too weak to be moved and I wondered what exactly I could do to help him. His wounds had apparently mostly been dealt by an over-zealous master, though I knew that malnourishment amongst some other not so apparent injuries were also playing a huge part in his presentation.

If he had simply been stabbed or sliced by a gladius, I would've known what to do with him, but in truth I was no physician. I was highly skilled at my art, and that was healing obvious and bloody wounds, not dealing with long term maladies or the like, but I knew that there was one thing that I could do for the man that no physician that I knew could have - I could bestow upon my latest purchase the fortune of the Gods.

I needed to ensure that nobody saw what I was doing, otherwise I could've landed myself in more trouble than I'd bargained for.

"I need to get you off of the stage. I want to help, but I cannot do it where people might see us, OK?" I asked.

The man made no move to respond to me but I didn't hold it against him. To him I was just another master and for all he knew I could've been the same as, or perhaps even worse than the ones who'd come before me.

"Listen, all I want to do is help you, so if there is anything you can do to try to move, then please, just do it." I practically begged the man.

He turned his head to face me, and perhaps this was the first time that he'd ever seen a master actually down on his knees before him. Whatever the reason, he shifted his weight and rolled himself off the platform and onto the hard ground. I imagined that it would've hurt him. Hell, it would've hurt me if I'd fallen that short distance onto that ground.

I followed the man and he wedged himself up against the wooden platform. Between the construct and Dinari and me, there was little chance that what I was about to do would get seen.

I then started to do something that I had only done once within the last ten years; I pulled the sharpened stick from inside my new robes and dipped it in the man's fresh liquid blood.

I always carried the stick with me, or some other item that I would be able to draw sigils with if ever the situation arose, but I had made the promise to myself that I would only ever call upon the Gods for help, if the situation meant that someone that I was sure was a worthy person, was going to die without them.

The man's bare chest was concave and I could see almost all of his ribcage once I'd turned him onto his back. His sunken eyes failed to focus on me properly now and his skin was grey. He looked as though he was just moments from death and I wondered if that final short fall would be his downfall.

I drew the sigil of Mercury's caduceus with all of the expertise that I had ever had and it took me less time than anyone watching might have believed possible. The moment I finished drawing it on the man's chest, it glowed a bright blue as I had been expecting, then faded back into the red of the blood that it was drawn with.

I watched the man's eyes as the sigil was completed and saw the blue glow replicated within them. I watched as his chest rose and fell as though it was artificially inflated with more air than he'd been able to inhale in years. I watched as his back on the ground straightened, as though a huge weight had been removed from his shoulders and now, if anything, he looked both peaceful and comfortable.

I decided not to push the man's recovery. I knew from the few times that I'd drawn a sigil in the past, that the magic would take its time to carry out the work that it needed to do, but I didn't know what it would do for a body that'd been so abused such as this one. Dinari and I simply sat with our backs against the auctioneer's platform and waited for any sign that the man could move, or at least would be strong enough to be able to be helped onto a cart or something that we could travel upon. I was under no illusions that

I would be able to walk for a day whilst carrying this individual, slight as he was.

"Are you a God?" I had been daydreaming about my home, sleeping in the bedroom that I had grown up in when the voice snapped me back to reality. The man who I'd drawn the sigil on was now sitting next to me with his back pressed against the platform.

I looked at him for a moment before I responded. His skin had regained its paler complexion in lieu of the grey that it had been displaying. His eyes were no longer sunken though they glowed a bright blue now and seemed so full of life. I was unhappy to note though that he still looked malnourished, though everything about him no longer presented as though he was on the brink of death.

"No," I replied simply. "I am just a man and his dog."

The man looked at Dinari and once again placed a hand on the dog's head in a caring gesture.

"When I saw this little creature back there, I knew that he had been sent to save me. There was just something about his face, you know…" the man said.

At the man's words, Denari placed his front paws on the man's hips and reached up to lick his face. He didn't seem to care and again stroked Dinari's fur softly.

"My name is Titus," I announced. "I know it looks like I just bought you and all that, but I have no intention of… that is to say that I do not want…" I struggled to find the right words as in truth I hadn't thought this far ahead.

"It does not matter," the man interrupted me struggling to find something appropriate to say. "I understand how all of this works. You are the master and I do what you say; I have no qualms with that."

"No, that is what I was trying to say," I protested. "I did not buy you to gain a slave, I bought you to give a man the freedom to choose to live his own life the way that he sees fit. I have a house, though at this precise moment it is just myself who resides there, and if you would like a place to live and a free life to live, then you may come with me. All that I ask is that anyone who resides within will pull their own weight to contribute to the costs of the ludus."

The man narrowed his eyes at me as though what I had just said was total bollocks. "You said, ludus?"

"Ah… well, yes. In its first incarnation, my house was a ludus and it was run by my family. That was a long time ago though, so now it is simply my house," I explained.

The man thought again for a moment before he asked me his next question: "I can live any life I so wish?"

I nodded.

"Can you make me into a gladiator?" he asked.

I was about to laugh, though in the split second before I responded, I could see that he was being serious.

"I have longed for the glory of the sands of battle ever since I was a young boy. I know that I don't look it now, but my body was once strong and agile and I know that with proper instruction, I will one day hear the crowds cheer my name." Then he realised that he actually hadn't told me what his name was yet. "It's Marcus, by the way."

I shook my head slowly. "The house is a ludus no longer and I have no facilities for training, or even a Doctore or coaches to aid you in your endeavour."

"But it was once a ludus of note?" Marcus asked with hope in his eyes.

"It was once a ludus, though of note I would not be so brash. It was respected in Liternum over a decade ago, but those days are long gone," I protested.

"You told me that I would be free to live the life that I so choose, and this is what I would like. I would give my life in the arena if it meant that I could repay what you paid for me, though I will make you this promise: help me to become the best gladiator that Liternum has ever seen and I will repay you tenfold. If I perish, I will do so with honour and bring glory to your house."

To be fair to Marcus, it did seem like a good deal, though I had reservations about sending men to die in the arena on my behalf. I thought long and hard about how this could be done whilst still sticking to my principles and I came to just one conclusion.

"I am OK with you being a gladiator, though only if it is truly what you want. I will do what I can to help train you though I can make no promises past being able to feed you properly and doing my best to find you a trainer. And lastly, I will not keep the coin that you receive from your fights, you will fight as a free man and we will share everything that you earn equally. How does that sound?"

Marcus didn't even need to think about the deal that I had proposed. To me it sounded fair, though to him it looked as though it was the most one-sided deal in the history of slaves and their owners.

"I will bring you glory, dominus," he announced rather quickly.

"No, you will bring glory to yourself, if that is what you wish, and please, call me Titus." I replied with a smile. "And this is Dinari." The dog's ears raised at the mention of his name and he opened his mouth to pant. Things like that always reminded me that Dinari was certainly more intelligent than I usually gave him credit for.

"I think I can stand now," Marcus announced shortly after we'd made our proper introductions. "My legs feel stronger and my stomach doesn't feel as though it is going to cave in on itself any more. Can I ask what you did to me?"

I pursed my lips and wondered exactly how much I should tell my new friend (friend being the only way I could describe Marcus without using the word 'possession' or 'slave'). In the end I decided on a slightly condensed version of the truth.

"I worked as an arena healer for ten years and have treated almost every wound that you could imagine that is borne of steel, fist or foot. In that time I have also picked up a few tricks that allow me to heal people at an accelerated rate."

Marcus, if he had seen any deception in my words, didn't show it. "I have never seen anyone heal anyone the way you healed me, though it truly does not matter. It is just another reason that I know you were sent to turn me into a glorious gladiator; the fact that you are a skilled arena doctor is just further proof."

I didn't want to rain on Marcus' parade and tell him that this was just all because I wanted to help people with the coin that Ovidius had left me, so I kept my mouth shut. It did occur to me though, that all of these events were extremely convenient, as though they had been scripted to happen in some way. I thought that if I ever saw Mercury again, I would ask him if there was any divine hand in all of this. The answer to that question though, may have come in the way of the result of the first fight that Marcus would have in the arena; if he perished, then it would be obvious that this life was not meant to be for him or for me.

Because Marcus had been so cheap to purchase, I was able to afford a room for the night within Neapolis and, by all accounts, it was so much more opulent than Ovidius' room that I had called my home for a short while.

The rooms in the city had been primarily created for labourers that were needed to make the city what it was and then for later maintenance, though later the rooms also became available for visiting dignitaries who either didn't own a property in the city, or simply didn't own one *yet*.

It was the most luxurious night sleep that I had ever had, and it made me happy to think that if Marcus wasn't in the same boat as I was, at least this was probably a luxury that he hadn't had for a long while either.

When I awoke to the bright sunlight the very next morning, Dinari was still curled up in a ball atop my feet as he was every single day. I sometimes wondered how much of a difference to my sleep pattern he made, knowing that my subconscious would've detected his weight upon me and declared it as a safe environment. I didn't want to think about the alternative.

There were two beds in the room though, and when I looked over to where Marcus had slept, I could see that his bed was empty. My latest purchase had disappeared without a trace.

I got out of bed slowly and dressed myself; it didn't matter if Marcus had decided to go out alone into the world, after all I had told him that he was free to do so if he so wished, though I had to admit that I felt a little disappointed by that fact and also because he had cost me almost all the coin I'd had left to my name.

I knew that my plan was kind of risky, and it had hinged on the fact that a person who didn't want to be a slave would rather be a free and housed labourer, but when I thought back over the last ten years, it was exactly what I had been doing myself – I worked to live and that was about it. The only difference was that I was now offering a real home, and not a blood-stained hall of death for the person in question.

Just when I was about to leave the room, Marcus appeared in the doorway with a grin on his face and bread in his hands. He handed one to me then tore the other in half and offered half to Dinari and kept the other. I was amazed at the fact that he was willing to share, though once Dinari had swallowed his half of bread in one gulp, I tore a small portion of my own bread and handed it to Marcus.

"We are all in this together. There is no reason that I should have any more than you when it comes to food. Also, Dinari prefers fish if you are offering, apparently too much bread is bad for him," I announced with a smile.

"Oh…" Marcus said, peering down at the dog who was looking up at the rest of the bread with a loving smile and wide eyes. "I thought that we could just all do with a little breakfast, no? I must admit though, I did have to borrow a few asses from your purse."

That statement made my heart sink a little. Marcus had helped himself to my money. I would give him the benefit of the doubt for now as I had said we were to share everything, but if there was anything more missing, I would have to re-evaluate my relationship with the man.

The bread, however, was delicious. It was somehow softer and lighter than the puls that I had become used to back in Liternum, and I savoured every mouthful.

"This bread… it's amazing," I announced thankfully to Marcus. "Where did you get it?"

Marcus seemed as though he was similarly taken by the bread and spoke with his mouth half-full. "A bakery just down the way. If you follow your nose you'll get there," he said.

I didn't really need to know where the stuff came from, but I thought it would have been nice for Marcus to hear that he had done something good for us.

The following day was spent on the long walk back to the ludus in Liternum. I had warned Marcus that the journey could be brutal in the heat, although we had stocked up on water and bread before we left so that we were sure we could make it without succumbing to exhaustion along the way. I'd brought a fish for Dinari to eat too, just to ensure he was properly fed on something other than bread.

Whilst we walked, the time simply flew by and before I knew it, I could see the ludus atop the hill on the outskirts of Liternum. The journey had been much more pleasurable with someone to talk to, and as I gave Marcus the unabridged version of my life (without the mention of the Gods), he gave me the details of his own.

Marcus had been a legionnaire in the Roman army, though he had lied about his age to gain entry at just sixteen rather than the required seventeen. He said that he was tall for his age and although there were some questioning glances in his direction, the gambit had proved successful. His family had always idolised soldiers, so when he had thought he looked old enough, Marcus had left the family home to join up for the twenty-five years' service that the post demanded. After just a few short years though, Marcus had begun to realise that the army and its legionaries were not heroes that lived the life of luxury and admiration, rather it was the opposite. The pay was low and opportunities to spend it were far and few between. Units of soldiers were sent out to either do the 'dirty work of politicians' (as Marcus put it), to guard some noble 'shit-head' (again, his words not mine), or to stand guard at the gates of some town where the population had started to become a little unruly. It was not the life Marcus had expected, and so one day he simply removed his uniform and left.

I knew that deserters from the army faced a death sentence when they were caught, so I asked how he had managed to avoid such a fate.

"When I was caught, it wasn't because I was a deserter. It was because I was carrying a legionary's weapon without being in the service... I hadn't really thought about it and had kept hold of my gladius because I thought it might've come in handy. What it actually did though, was to cement me as a thief in the view of the guards that found me with it strapped to my side. I was offered either a lifetime of servitude for my crime, or a lifetime without my right hand… sometimes I wonder if I made the right choice, though other times I am grateful that I get to live without such a handicap."

Marcus then went on to tell me about how he had been bought and sold by masters in both Rome and Neapolis and how not a single one of them showed any real regard for another human being. The best scenario that he had endured was a single small room shared by no less than twenty slaves at any given time, and the worst was his last master, who had fed his slaves just one small meal every two days and beat them regularly. His story made me sick, and once again I felt as though I had done the right thing in taking this individual on.

Marcus and I entered into my house through the main door at the front of the property and the bliss that I felt in having my home back once again took my breath away. I could also see Marcus looking about the building as we walked through the entranceway and I could tell that he was impressed. Eventually he spoke without looking in my direction.

"OK, so what is the catch here?" he asked.

"What do you mean?" I replied cautiously.

"This house… and everything you say you will do to help me… it just seems too good to be true, and I know that if something seems too good to be true, it probably is," Marcus said.

"Nope. It is just like I said; half of what you earn and a little help around the house when it's needed. Though I suppose if you really are set on becoming a gladiator, we can probably go ahead and call it a ludus again and not a house.

XIV – Semper Paratus.

"Always prepared."

Despite having all of the available rooms within the house to choose from, Marcus decided that if he was to become a real gladiator, he would live in the gladiator pens just off of the training sands outside the ludus. I did try to dissuade him, but his decision was made and his mind stalwart.

I had imparted as much wisdom as I could to the man, the way in which my father had trained his gladiators physically, though I knew that he had never tried to teach technique in any meaningful way and if I was to follow in his footsteps, I knew that soon I would have to arrange for a real Doctore to be present in my ludus.

Marcus must've been used to training his physical condition however, and that surprised me. His days within the ranks of the Roman legions had very obviously given him some insight into conditioning his body to be able to withstand a tremendous amount of physical exertion.

I was yet to buy or arrange for any real training apparatus for the training sands, though Marcus was apparently extremely resourceful when it came to repurposing everyday items to his cause. He had dragged a huge tree trunk up the hill and onto the training sands so that he could pick it up and put it back down over and over. Then he would hoist it onto his shoulders as best he could and walk it around the sands until he could take no more, and then finally he would drag it until his legs gave out.

I made sure that I kept food and water always available for the gladiator in training, and by all accounts after just a few days, Marcus looked as though his body had begun to repair itself, the malnutrition that hampered it a thing of the past.

At night, Marcus slept soundly in his small cell. It wasn't a cell in the strictest sense of the word, though for all intents and purposes that was exactly what it was. I spent a lot of time inspecting every nook and cranny of the ludus when I wasn't in the town picking up food or water for the next few days as I wanted to know every single inch of it. My mother and father had loved this place, and it did their memory the service they deserved to appreciate everything they had ever done for me.

Dinari had been his usual beautiful self the whole time. I kept him well fed with fish and bread as much as I could, though I knew that the money that I had was soon going to run out. Truth be told, if I had spent what I had planned on spending for Marcus, it would've already dried up, but it seemed as though it was the will of the Gods once again that we had a little breathing room before we had to do anything drastic.

Marcus had beseeched me to enter his name into the gladiator roster with the arena master and although I had my reservations about how ready he was, I had done as he asked. He was a free man after all, and I had promised him that I would do everything I could to make his dreams a reality.

Thankfully, as an unknown entity (both myself and Marcus), the arena master had told me that we would be waiting for a month before he would be placed upon the sands in front of a crowd. This seemed odd to me, but, as the games had become far more civilised than they once were, it did make sense. People now wanted to see longer bouts filled with technical expertise, much more than they wanted to see a gladiator swiftly decapitated and his head paraded around the sands as though it was the most amusing thing in the world.

The only problem that I had with all of this, was that Marcus was not a trained gladiator, and when asked what style he would be using by the arena master, the only thing that I could think of to say, was Samnite. It was not a popular class and was seldom used following the changeover from the Roman Republic to the Roman Empire around five decades ago, but it was both the closest thing that I could think of to how legionaries would've been trained, and they also had the best shield and sword of all of the gladiators in the arena – even more so than the mighty Murmillo. They were rare to see in the arena nowadays, and the fact that Samnites almost exclusively fought against Retiarius was just another reason why Marcus would have to wait so long for a pairing. It suited me down to the ground though, as it would give me the chance to find a trainer for him to give him the best chance possible for victory in the arena.

After the first couple of weeks of allowing Marcus to train his body in strength and endurance alone, I decided to make my way into town to find him a trainer. Honestly though, I had no idea where to start.

I took Dinari to the arena and as always the thoughts of making this very journey with my father, the very last time he had taken Dinari, Vettius and me to the games were present in my mind. The building, roads and people had all changed over the last decade, but the feeling it gave me remained, and I imagined that it would remain there until the day that I died.

I thought to approach the arena master first, as I knew that with the games scheduled to happen that very day, he would already be sitting in his own personal seat in a private section of the stands. He would always be first to the games so that he didn't have to deal with the crowds, and being the same arena master for over a decade his habits had become well known: arrive early, drink wine and leave late. He did have guards, but once I'd told them that I had a gladiator that was participating in the games, I had been let through.

"Ah, young Titus. Here to remove your gladiator from the games already?" The master asked sarcastically. He was an older gentleman with a greying beard and a fat belly. The lifestyle had apparently caught up to him and he could no longer escape what time did to a person who lived mostly in luxury.

"No not at all, arena master," I said quickly.

"Please, call me Galerius," he interrupted me before I could make my speech.

"Galerius," I repeated with a slight bow. "I am in search of a trainer for my gladiator so that he may provide the crowds with the best possible showing. I ask you, do you have a list or could possibly point me in the right direction to find such a man?"

Galerius practically guffawed at my question. "For a Samnite? You are decades too late my boy! If you wanted a trainer for Murmillo, or Retiarius I could give you a list of ten! But a Samnite? I am afraid that with this one, I cannot offer you any aid."

My heart sank a little. "Do you think it would then be appropriate to change my man's class?" I asked.

Galerius stroked his beard, though I could see he had a smile on his face. "No boy, the casting has been made, your man will revive the class of Samnite and it will either cause others to follow suit toward victory, or it will be a lesson as to why things that are dead and buried should remain so."

"But the show…" I started to protest, though Galerius held up a hand to silence me.

"I have spoken, boy. Now go, I have wine to drink and gladiators trying to kill each other to watch!" Then he added in a slightly lower tone: "though it is not like it used to be…"

I didn't protest any further; it was clear that Marcus was going to be at a clear disadvantage in all of this. As I turned to walk away though, Galerius called out one last nail in my coffin:

"Your man is going to have to provide his own arms and armour too! We do not keep extinct sets around here on the off chance!"

I gritted my teeth but said nothing; we were already in enough trouble as it was.

Dinari had kept by my side throughout the entire conversation although he hadn't made any noises or movements towards the man one way or the other. As usual his reading of the situation had been correct; he knew that anything aggressive would've landed us in trouble, and the man did not deserve anything positive from him. It was funny as although he was the most loving dog in the world, when it came to people who I didn't like, Dinari seemed to share in that sentiment.

We picked up some bread and a handful of fruits from Liternum before we returned to the ludus. I knew that without adequate training in his art, Marcus was going to be at a significant disadvantage in the arena against whoever this Retiarius was going to be. The good thing, though, was that because Marcus was an unknown entity, it was likely that he was going to face off against a gladiator of little note – which could mean little skill too. Thankfully, I'd seen more than a few Retiarius fight in my time, and I knew where they were going to be most vulnerable.

When Dinari and I arrived back at the ludus, I joined Marcus on the training sands in order to impart what knowledge I had gained during my time inside the arena.

"The Retiarius has three main ways in which he wins his fights," I explained as Marcus continued his training regimen with a heavy-looking branch. He was lifting it above his head and pressing it over and over as I spoke.

"He has the trident as his main form of attack, he is only lightly armoured so he will try to move in quickly. From what I have seen, when the trident's range has been eliminated, the gladiator will be easily attacked as his armour is so light. Then you have to deal with his net. It will be weighted and generally it will slow you down so that the Retiarius can attack with his knife if the trident had been eliminated already, if not, being caught in the net and having a trident thrust at you will end you. Do not get caught in the net." I thought about the Retiarius that I'd seen in the healing room as I'd worked at the arena.

"Retiarii are almost always wounded in exactly the same ways: they get small cuts and gashes to slow them down before deeper wounds can be made once they become desperate. In my opinion, the best way to beat them is to use their overconfidence in their speed against them. Make your opponent overreach, thinking he has bested you from the beginning and attack on the counter. You have a shield and more armour to work with, though you must ensure that you do not tire quickly." The knowledge that I had was everything I could do for Marcus, and I could tell that he understood my words and would heed them.

Marcus had gained a lot of muscle in a very short amount of time and I didn't know if it was his muscle memory, diet, training regimen or more likely a combination of all three that was to thank for this. Physical stature, though, I knew was only going to be half of the battle and if Marcus had previous training to call upon with sword and shield, it was the thing that was going to make the biggest difference when he entered the arena as a new gladiator.

I spent the following weeks doing my best to work with Marcus and impart all of the knowledge that I had gained about gladiators and their styles. Of course he knew how gladiators fought, the equipment and armour that they had, but I knew where each gladiator would carry the most wounds and therefore would be most likely to be injured. Samnites, though, were a mystery to us both and I hoped that this could've been an advantage as Marcus' opponent would similarly have little experience in dealing with that style of gladiator.

I had tried, tried and tried again to bring the services of a Samnite trainer to my ludus, but it seemed as though it was perhaps too much of a request, as although I did manage to speak to a number of trainers willing to teach Marcus how to survive in the arena, not a single one of them had even seen a Samnite gladiator fight. I hadn't brought any trainers back: I didn't have coin to waste on one that didn't understand how my man was going to fight.

XV – Deos Fortioribus Adesse.

"The gods are on the side of the stronger."

The day of Marcus' first battle came around all too soon. I felt as though he wasn't ready to face another gladiator in a fight to the death yet, though I didn't know if I would ever feel he would be. The truth was, I just didn't like death. I liked the arenas, the sands, the contests and the techniques, but with age, I had no lust for blood.

The journey to the arena in Liternum once more echoed of the same trip that my father, Vettius, Dinari and I had taken, and from my new position within the party – the one that my father had filled as a Lanista – I had a new appreciation for just how difficult his task must've been.

I went with Marcus into the prep area and I was happy to note that the armour that I had arranged for him to wear was awaiting him there in a pile. He would hold a short gladius and a rectangular wooden shield and wear a singular metal grieve along his sword arm and a leather shin pad on his left leg. He also had a plumed helmet for his head, though without a full face covering it meant that he would be able to see more than the traditional Murmillo-style helmet would afford. The last piece of armour that he would be wearing would be a triple-disc pectoral cuirass to keep his trunk well protected from the deadly spear of his Retiarius opponent.

The arena hands that had brought the equipment awaited Marcus in the prep room to cover the gladiator with the oils that would make his skin glow in the hot sun when he took to the sands. When I observed Marcus in all of his gear, I had to admit that he had transformed his body from a ghost of a human into somewhat of a muscular man. He hadn't grown into the kind of beast that I had seen out there on the sands, he simply hadn't had enough time or food to make that kind of change yet, but he was certainly a totally different man to the one who I'd paid for not too long ago.

I waited for the arena hands to disappear so that I could impart my last knowledge and action to my man.

"Listen, Marcus… there is something I need to do and I am going to need you to trust me." I said slowly. I had already made up my mind about what I was going to do, and I knew that I had to tell Marcus the truth as I did it.

Marcus nodded, his head apparently already out there on the sands.

"I need you to take your breastplate off."

The gladiator gave me a sideways glance but started to unbuckle the leather straps that held his breastplate in place upon his chest.

"There is something that I have not told you," I said as I pulled my sharpened stick out from within my robes. I had also prepared a flask of ink to use when carrying out my secret art. "The day that I rescued you from your slavery, you were close to death…"

"I remember," Marcus said. "You did… something to heal me. I know it was not something that was normal nor that would be accepted, but I have never asked you about it. Some things are better left unsaid…"

"Right… but this is something that could help you right now," I spoke as I drew the sigil onto Marcus' chest, right above where I knew his heart was. "This is the caduceus of Mercury. It will bestow upon you a healing power of the Gods. You will not be invincible, but small wounds will cause you less problems whilst you are out there on the sands, and heavier wounds will close quickly. If you do lose this battle and are rendered in a bad way, this sigil may save your life as it once has before."

"Do you really believe in such things?" Marcus asked, looking down at the unfinished sigil, but I didn't have to answer; as I formed the last stroke, the sigil glowed brightly, illuminating the entire room and I simply smiled.

"By the Gods," I managed to hear Marcus whisper, and I couldn't help but feel a little smug at that.

Marcus took to the sands after he'd refastened his breastplate and I followed him to the iron gate that I had stood behind on so many occasions. I didn't want to take to the stands just in case I was needed to help the arena doctor if Marcus fell and I knew that my replacement – one of the former hands – was not as skilled as I would've liked from a doctor. Within a moment, Marcus' opponent joined us at the gate and awaited the call from the arena announcer.

"It is a good day to die, no?" the Retiarius said without looking toward either of us or Dinari, who sat patiently by my side.

The Retiarius looked as though he was in good shape. He was dark-skinned and fairly lean, and was taller than Marcus, which I knew would only aid his reach advantage.

Eventually, the two gladiators moved through the open gate and took to the sands and as Marcus walked away from us for what could've been the last time, I heard Dinari make a noise not unlike that of a seal at the sight of his newest best friend walking away. I wondered how much Dinari knew about what was happening, but as usual the way he was acting told me that he knew a lot more than I was giving him credit for.

I could tell immediately that Marcus had listened to my words as he and his Retiarius opponent faced off against each other from across the sands. I could also tell that my man had also been trained well as a soldier, as he held his wooden shield up just beneath his eye line to protect most of his person from any wild attacks from the Retiarius.

Conversely, I could see that the Retiarius now looked as though he wanted to use all of the advantages of his equipment: the lighter weight of his armour and the longer reach of his trident, to try to best Marcus. I pondered on the weight of equipment versus skill and training, though I knew I wouldn't have to wait very long for an answer.

"Let battle commence!" the announcer shouted loudly and his voice travelled around the amphitheatre in a moment. His words echoed in my mind and my pulse quickened at the sight of both of the gladiators becoming rigid, ready to make the opening moves.

The Retiarius immediately moved to press the advantage that he had via speed, reach and agility. He leapt up into the air and thrust his trident at Marcus, who planted his back foot on the sands and lifted his shield to defend himself. My heart skipped a beat as I immediately worried about how strong the equipment was that I had bought for him, but thankfully the shield held. The trident was deflected to the side though the noise that the contact had made was deafening.

The Retiarius pulled the trident back and clasped it in both hands before launching another strike at the shield, though this time with a lot more force. Again, Marcus blocked the strike and deflected it, although as he did, the Retiarius let go of the trident with his left hand and swung it *underneath* Marcus' shield at his shins. The trident, which was not traditionally a slashing-type weapon did have a little in the way of edges to its tips and I watched in horror as the centre tip of the weapon bit into Marcus' leather shin guard and a trickle of red blood fell from the wound and onto his sandals.

To his credit Marcus did not make a sound, though in the moment that it took for him to right himself, his opponent was on him again with strong and straight attacks that Marcus was barely able to block. This Retiarius was extremely fast and it was all that Marcus could do to keep his shield between himself and the tip of the trident.

I did not hold out much hope in this fight for my gladiator. Marcus had barely even been able to fend off his wild opponent, let alone throw any attacks of his own.

Then I saw what legionnaire training could do when presented with an opportunity. The Retiarius over-extended his reach as he strode in for a finishing blow and as Marcus deflected the trident with a strong backswing of his shield, he followed it up with a straight stab of his gladius. The attack caught everyone in the arena off-guard and the crowd fell silent, unsure of what had actually happened. That was of course until Marcus pulled his sword back and a spray of red blood coated the inside of his shield.

The Retiarius looked stunned and he actually had to inspect the wound to the side of his stomach before he would believe it for himself, and in that moment of distraction, Marcus followed through with a hard front kick to the gladiator's stomach that sent him flying backwards and to the ground.

The Retiarius, who I'd presumed was a lot more injured than he actually was, rolled as he landed and righted himself as though he had never been hit at all. In the act of being hit though, the gladiator had lost his trident, and it lay out of reach, closer to Marcus than to the Retiarius.

Marcus stepped forward, keeping his shield at eye-level once more and the Retiarius drew his dagger and the weighted net from his belt. The gladiator once again darted forward and leapt high into the air with dagger outstretched. Marcus simply shrugged the dagger off with his shield as the gladiator impacted his defences, though I had seen what Marcus had failed to: the dagger had been a diversion and snaking around his shield to the far side of the wild attack, the Retiarius' weighted net entangled Marcus, catching on his shield and the metal of his gauntlet. Marcus had had his hands tied, and there was nothing that he could do about it.

The Retiarius pulled his net tight and Marcus fought against it to free at least one of his hands although the task looked difficult. The dark-skinned gladiator then moved in so quickly to dagger range that Marcus could do nothing. He took the first cut to the top of his arm well, though the second strike sliced into his collar and my breath caught as I worried that it was the killing blow. Dinari whimpered and raised himself to his feet, his tail hanging limply between his legs.

Marcus fell.

Then, in his moment of quiet calm, he rolled away from the Retiarius and out of the entangling net. As he raised himself back to his feet I could see that his wounds had already stopped bleeding and I thanked Mercury for caring for the man.

Now without his net and trident, the Retiarius had nothing but his dagger to keep him alive in this fight, whereas Marcus still held onto everything that he had walked out onto the sands with.

The Retiarius knew that he didn't have many options left to him - he could either fight for his life or simply lay down and die. I was not surprised to watch him take the first option.

The gladiator grasped his dagger and ran at Marcus. Marcus did not flinch, he simply held his shield before him and when his opponent reached striking range, Marcus forced his shield outward, hitting the man with all the might he could muster with the wooden shield.

The Retiarius' nose exploded with a cloud of blood as he fell backwards and to the ground once more.

Marcus moved over his opponent and kicked the dagger away from his hand. This was it, the end of the fight and everyone in the arena knew it.

The Retiarius, disarmed and entirely at the mercy of Marcus, raised a finger to the air to signify his 'missio', or surrender.

I knew that ten years ago, this very act would've incited a riot in the crowds who wanted nothing more than to see a gladiator cut down in the prime of his life. Now, though, the crowd cheered for Marcus as the technically superior fighter, and he stepped back and away from his defeated opponent to the applause of the crowds.

The arena announcer was quick to announce Marcus as the victor, though to my ears it didn't sound as though he was very happy about it. The last thing that the arena wanted was for an extinct gladiator class to prove that it had been worthy all along. I didn't care though, Marcus could fight as a Cestus for all it mattered, I just wanted him to live, and to a lesser extent to win.

Both gladiators walked off the sands under their own effort. I could see that Marcus had all but healed, although the Retiarius would require tending to by the arena doctor.

I made sure to hang about near the healing room just in case the new doctor was a little frivolous with the blade, though I was happy to note whilst listening to Marcus recount his glorious victory, that the Retiarius' wounds were cleaned and coated so that they would be allowed to heal properly. I wondered what it had done for his pride though, losing to an unused style and untested gladiator.

"It'll be sooner rather than later that the crowds will be begging for the arena master to schedule matches against me!" Marcus was saying and I was only half paying attention to him. His victory had been a good one, though he was a long way from the grandeur of some of the more well known gladiators out there.

"Do not go getting ahead of yourself Marcus, I replied. "It was a closely fought match and if you hadn't have had that little advantage of yours…"

At that moment, my sentiment was interrupted by a hand on my shoulder. I turned slowly to regard whoever it was, either hoping for payment from the arena master, or a congratulating handshake, although a part of me worried about the sigil I had drawn and how it could've been looked upon as cheating by any of the other gladiators or indeed the crowd.

The man who had interrupted me, although now clean shaven, much larger and more muscular, was Vettius: the very man who had fought on behalf of my father before both he and my mother had been killed.

Vettius was wearing a robe rather than a gladiator's attire so it was evident that he had joined the contest as a spectator rather than a contender. What flashed through my mind immediately, though, was the memory of the bright blue sigil that Vettius had carried upon his body the last time I'd seen him fight.

I took a step back from the man.

"V… Vettius!?" I exclaimed loudly. The gladiator smiled and gestured to Marcus.

"Your man did well today, Titus. He fought as a legionary would… more than a gladiator… though skill is skill it seems. I did not expect to see you here with a gladiator though, and I would have questioned the fact that it was actually you, until I saw what lay hidden beneath solid armour," Vettius said.

"It has been a long time," I replied quietly. "But what happened to you all those years ago? I came to look for you but you had already left the arena by the time I had arrived."

"I remember the day well," Vettius replied. "Everyone remembers their first victory…" he shot a knowing glance at Marcus, who was still beside himself with delight.

Dinari barked loudly and stood on his hind legs for Vettius to stroke his head.

"And I would never forget you, furry one," Vettius said in a much softer tone. "The day of my first victory was a day of change for me. Your father had adorned me with his latest work…" he gave me a knowing stare that said 'we will discuss the sigils later', then continued. "When I had defeated my opponent upon the sands, I was taken to have my wounds tended to as some were taking a while to heal on their own. The doctor kept me still until he was happy that he had cleaned and treated the wounds properly, but by the time I was allowed to move, word had arrived that the ludus that held my servitude had been burned to the ground, and the master and mistress were missing. I waited for clearer reports, but the only word that reached me was that everything was gone… So I took the coin that I had won in the arena and set out to forge my own path. Had I known that you were still alive, I would have returned to you as my master."

My mouth hung open at Vettius' story. I knew it was the truth, but for him to have heard about the events of that day so quickly just didn't sit right with me. Of course I didn't suspect him of any wrongdoing, but something untoward had certainly happened and I wished I could unravel the mystery a little further.

"So where did you go?" I asked, deciding to ask more about the gladiator rather than ponder my own mortality, or my parents' deaths.

Vettius smiled as though internally recounting all of the years, and I could tell that they had been good to him. I was happy for that fact; in my eyes everybody deserved a good life.

"I travelled across the empire to fight in arenas as a free gladiator," Vettius announced. "I fought as Retiarius and my opponents quickly learned to fear me. In the last decade, I have fought and won over twenty contests… I was beginning to gain fame wherever I went…

"Is that why you are back now?" I asked. "To fight in Liternum again?"

I could see that my words hurt Vettius, though he didn't shy away from a response.

"I… am afraid I am gladiator no longer…" the man said, sliding his dark robe off of his left shoulder. Underneath, his arm was as it should've been - for the first five or six inches that was. The rest was missing and had healed into a rounded nub. It was immediately clear that he had lost this arm and for a gladiator, that was the end of his career.

"No matter the speed, perception or healing that the Gods bestow upon a mortal man, that is precisely what he remains: mortal. One fleeting moment allowed for a superior opponent to take his advantage is all that is needed."

I peered at where Vettius' arm should've been and a part of me felt his pain. This was the kind of injury that nobody could do anything about and one that could happen in an instant when upon the sands. Some gladiators would've preferred to have been killed with honour, rather than carry this injury for the rest of their lives.

"But beside all of that! I have just arrived in Liternum and am yet to discover a bed for the night. Tell me, Titus, what has life done with you for the past decade?" Vettius asked, his smile and positive demeanour having returned.

"Well actually... I now own the ludus that you know to have burnt down. I rebuilt it from the ground up and Marcus here," I gestured to the victorious gladiator who had taken to squishing Dinari's face between his hands, "lives and trains there. I must admit though, there is yet another to call the ludus home."

"Then I have a proposal for you," Vettius announced.

XVI – Non Omnis Moriar.

"I shall not wholly die."

Vettius' proposal was a simple one: he wanted me to allow him to live within the ludus as he had once before (though possibly inside the house proper this time), and keep him fed and clothed. In return he would train Marcus to be a Retiarius. I had tried to get him to leave Marcus as a Samnite, as he had already won a fight under the title and as I had bought all of the equipment he would need for that role, but as usual the answer to me was that he had never actually seen a Samnite on the sands, let alone knew how to teach one effectively. He did assure me though, that the equipment I'd bought could be used as a training apparatus, so it wouldn't be wasted.

I initially thought that the arrangement was a little too good to be true, though Vettius told me that as he could no longer fight in the arena due to the loss of his arm, many ludus' across the empire would not even take him seriously as a trainer. Also, as Vettius had never technically been freed from his service to our ludus, he felt as though he had a personal debt to my family, and therefore to me.

Of course I had tried to dissuade him from such feeling, but the former gladiator had made up his mind, and had asked that in future he be referred to as 'Doctore'. I gave up and agreed to his terms.

I showed Vettius around the house once we had returned one man heavier. It was kind of moot because he'd lived there before, though I suspected that he had never had the chance to sleep inside, having briefly lived in one of the cells next to the training sands. This was a luxury that I didn't want taken from the latest member of my household, and Vettius didn't object at all to a warm room and a comfortable bed.

"There is one last thing that I need to know," Vettius said once we were alone in the entrance foyer to the house. Well, we weren't strictly alone as Dinari was predictably by my side, biting his nails with loud crunching sounds as though it was the most important task in the world.

"How many sigils have you learnt so far? And how much power can you impart to your gladiators?" Vettius' eyes were wide with wonder, and I hated to disappoint, but I couldn't lie to him.

"I only know one - Mercury's caduceus," I answered honestly.

"One?" Vettius sounded shocked. "How can this be, when your father knew three that I knew of!"

"Three!?" I asked in astonishment. "What do you mean he knew three?"

"Did your father never impart the knowledge to you? I had just assumed that because you had drawn a sigil on Marcus, that you had been taught…"

I let my head hang a little at the thought of my parents, and how much they should've been able to teach me, had they not been so cruelly taken.

"He never really… had the time…" I said slowly.

"But your father must have left you something that would teach you everything that you would need to know. I had not been with the ludus for very long I must admit, but I knew your father and if he was the man that I thought he was, then he would have made sure that you would not be left without the knowledge that he had been learning. Are you sure there is nothing that you can think of, anything at all?"

I thought about that for a long moment and I knew that Vettius was right; my father would've done anything to make sure that his family was cared for, even if he wasn't there to ensure it.

"The only things that I managed to save from the fire were two books from my father's office, though they are both empty. I would not still have them but an old friend of mine saved them for me. I was going to sell them actually, though I never got around to it."

"Show me the books," Vettius said sharply, which took me aback.

I retrieved both of the empty books from my room and brought them back to Vettius, who turned them over in his hands as though there was something on them that I wasn't able to see. His expression gave nothing away and I half expected the former gladiator to throw them to the ground, though instead he started speaking again.

"I saw your father writing in one of these books once. Making notes of some kind, but when I looked down at the page there was nothing there. I have heard on my travels across the empire of ways to conceal writings from those that are not permitted to see them…" Vettius trailed off conspiratorially. He then walked with the book in hand to one of the burning torches along the stone walls. He held the book open so that just the first page was near to the burning flame and my mouth hung agape as the blank page began to fill with my father's writing.

Vettius walked back to me and handed over the book for me to read the words. I didn't think he read them himself, although I wouldn't have begrudged him the fact if he had. The words on the page hit me as though they had a physical weight behind them:

My son, Titus. I fear that the time is running short for me to be able to teach you the things that I have learnt over the past few weeks. I have discovered a technique that can make gladiators better in the arena, though I am only at the beginning of my journey.
I do not know the limits of this power and I fear that discovery of the art could lead to dire consequences. You are but a child and I do not wish for you to worry about such things, but one day you will own everything that we have built as a family.
My biggest wish is that you are afforded the luxury of a name that speaks for itself, without having to prove yourself through bloodshed and battle.
There are magical symbols that, when drawn upon an individual, bestow upon that person enhanced abilities. I have discovered some of these symbols and if they continue to be effective, I will dedicate my life to finding more.
Titus, my son. If anything happens to me, I bestow upon you in the following pages the knowledge that I have learnt in this task, and hope that one day you may also see the value in their usage.

I turned the page to the next and when I saw that it was blank, I walked over to the torch as Vettius had done and held the book up to the flame until it too began to change, showing what my father had drawn there.

This symbol is the caduceus of Mercury. It will bestow upon its wearer the power of enhanced healing.

The page was filled with the sigil that I had already mastered, the winged staff of Mercury with intertwining tails down the length of its shaft. There were also some notes on the page about how effective the enhanced healing was, though it was information that I already knew.

My hands began to shake as I turned to the next page, and I wondered what else I could possibly learn next from my father.

The next page filled with another sigil, and I immediately recognised it for what it was. It was something that I had seen before, though not something that I had ever put much stock into. Upon the page, was a perfect drawing of Mercury's winged cap: petasos.

The notations that sat around this sigil informed me that this sigil would bestow an enhanced sense of perception upon the gladiator who wore it. The gladiator would be able to anticipate attacks as they came at him, as though he had the ability to slow time. I wondered if Vettius had worn this sigil upon his body when I saw him fight in the arena all those years ago but it was a question that could be answered later. Right now I needed to know everything that my father could do, and had wanted me to know.

I turned the next page and wondered exactly how far my father's notes could take me. I followed the same pattern as before and heated the page to reveal the sigil.

I recognised this sigil too, though again I hadn't been aware that the image held any power. This one took the form of a single winged sandal and I knew without reading the description that my father had left, that this sigil would impart the bearer with enhanced speed as it was without doubt Mercury's Talaria.

I took in all of the information on the page before I made a move to walk back to the flame with the next page of the book in hand, but before I could, Vettius took a firm hold of my forearm.

"This is everything that I had ever seen your father create upon a gladiator. I do not know if there is more to be learned from this book, but do not be disappointed if there is no more."

I nodded at the man though I wasn't yet ready to make eye-contact with him. In my mind, what was happening was between me and my father. I knew Vettius was involved, but at that particular moment, I thought it would do my father's memory the best honour to keep this between the two of us.

I held the next page of the book up to the flame, and then the next and the next, but there wasn't a single other mark in the entire book and I realised that this was the point at which my father must've been killed – before he could impart any further knowledge to the book... and then to me. I dropped it to my side almost defeated, though I knew that I had just tripled my arsenal of sigils that would help Marcus in the arena, and combined with the fact that he would actually have a proper teacher now, his chances of survival had gone through the roof.

I checked the second book against the flame, though this one was entirely empty from start to finish no matter the heat that I applied to it. I wondered if my father had thought that he would have a lot more knowledge to impart, but there was no way for me to know. As it was, I needed to master the two new sigils as quickly as possible so that when I drew them onto Marcus' skin, he would benefit from their divine power.

"In the morning, I will begin training with Marcus, though I make no promises that it will be easy for him. I do promise though, that it will make his time in the arena easier, one way or another. Is there anything else that you require of me?" Vettius asked.

I shook my head but remained silent. I wanted to be alone for a while so that I could gather my thoughts properly. This whole ordeal had been far too much and the memory of my parents and their untimely deaths was once again fresh in my mind. I wondered just what the reason behind their murder had been, and then thought that if my father had really known that something bad was going to happen to him, why hadn't he done more to prevent it? There were so many questions and so few answers and a big part of me knew that I may never find them.

With just one single sigil – the caduceus of Mercury – in my arsenal, I'd never felt as if I was very much of a Sigilarius. I hadn't really ever done very much with the skill that I had practised over the years and a big part of that still ate away at me, including the fact that my skill had almost led to the freedom of one of the men that had killed my parents – and possibly contributed to the deaths of two innocent legionaries. I had managed to shake that guilt off though, when the skill meant that my man Marcus was afforded divine intervention in his own battle upon the sands.

I retrieved the single pot of ink from atop my desk, exactly where I had left it, and pulled a few sheets of parchment from their place on the bookshelf. Parchment being cheap where books were not, I had made sure to buy some for the very task of practising my drawings, although I had never imagined that this would be the parchment that I would be practising *two* new sigils upon.

I chose to work on Mercury's winged cap first. There was no reason to particularly choose either of the new sigils, it was just that I had seen that one first, so that's how it was.

Penmanship had become a somewhat natural art to me as I had practised it so much over the last decade. I was never really *in training* to become a Sigilarius, and a part of me knew that the skill was transferable. Rather I just enjoyed creating art, and that enjoyment had meant that now I was a master of sketching.

Mercury's cap shimmered blue as I had completed it without missing a single stroke or misplacing an errant line. It was easy for me and as usual as I drew sigils, I felt as though my hand was being guided in some places by the Gods themselves. I turned the parchment over and repeated the process on the back with the sigil for Mercury's winged sandals. Again, it glowed brightly as it was completed and I smiled to myself for my accomplishment.

I knew that creating the sigils when I didn't have the guideline of my father's book handy was going to be much more difficult, but I also knew that with a fair amount of practise, drawing the sigils perfectly from memory was going to be a task that I was entirely capable of.

XVII – Ars Longa, Vita Brevis.

"Art is long, Life is short."

I spent a long time alone learning the two new sigils (well alone as anyone could be when in the presence of Dinari, the most lovable dog in the world). I also practised the caduceus every now and then to ensure that I wasn't forgetting anything, though thankfully the images in my mind remained both separate and clear.

It seemed as though we were all simply going through the motions once I'd arranged for Marcus to have his second fight in the arena. Vettius had told me to ensure that the battle was not to happen within the next month so that Marcus would have adequate time to train and I agreed. Marcus wanted to take to the sands sooner, though with there now being three of us and Dinari not having a vote, he was outnumbered and had to obey the ruling of democracy.

The arena master had evidently been surprised at the skill of the gladiator in his first fight, though was happy to see that the more conventional style of Retiarius rather than Samnite had been chosen for the next battle. It was nice for something new and interesting to happen in his arena, but unknowns could be dangerous.

We had been offered a purse of twenty-five dinari for the second fight as Marcus already had a victory under his belt. I didn't care much for the coin, though if it kept increasing as Marcus won battles – which I was sure that he would – then I was happy with that. When I said I didn't care for the coin, I knew that it was a necessity, though there were more important things to be done in the world. My mind had already turned to the next person that I could purchase from nearby Neapolis, and for that I needed more coin, much more. I had actually toyed with the idea of purchasing a tested gladiator so that I could multiply my income and help even more slaves become free, though I remembered that seasoned gladiators could range from the tens of thousands of dinari to the hundreds of thousands and that was simply out of reach for someone of my standing.

I had not needed to buy equipment for Marcus for his upcoming fight this time either, as the arena provided such materials for the more regular classes and Retiarius was one of the most common. It suited Marcus too, his build was not overly large or muscular – though he was still strong – so he was more suited to a role that required speed and agility over stalwart power.

I hadn't interfered with Vettius' training regime with Marcus although I had watched the pair on the training grounds from the ludus on a few occasions. Sometimes Marcus was working with the heavy tree trunk, or rocks that the pair had gathered to work on his strength, sometime Vettius had him running laps on the sands, and other times they had been working on technique both with and without weapons. Retiarii, after all, were often left empty handed once their trident and net had been thrown, although he would have a short dagger too, but that would be mostly useless against a Murmillo with even a minimal amount of skill.

As the pair trained their art, I trained my own and by the time the day of the fight had arrived, I was confident that I could draw the sigils onto Marcus both accurately enough that they would work as intended, and small enough so that I would be able to hide them under the minimal armour of a Retiarius.

Marcus would be wearing a 'manica' and 'galerus' – arm guard and shoulder guards - and nothing else apart from his loin cloth and the thin belt that held his dagger for when the time came that he could use it. I hoped that he wouldn't have to ever even draw the thing, though I'd seen enough Retiarii fight to know that it was a distinct possibility.

I could fit the three sigils along his left arm perfectly as I'd already practised drawing them smaller and smaller, so that is exactly where I placed them as I joined Marcus in the gladiator's prep area attached to the arena.

Vettius had taken to the stands to watch the fight from a vantage point that would be useful for recounting the actions taken in the fight later in training. I would wait by the iron gate with Dinari as I had done before, in case I was needed once the fight was over and either of the men required medical assistance over and above what the new arena doctor was capable of. I told myself it was for both gladiators' benefits, though I knew that what I really meant was that I was there in case Marcus needed my help.

The sigils glowed a bright blue as I drew them with ink instead of blood onto Marcus' arm. From what I could gather, the medium didn't particularly matter, it was the skill and the intent that channelled the power of Mercury into the bearer of the sigils.

I fastened Marcus' armour back onto his arm and he picked up his trident and net to make his way up the tunnel that led to the iron gate separating the golden sands from the world beyond, where gladiators were mortals and not Gods.

Marcus, Dinari and I made our way as a trio to the gate and as we walked, his opponent dressed as Murmillo pushed me aside with a strong arm before he came to the iron gate himself, not turning to look at us.

"To think I have to fight piss stains like this," the Murmillo said as though to himself. "One victory fighting as a nothing class, and he gets the glory of dying at my hand. Next battle I shall rather fight a gladiatrix than another of these weak shitheads."

I didn't need to say what I was feeling, because at that moment Dinari growled at the gladiator. It was only the second time that I'd ever seen him take an aggressive stance, though it was clear that he had noted the gladiator's mood and insult, and had taken offence on Marcus' behalf. Before I could do anything to pull Dinari back though, Marcus stood before the dog in a protective stance.

"We will see who is the shithead, once we take to the sands. Until then, I suggest you shut your mouth, before I shut it for you," Marcus said flatly in a happy yet cocky tone.

The Murmillo seemed so stunned, that before he had the chance to reply or retaliate, the gate began to swing open and the two men walked out onto the sands, Murmillo with his arms raised aloft to the cheers of the crowd who evidently recognised the gladiator, and Marcus without any fanfare, though I could tell from his gait that he knew exactly what he planned on doing.

The arena announcer introduced Marcus as the previous Samnite, to which the crowd responded with a not insignificant cheer, though he didn't allude to any other victories or the man's past.

Then, the Murmillo was announced as the 'Serpent of the Seas', 'Hunter of the Hunted', with six victories beneath his belt, all against Retiarii. I clenched my jaw at the announcement of the gladiator's titles; it seemed that as usual, someone, somewhere had dealt us a hand of shit.

The gladiators stood to the ready and the arena announcer called for the beginning of the fight. While Marcus immediately stood to the ready, Murmillo dropped his shield to the ground and removed his helmet for all the crowd to see him in all his glory.

The gladiator had short black hair and a chiselled jawline. He looked strong, determined and fierce and, above all else, fearless.

I thought it reckless to remove an item of armour when fighting in the arena, though I knew that the full coverage helmets that Murmillo wore restricted their vision somewhat, so this could've been a tactical move rather than one of vanity.

The crowd, however, seemed to adore the actions of this gladiator.

"I am the Serpent of the Seas!" The gladiator shouted into the crowds, who fell silent to allow him to speak.

"I will destroy this tiny human, and return again to feed on whoever dares to grace my waters!"

The crowd went absolutely berserk; they pounded their feet on the ground, cheered and whistled for the overzealous gladiator. They loved a good show, and this Murmillo was certainly an impressive showman.

Then the fight abruptly began.

The Murmillo hoisted his gladius and shield to the ready and moved into range with Marcus, who began to strike out with his trident, though the Serpent simply batted away the weapon with his sword and shield over and over. He moved and swatted as though he was following dance steps and all the while, he did it with a smile on his face. In fact he was almost laughing.

Marcus was forced to move back further and further as the Murmillo proved almost entirely unbreakable in his defence and movements. Then, Marcus simply stopped attacking and without missing a beat, the Serpent opened his guard that'd been afforded by his shield and followed up with a deadly swipe from his gladius.

I saw the attack coming. I thought most of the crowd had too, but I couldn't have been sure that Marcus could've seen it, as up until now the wooden shield had always been between the two gladiators.

Thankfully, Marcus had seen it. His upper body zipped backwards and out of the path of the swipe, and when the gladius came back at him in a fierce backhand, he ducked under it.

Three more attacks came at Marcus and all three found nothing but thin air before or above him; the gladiator was just moving so *fast*.

On the fourth attack, he aimed a stab at Marcus' stomach, who spun to the side of the pair and to the rear of the Murmillo before he could do anything about it. When the armoured gladiator turned to see where Marcus had disappeared to, his mouth shot open, ready to shout as he was confronted with the tip of the centre spire of the Retiarius' trident.

One single thrust was all it took from Marcus and the tip of the trident shot through the Serpent's mouth and out the back of his skull. There was no way that the gladiator could have survived that blow, and as he fell to his knees with the look of sheer surprise still etched upon his face, the amphitheatre erupted.

The noise was deafening to my ears but I didn't care. Marcus had lived to fight another day and this time I had seen the divine power that the sigils had imparted onto his physical body. I was a little conflicted though about just how brutal the Murmillo's ending had been, though that was a demon to be dealt with at a later date.

Marcus had become the Slayer of the Serpent and I couldn't be happier about it.

My gladiator made to leave the arena sands as the crowds chanted 'Retiarius!' over and over but before he made it to the iron gate and his ultimate exit, he removed his helmet and turned to the crowds, who fell silent.

"My name is Marcus Demitrius, of the ludus Brutus! And I am the Slayer of Serpents!"

The crowd once again erupted into cheers for Marcus, though now they used a combination of 'Marcus' and 'Slayer' in their chants.

"Did you see that?" Marcus asked me as he began to remove his armour. The look of absolute glee on his face was a sight to behold - it was so powerful that it made me smile.

"I saw… that Murmillo had no chance," I said whilst trying to forget the gladiator's astonished expression as he has fallen.

I quickly wiped away the sigils from Marcus' arm once it was free of the armour that hid them; the last thing I needed was for anyone else to see what I had done to help my gladiator out on the sands.

"Maybe next time they shall give me a proper gladiator to fight!" Marcus said, though I could tell that his arrogance was borne from the flames of victory and not a character flaw on his part.

Vettius' voice came from behind us as he entered into the prep area, "I knew of the Serpent, he was a skilled gladiator, though far too overconfident. You do not need to fight a more skilled gladiator to be on level footing, just perhaps one that keeps his helmet atop his head."

Vettius then took a hold of Marcus' forearm in polite congratulations and both men shared a short laugh.

Dinari made a noise again, not unlike that of a seal, and attempted to leap up to add his own hands to the gesture, though when it was clear that he couldn't make it and he began to look a little upset, Marcus picked the dog up and held him under one arm. Dinari looked absolutely delighted with the action and tried to lick at Marcus' face, though he couldn't reach.

"Celebrations are in order then!" Marcus announced happily and neither Vettius nor myself were in a position to object.

We spent some of the coin from the fight purse on wine to be taken back to the ludus. Marcus had wanted to stay in the town for a while, though this time Vettius and I both objected, as we didn't want to cause any trouble in a drunken state, or otherwise gain looser lips than we would have liked. In the end, the three of us and Dinari headed back to the ludus and lit a fire atop the training sands, where we drank, told stories of the past and I had to admit, sang songs merrily, late into the night.

The next morning, the first sight that I awoke to was Dinari licking Marcus' ear. Marcus, who I was sure would have been cursing the entire world for the almighty hangover that he was feeling, just let it happen. It made me smirk, though when I saw Vettius appear from one of the gladiator cells in his training attire, I immediately felt for Marcus.

"Up, NOW!" Vettius commanded and I almost obeyed his word myself. Of course I knew that the instruction was for Marcus though, who opened his eyelids to reveal two bloodshot eyes and the look of both sheer pain and dread within them.

Vettius, who was holding a wooden sword, smacked Marcus hard on the side of his ribs with it.

"I said UP!"

Marcus mumbled, then raised himself into a push-up position, and promptly vomited. It was red like wine and the smell of it made me stand up and back away. I almost tripped over Dinari, who was now hiding behind me.

Vettius again hit Marcus with the wooden sword.

"This is to be your next lesson. Sometimes, you will not want to fight. Sometimes you will be sick or have a headache. Sometimes your wounds will hurt so much that the last thing you want to do is raise yourself to your feet to meet your opponent. These are the times that a real gladiator is separated from a man who simply stands upon the sands to fight. Get up off your knees and fight, or are you a coward who refuses to meet the challenge of a man with just one arm?"

Marcus, buoyed by Vettius' words, raised himself slowly and unsteadily to his feet. He looked shaky at best, though without a weapon to hand, he did what I hadn't expected, he raised his fists and stood to the ready.

"Fight!" Vettius ordered and Marcus shuffled forward. He could barely lift his feet from the sand and when he swung wildly at Vettius, his Doctore simply moved out of the way and slapped the wooden sword onto the back of Marcus' shoulder. Marcus yelped and moved back and away quickly. I wondered if he was still drunk.

"You fight in the arena like that?" Vettius asked. "I would not have even needed two arms to kill you out there in my time!"

Marcus moved in again and swung hard. I could tell that he was slightly angered by the situation but again his wild swing missed, and Vettius brought a knee up into Marcus' stomach. Marcus doubled over and vomited again.

"A seasoned gladiator does not always fight at his best," Vettius explained calmly. "If you have one hundred fights in the arena, how many do you think you will partake in whilst you do not feel your strongest? This is where the gladiator is tested, and made."

Marcus eventually pulled himself to his feet again and moved toward Vettius, though this time much more cautiously. He leant in to grab his Doctore into a grapple, though Vettius cracked the pummel of his wooden sword into Marcus' back, causing the gladiator to slide down Vettius' body and onto the ground in a heap.

"You do not have to stay to watch, Titus," Vettius said to me as he readied himself for another round with the seriously hurting and hung-over gladiator.

"Could I not heal him with a sigil?" I asked almost pleadingly on Marcus' behalf.

"No. The reason I lost my arm in the arena was because I relied too heavily on the power that these sigils provided. I became cocky and complacent, believing myself invincible. Marcus needs to know how it feels to fall from elation, to panic. From invincible, to begging for death. These are the lessons that would have saved me my injury, and they are lessons that Marcus will learn, whether it be against his will or not."

I saw Marcus turn to me with tears in his eyes. "Titus… this… I must learn," he almost choked out. His mouth was filled with blood though I could now see the determination in his face.

I turned away from the pair to leave them to their barbaric training and Dinari and I walked back into the ludus in search of water, and a proper bed to rest in.

I awoke in the early afternoon, once the sun had passed its highest point, and I ventured back outside onto the training sands, where Vettius and Marcus were still sparring. It looked as though it was a much more even affair now though; either Marcus had vomited up all of the wine that had been poisoning his body, or he had simply returned to himself through sheer willpower. One thing I did think, though, was that Marcus would be in no hurry to get *that* drunk on the wine again.

XVIII – Ad Astra Per Aspera.

"Through adversity to the stars."

I both allowed and encouraged Marcus and Vettius to train together for as long as they needed, so over the next few weeks it was not surprising that I didn't see much of either of them. The training was gruelling for Marcus, though I could see that it was also taking its toll on Vettius. The Doctore, when I saw him on the odd occasion, had been covered in sweat and was panting as though he'd just run a marathon. When Marcus was not hungover, I was sure that Vettius had his work cut out for him out on those sands.

Something unexpected happened this day that had taken me by quite some surprise: the Liternum arena master, Galerius had knocked on my door.

When I had allowed Galerius entry into my home, it took me a moment to place the ageing, fat man, though once I did, my mind filled immediately with a deep foreboding.

"Good Galerius!" I announced happily. "What can I do for you on this fine day?" My father had always said to be kind to the hand that feeds, and in this case, this very man decided on the battles that Marcus would be fighting in.

"The ludus Brutus…" Galerius said almost in wonder as he peered around the building. "I never thought I would see the day that this house would once again grace the town of Liternum with its gladiators… as if by some divine intervention, no?"

The raised eyebrow that punctuated the man's sentence gave me cause to be cautious and I immediately wondered if he had chosen his words carefully, or if I was reading too much into things.

"I... worked hard and rebuilt the ludus with the help of the good people of Liternum," I explained with my smile still plastered on my face. "I do not know of the Gods and their interventions, though will praise them if praise is due."

Galerius eyed me before stepping past me without invitation into the entrance foyer that was open to the elements.

"This was a wondrous ludus a decade ago," he said as he walked. "It was such a shame that it fell so tragically. Tell me, do you know what happened here?" The arena master asked rather rudely with his back to me.

"It... was burnt down... by two assassins," I said simply. "I do not know why." The screams of my parents' deaths rang loud in my ears, though their plight was interrupted by Galerius.

"The Gods do tend to work in very mysterious ways... though if you would like a piece of advice that I may impart upon you for this ludus and the gladiators that you train here: do not tempt the Gods, and always teach your gladiators to fight a fair fight, else they may see it fit to befall the same fate to your home, for a second time."

My mouth hung open. Was this a threat? Did the arena master know something about my parents, the ludus, the sigils, the Gods or Marcus? I knew I simply couldn't ask, and I really wasn't that stupid, but the man had been less than cryptic with his warning, almost to the point of obviousness.

In the end, I managed to arrange my thoughts so that I could form proper words. "My gladiators will be taught properly, and with proper respect I can assure you. There will be no falsities here."

"That is... good to hear," Galerius replied as he turned to face me again and clapped his hands together once. "Now to business! I presume that your man, the Retiarius, would like to fight on my sands again?"

I nodded. "He is already itching for his next contest."

"Ah, then I have the perfect match for him in the coming week. I do not remember him suffering any injuries in his previous bout, so I presume the timing is not an issue?"

I wanted to object, though I got the distinct feeling from the arena master that saying no to him would be a very bad idea, so instead I simply nodded.

"The purse to you, should your man prove victorious, would be one hundred dinari."

I forced my eyebrows not to raise though it took a little effort; this was quite the jump in coin from the last fight, though a part of me still thought that I was being led in this conversation.

"We share the coin," was the first thing I could think of to say, "and I will with any gladiator who fights for this ludus."

Galerius stroked his beard with a look of intrigue on his face. "That is... unorthodox," he said eventually. "Though who am I to pass comment, as a simple arena master..."

I didn't reply, nor did I make any moves to stop Galerius from peering around my house with a fair bit of interest.

"Anyway," Galerius finally announced. "I must be going, I have other business to attend to and I am sure that you have preparations to make for the upcoming battle. Good day, master Brutus."

"It's Titus," I said automatically.

"Titus... it was good speaking with you, and I am happy to see that the ludus Brutus is back on solid foundation..." Galerius made the effort to make it sound as though his words were contrary to his feelings, but I ignored it and bade the man farewell. I could tell that he wasn't on my side in any sense of the word, and the last thing I wanted to do was make an outright enemy of him.

When I told Vettius and Marcus that the next fight was to happen so soon, Vettius looked pensive where Marcus looked determined. I shared in Vettius' sentiment; there was something a little off about how the fight had been scheduled so soon.

"I do not like this," Vettius said. "The arena master is up to something for sure. No gladiator should be expected to compete with such regularity."

"Maybe the people simply want to see me take down another gladiator?" Marcus announced.

"Maybe he thinks that you will tire easily so soon after your next match, and then the ludus will have a losing gladiator... Galerius did not seem as though he was fond of the place at all," I offered.

"No, I fear it may be more than that. If he simply wanted this ludus to disappear from the arena, then he would just ensure that Marcus would have no match at all. I would rather say it sounds like a test," Vettius said thoughtfully.

I had to agree with Vettius. If Galerius did indeed know more than he had let on about the Gods and the sigils, as I suspected he did, then he would no doubt want to make sure his assumptions were correct before he took any action upon them.

"Either way, the reason does not matter," I stated simply. "I had no choice but to accept the match, so all we can do is train as much as possible and try not to think about any ulterior motives that the arena master may have."

Marcus and Vettius both agreed and turned their attention back to training.

Then Vettius turned back to me again before I left. "Do you know what kind of opponent Marcus is going to be placed against?"

"Nope," I said with a smile, "just train him up to deal with them all." I waved a hand over my shoulder as I spoke as though to punctuate my statement with nonchalance.

Vettius was about to retort, but I had already begun walking away, when he shouted towards me: "He's going to die, you know?"

Then I heard the clash of wood on wood and I could tell without looking that Marcus was doing his best to prove Vettius wrong.

~

I wished that we had had more time to prepare. The day of the fight had come around so quickly that I was unsure if Vettius could've possibly given Marcus enough direction so that he would be safe out there on the sands. What we saw though, as my group of Vettius, Marcus, Dinari and I stood behind the iron gates, sent a chill down all of our spines.

The absolute beast of a gladiator that stood awaiting Marcus on the stands dwarfed my man by at least two feet. He was muscular beyond all belief and his armour was nothing more that leather wrappings around the top of his arms and his shins. In each hand he held a long, curved blade that looked as though each could behead a man in a single swing. I was also sure that beneath one of the leather wrappings on his arms, as he moved them up and down to rile up the crowd, I could see a faint red glow, the telltale sign of some divine magic.

The gladiator and the spectacle before us all reminded me of the Cestus that Vettius had fought all those years ago, but before I could turn to him with my question, Vettius placed a hand on my shoulder as if to keep me quiet.

"You think I can take him?" Marcus asked quietly and I could hear a little fear creeping into his voice.

"The bigger they are, the harder they fall," was all that Vettius could say and I knew that he meant it motivationally, though I didn't know how far that it was going to go – I certainly wouldn't want to get out there on the sands with *that*.

Dinari must've picked up on the tension just then, because before anyone else could say anything, he leapt up at Marcus, placing his paws on the gladiator's knees. Marcus picked up the dog and brought him up to eye-level.

"Do you think I'll be ok?" he asked Dinari.

The dog barked loudly, then looked as though he was pointing his nose to where I had drawn the sigils onto the gladiator. Marcus smiled as he caught Dinari's meaning: he had the power of the Gods within him, so how could he possibly lose?

Our small group then listened at the iron gate as the arena announcer took to the sands to prepare the crowd for the upcoming bout.

"Today we have a special treat for you! All the way from Rome, this gladiator has decided to show us exactly how arena matches are supposed to be fought! A brand new class to be tested here on our sands today against a Retiarius who has been winning matches as you all have seen. Who will survive out in the games today? Hailing from the ludus Magnus in the capital, I present to you: Dimachaerus!" The gladiator raised both his swords high above his head and the crowd made it clear with their reception that they absolutely loved him. "And the very man that you all seem to enjoy here in Liternum, a local gladiator hailing from the recently rebuilt ludus Brutus, I present to you: The Slayer of Serpents, fighting as Retiarius once more - Marcus!"

The gates opened quickly and Marcus jogged out onto the arena sands to cheers and applause from the crowds. I could tell that the people did seem to like him, though seeing these two men side by side looked like it was a death sentence for Marcus. *Did people really grow that big?*

"Today's fight, as directed by our illustrious arena master," the announcer gestured towards Galerius, who sat in his own private section of the amphitheatre eating grapes, "will be a battle to the death with no quarter given!"

The crowd cheered and I even heard some 'ooh's' and 'aah's' from the bloodthirsty mob. They'd grown as a people over the last decade, but they hadn't yet managed to pull away from all of their belligerent roots.

Marcus turned to look back at the iron grate as though to ask what the fuck was going on, though I could do nothing other than shrug.

"He has set this up!" Vettius growled angrily. "There are never matches prescribed to the death any more, and that gladiator from Rome? I have a bad feeling about all of this, Titus."

"So do I, but we must have faith in Marcus," I said. "He is equipped as best he can be for this fight, so let us believe that he will win, rather than ponder on the unknown."

My words seemed to settle Vettius down somewhat, but my heart was beating faster and faster as though it was anticipating the beginning of the match.

Then, all of a sudden, it began.

XIX – Cogito Ergo Sum.

"I think, therefore I am."

It did not seem that the Dimachaerus viewed Marcus as any cause for concern; he stood in the centre of the sands unmoving as Marcus practically danced around him, though my gladiator was yet to launch a single attack. I worried that Marcus was just going to tire himself out, though it was way too early to harbour such thoughts and I knew that.

The huge gladiator holding two swords didn't even raise his weapons to the ready, and eventually Marcus knew that he had to do *something*, otherwise the crowd were going to turn on him.

Marcus stood firm and stepped into range with his trident, and although he looked menacing, something happened that I hadn't been expecting; the Dimachaerus swung a deadly blade around and directly into the path of Marcus, who also hadn't seen the attack coming. Where he and I had both had clearly thought that the range of the trident would be longer than the range of the huge gladiator with just swords, we were sorely mistaken. The crowd gasped as Marcus folded backwards over his own legs to dodge the deadly strike.

I didn't know how Marcus was possibly going to win this fight; he had no range or size advantage as a Retiarius should, and this thing that opposed him was definitely some sort of half-ogre.

I could see that Marcus held onto his trident with as much force as he could possibly muster as his knuckles had begun to turn white. I wanted to call out to him, to tell him to relax but I knew that Vettius would be doing so if it was required.

Then the Dimachaerus began to walk slowly forwards, towards Marcus. My heart beat so quickly I thought it may stop and my hands were pools of sweat. I needed to remember though, Marcus had the divine will of the Gods on his side – he was safe, I was sure he was.

The behemoth began to slice his blades through the air at Marcus and it was all that my man could do to simply dodge the wild attacks whilst still moving back and away from the advancing man. It didn't look as though the Dimachaerus had much skill though; his attacks were uncoordinated and although he was pretty fast for his size, he seemed to be relying on his strength and size a little *too* much.

"Cut him down to size!" Vettius shouted from my side and it made me jump. Then Dinari barked as though he was agreeing with the Doctore and I wondered if Marcus had heard the instruction.

I didn't have to wonder for very long. Marcus changed tact with his trident and instead of going for his opponent's torso, which remained mostly out of reach, he waited for an opening and thrust his weapon at his opponent's leading shin.

The huge gladiator roared as the trident made contact, though his swinging swords did not alter their path which meant that Marcus had to let go of the trident to quickly dive out of the way. Then when he righted himself and looked back at his opponent, he could see that his trident was *sticking out of* Dimachaerus's shinbone – strong and dense as it was.

The gladiator simply didn't seem to care and he carried on moving as though the weapon had been there all along.

Marcus looked to the iron gate for a fleeting moment as though to ask what exactly he should do next, though Vettius simply shrugged. I had nothing to offer either.

I tried to imagine what I would do if I was in that situation, though other than trying to retrieve the trident. I couldn't come up with anything other than 'run'.

Thankfully, Marcus attempted my first thought; he moved in toward the Dimachaerus, who allowed my man to take a hold of the trident with both hands and attempt to yank at it to break it free. It seemed though, that it wasn't going to budge an inch.

The huge gladiator then smiled and *laughed* loudly at Marcus' attempt to pull his trident free, which seemed to anger Marcus, who pulled his dagger from his belt, and jammed it into the side of his opponent's knee.

This time, the larger gladiator roared in pain and I didn't blame him one bit. Even from where I was I could see the bone as the man's flesh tore away where the dagger cut and Marcus twisted the blade mercilessly.

Then the behemoth, somehow gaining some strength from places that I was entirely unaware of for a human being, raised his injured leg, trident still protruding, and kicked Marcus square in the chest.

Marcus flew backwards at least ten feet at the brutal attack and I was sure that I had heard his ribs crack and break. This time he did not roll and regain his footing, he stayed down with his eyes closed.

This was surely the end of my man and I readied myself mentally to have to deal with his broken body once it was to leave the sands.

The huge gladiator walked slowly to his unmoving opponent, visibly chuckling as he approached, and the crowd went silent so that they may be able to hear the killing blow for all that it was. He then pulled the trident from his own leg with somewhat ease, and snapped it over his knee.

The Dimachaerus stood over Marcus and raised a single curved sword into the air, ready to strike, but as he did so Marcus' eyes snapped open and he rolled underneath his much larger opponent. By some divine boost of speed and perception, he pulled off the impossible: he dodged the final blow from taking his life while at the same time using his net to relieve the gladiator of the sword that he held by his side, forgotten as he was carrying out his deadly task.

The giant gladiator did not seem to care. He looked at the sword that had become entangled in the net and shrugged. I couldn't say I blamed him; he looked deadly enough with just the one of the weapons in his hand. Marcus though, he looked pleased with what he had managed.

Again, the Dimachaerus bore down on Marcus. He still looked so menacing, even without both of his swords in hand, but Marcus was buoyed by the way he had removed one of the weapons from the fight. He dodged a swing from the curved weapon and deftly stepped back and out of reach of the weapon.

The Dimachaerus then *ran* at Marcus, bridging the distance between them in a moment. I wished that Marcus had still had his trident so that he had something, anything, to block the following attacks with, but it simply wasn't the case. Marcus' huge opponent once again kicked him in the chest, though this time with the additional force of his momentum and I watched Marcus fly through the air and land on the sands once more. He didn't lie still this time though, he brought himself to his feet gingerly, holding his stomach as though he was going to vomit.

The behemoth laughed loudly for all to hear and the crowd began to boo as Marcus promptly turned tail, and shuffled away from his opponent in a half run, half stumble. I couldn't blame him; this thing that he had been placed to fight against was not human.

The Dimachaerus slowly followed Marcus as he moved to the edge of the arena wall and began to skirt it. I could see that he seemed to be enjoying the gladiator's dishonour as he feebly attempted to keep his distance. The Dimachaerus did not make any move to try to chase properly; he knew that the fight was all but over so why waste the energy?

That was when I saw where Marcus was headed. His trajectory around the arena was not a way to escape from his opponent; he was trying to move the overpowering brute away from the discarded weapons upon the arena sands, so that he would have something to attack, or defend himself with again and eventually the crowd hushed their loud displeasure as they realised the very same thing.

Marcus reached the net that held the entangled sica sword that he had removed from the Dimachaerus with his net earlier in the fight and took the time to calmly unfold the net around it so that he could pick it up. I wondered if he was going to go for the trident, though the two halves looked way too short to have been effective against this enemy.

The Dimachaerus, who had seen all of this happening, just didn't care. He walked calmly towards Marcus as though he was letting him retrieve the weapon, and once he arrived within range he swung his sword at Marcus. The strike was so quick and unexpected that I almost let out a shout, but Marcus managed to dodge the attack just barely, a thin trickle of blood appearing down his arm where the blade had bit in so slightly. To his credit, Marcus didn't scream or shout, he simply readied himself with his new sword and stood to face his opponent once more.

The giant gladiator raised his arms to the air and shouted a blood-curdling scream and as he did so, I was now certain that there was a red glow emanating from beneath his bindings. I spared a look at Marcus, and where his own sigils lay, though they had been hidden well and there was no sign of the bright light that they oft produced.

The Dimachaerus swung his sword again from high to low and I could see the murder in his eyes. Marcus though, *blocked* the attack with his own sword. Granted, he had two hands on it where his opponent had just one, but I couldn't believe that he was matching his own strength against that of the ogre he stood against.

The pair faced each other as though locked in some unarticulated battle of wills and I watched as Marcus' arms began to fall to the ground as his strength and endurance simply wasn't enough to match up to the Dimachaerus.

Both gladiators refused to cede to their opponent but it was clear that Marcus had to do something before he was soundly bested. Then the

Dimachaerus brought his other hand to bear on his weapon and the contest was all but done: the blades hit the ground and I knew that Marcus had but a moment to get out of there. He did not relent though.

Marcus released his right hand from his sword and punched blindly around the duelling blades, directly into the wounded leg of his opponent. He punched again and again though no effect could be seen until he hit the ruined knee, where his dagger had caused the brutal damage. The Dimachaerus' leg folded as he howled. Marcus took this new opportunity without hesitation.

The blades all but forgotten about by the injured man, Marcus slipped his own from between the ground and the Dimachaerus' and swung it upwards with all his might. This blade did not get stuck in the gladiator's apparently impenetrable bone though, this time it cut *straight through* the flesh and bone of the gladiator's arm and it fell to the ground with a thud.

Marcus didn't stop there. Buoyed by the successful attack, he rolled on the ground to bring himself behind his howling opponent and sliced downwards now, this time severing the Dimachaerus' leg just below the knee with ease. I didn't know if this weapon was simply sharper than the trident had been, though where the man's physical body had created an issue before, now it seemed to pose no defence against Marcus' attacks whatsoever.

The Dimachaerus writhed on the ground in agony and it was the first time in the fight that he had actually looked as though he was mortal.

Marcus did not spare a moment of respite and as his opponent's attention was focused on his own ruined body, Marcus cut the man's head off without delay with one single strike. It fell to the ground with a thud and after a short silent pause from the crowd, the arena erupted.

XX – Damnatio Ad Bestias.

"Thrown to the lions."

"Did you see that!! I mean did you *fucking see* that?" Marcus practically cried as he reached the iron gates where Vettius, Dinari and I awaited once the arena announcer had closed the proceedings with a very colourful recitation of how Marcus had won against the much larger opponent.

I was about to congratulate the man, though as I was about to speak, the broken body of the Dimachaerus was dragged into the tunnel and away to the healing room by four arena hands. His severed arm and leg had been placed unceremoniously atop his lifeless body and I wondered if the brute deserved such treatment.

I needed to see if what I thought I had seen was true: did this gladiator have a sigil drawn upon his body? And one that shone with red power instead of blue? There was only one way that I knew of to find out, and so I began to follow the arena hands into where I knew the gladiator would be placed upon the stone table, awaiting the doctor's knife.

I could tell that the rest of my group followed as I could hear their footsteps, though none of them said a word as we followed the trail of blood on the floor that the body left as it leaked out from the wounds of battle.

When I arrived in the doctor's room, the healer that had once been a hand acknowledged my presence with a nod. I was half expecting to have to explain my presence in the room, though this man knew of both me and my skill as an arena doctor, so he moved out of the way without a word and left the room entirely. I didn't blame him; it was never a *fun* thing to deal with severed appendages, and the size of this gladiator meant that his body was going to hold a lot of blood – and that made for messy work.

I took a hold of the knife that sat out of reach of the stone table as usual and used it to cut the wrappings from the man's arms and stomach and as I did I could see the tell-tale sign of an inert sigil drawn onto his body.

At the top of the gladiator's arm, was drawn an unmistakable shield – a sigil that I had never seen before. I traced it with a single finger a few times, then repeated the action with my eyes closed to make sure that I understood its form properly.

"That is surely the symbol for Mars," Marcus announced as I pondered.

I whipped my head around. "What? How do you know?" I asked, astonished.

"When… when I was knocked out, back there on the sands…" Marcus said though obviously not totally sure of himself and not wanting to spill the beans all in one go. "I heard a voice… it told me that the only way to pass Mars' power was to use it against him… I wasn't sure what it meant, though I thought on it for a moment and guessed the only thing I could do was to try to take my opponent's weapon and use it against him. I guess I was right… though until now I was not sure if what I had heard was actually a voice, or if it was just my own dying mind playing tricks on me…"

It sounded right. The trident that Marcus had attempted to use against his enemy seemed so ineffective when compared to the curved sword that he had appropriated and I thought about just how effective that kind of skill could've been for a gladiator. I supposed that they didn't call Mars the 'God of War' for nothing.

"Well you have lost a bit of blood," Vettius said, gesturing to Marcus arm. "We will probably need to see to that wound before the day is out."

"It is already healing," Marcus said, "blessings of Mercury and all that…"

With the talk of the fight that had just happened, the mood had turned somewhat sombre. It was clear that the three of us were still somewhat in a state of shock that Marcus had managed to escape from the jaws of death with nothing but a simple scratch to remind him of that fact.

Whilst the two men spoke though, I had been drawing. I knew that the symbol would be easy for me to replicate and I spared no time in drawing it as I had once done with Mercury's caduceus, in blood on the floor of the healing room.

I finished the sigil and where the three that I had learnt for Mercury had shone a bright blue, this shield, the Ancile of Mars, glowed with a burning, deep red.

Then the very ground beneath us began to shake.

I looked at Dinari who was very interested in the sigil as I had drawn it and he met my eye contact with a kind of worried expression. Vettius and Marcus both looked down at me still crouched on the floor and before they even had the chance to ask what the hell I was doing, the roof of the doctor's room was torn off and flew upwards into the sky. The sky itself had turned black as night though I wasn't sure when it had happened.

All four of us looked up to the sky as it began to swirl as though a tornado had been angered and had roared into existence directly above us. The roar of the wind was deafening and the ground beneath my feet didn't stop shaking for a moment.

A face then appeared above the healing room, where the roof had once been. It must've been ten feet long and wore the helmet of a centurion atop his head. His beard was bushy and black and his expression was angry and it made me immediately fearful of what was to transpire.

"You have called upon the divine power of the mighty Mars," the God said and his voice boomed to a volume that made me fearful for my hearing.

"Tell me, Sigilarius, why is it do you think that you are worthy of my power?"

It took me a moment to figure out that the God was talking directly to me, and it made me stutter before I could form my words properly.

"I... I... I don't think that I am worthy... I would never use the power of the Gods for myself," I replied.

"And you, gladiator... I watched you kill my champion on the sands of this arena, and now you call upon me?" Mars asked Marcus.

"I did nothing but what I was supposed to do!" Marcus called up to the God in an assured and clear voice that I knew I wouldn't have been able to manage myself.

"This place *stinks* of the power of my brother..." Mars said almost as an afterthought as though he hadn't heard Marcus speak. He seemed as though he was distracted, though I didn't know if that was a good thing or a bad thing.

Mars then turned his attention back to me: "My power on the arena sands is unparalleled by any other. If I were to allow you to call upon it, tell me Sigilarius, what glory would I receive in return? What blood would you shed in my honour?" Mars asked, though before I could reply, Vettius spoke on my behalf.

"If your power is unparalleled, then why did your man get bested out there by one calling upon the power of your brother?"

I would certainly not have asked that question. Staring up at the giant, literal God, I would have known better. Vettius though, thought that he had apparently lived long enough.

"You dare speak to me in such a disrespectful tongue, mortal?" Mars practically boomed and a hand rolled into view above the healing room and *picked Vettius up*, taking him high up above us and into the sky. The God then placed my struggling friend into his open mouth and *ate* him in a single bite without a single sound.

Dinari barked loudly, over and over without stopping though I did try to shush him in case the God found it reason enough to end all of our lives. I was stunned though and I could tell that Marcus was also in two minds.

"You do not show me the respect that I expect from mortals," Mars said as though our conversation had not been interrupted by his heinous action. "You will need to earn the right to call upon my powers, if that is what you wish from summoning me here."

I wasn't listening to Mars properly now, I was in shock at the loss of my good friend Vettius who had simply been taken away from me without any sort of fanfare. It made me remember the feeling of the loss of everyone who I'd loved that had been taken away; my parents, Ovidius... I hated loss.

"Nobody deserves the right to the powers of the Gods," I said quietly, holding back my tears and the anger that had begun to brew. "There is no mortal being that should have the power to choose between the life and death of another..."

Mars looked as though this was an answer he hadn't been expecting and I watched the emotions playing out upon his huge face. Eventually, it landed on a look of calm stoicism.

"Your words are truer than you may know, Sigilarius," Mars said almost quietly. "Though the mortal realm can be unfair and unjust, I can feel your pain and I know your suffering. Do not let your principled mortal mind stand in the way of greatness beyond all reckoning. I tell you again, earn the right to call upon my divine powers on the sands of the arena and you will become an unstoppable champion of the entire empire!!"

I thought for a moment about what Mars was saying, and how he was saying it. Then it occurred to me that he may be testing me, or probing me to see how I would react to certain questions, ideas or simply the tone of his voice. He had challenged me, caused fear and upset, and now he was bargaining. I didn't know what this all meant, though I could tell that as this conversation had continued, Mars was almost baiting me into gaining his power for myself, and I alone knew that this was not something that I wanted. Everything I did and everything I learned, was for the benefit of others and not myself.

Somehow, knowing that this was some kind of game that the God was playing made my mind clearer, and made it easier to think about what I needed to say.

"What do I have to do to prove myself to you, Mars, God of war? What could I possibly do as a mortal to show myself worthy?" I asked.

The huge face smiled as though I had just asked the right question. It was not, however, a warm and friendly smile, it was devious and I knew that he was going to ask something that I wasn't going to like.

Then a spear and shield appeared by my feet, and when I looked at Marcus, an identical pair had appeared at his too. I made sure that Dinari hadn't been given some doggy-type weapons and armour too, though thankfully he had been left out of whatever this was.

"I require bloodshed," Mars announced simply. "The blood of life is the cornerstone of the mortal condition, and it is my requirement that you honour me with the shedding of it to prove yourself worthy of my power. Pick up arms and armour and fight now so that I may be entertained."

I didn't pick up the shield or spear, and when I looked to Marcus I could see that he hadn't made any moves to do so either. Internally I was a little thankful of that fact, partly because I knew that I wouldn't be able to best the gladiator in combat, but also because I wanted to be sure that Marcus wasn't some power-mad brute as his last opponent had been. The fact that he refused to fight me, though, told me that I had made the right choice in trusting him with the power of Mercury.

"Pick up your weapons and armour," Mars repeated sternly, though neither myself nor Marcus made any moves to comply with the instruction.

"We do not fight against each other, and I do not want your divine power if it means that I have to shed the blood of another whom I care about," Marcus announced. I gritted my teeth in anticipation of the God's wrath, though it did not become immediately apparent.

"They need not prove themselves to you, brother," a second, much softer voice boomed overhead, and I recognised immediately that it was Mercury's. I looked up to see where the sound had come from, though I could not seem to find the God anywhere.

"We do not pick who we impart our divine power unto; the mortals find us and that is the way it has always been," Mercury continued.

"DO NOT lecture me on playing favourites, brother, I have seen what you have been up to, and it is very different to what I am proposing here!" Mars boomed.

Mars certainly seemed angry again and it made me worry. I didn't know which of the Gods would be more powerful if they chose to make this a contest, though by the sounds of them and from what I knew of the

Pantheon, when it came to fighting, Mars was unparalleled.

"And I saw what happened in the arena as you tried to intervene to have this mortal removed from the world. Do not think me blind, brother."

I could tell that the discussion between the Gods was becoming heated and that there was nothing I could do… except for one thing… and as the Gods descended into a kind of divine sibling rivalry, I picked up the spear that Mars had provided for Marcus and me to fight with. Then I slid my open palm along its tip, to the sharpened steel point without any delay. I didn't even have to place the slightest amount of pressure onto the razor's edge and my palm filled with my own warm, red blood immediately.

Both of the Gods stopped talking mid-sentence and I saw Mars' face turn its attention back to me.

"What is this?" Mars asked forcefully.

"I have spilled blood in the honour of the Gods! Just as you asked!" I announced clearly. "I will not draw the blood of my gladiator, though my own is freely given."

Neither of the Gods said a word. I didn't know if it was because I had done something truly heinous, or that they simply hadn't been expecting me to harm myself before another. I knew Mercury would have known, though Mars was a God that enjoyed bloodshed and war, and self-sacrifice may not have been in his repertoire.

Eventually, Mars broke the silence.

"I accept your sacrifice of blood and will allow you to utilise my divine power as you see fit. If, however, you do not use my sigils in the search for victory, I may choose to rethink my decision."

The swirling mass of clouds overhead, the whooshing of the wind and the shaking ground all then dissipated and Mars' face simply disappeared. Above us remained only blue skies and the sun as it bore down on me before the roof of the healing room returned. Then I turned to see Vettius, standing right where he had before Mars had dispatched him so cruelly.

"Vettius!" I called out. "I thought you were done!"

"It takes more than the might of a God to kill me, Titus," Vettius announced calmly with a smile, though I could see some evidence of worry and fatigue upon his face.

"You should choose your words more carefully," the voice of Mercury carried through the roof of the healing room and I turned to see a very man-sized Mercury enter into the room.

The God was again wearing a flowing, bright white toga and a rimmed, metal hat, and his sandals were still flanked by the golden wings of his Talaria.

Vettius and Marcus, apparently both in awe of this more relatable God, fell to their knees as a sign of respect.

"To your feet," Mercury stated simply. "I do not wish for, nor do I need, your praise or servitude." As he spoke, the God picked Dinari up in his arms and brought him up to his chest, cradling him. Dinari panted heavily with a very smug look upon his face. Mercury scratched him behind his ears and I couldn't help but smile.

"Once again, you have surprised me, Titus," Mercury said. "I once told you of the reasons why I had bestowed my divine powers unto you and you have been truthful in both your words and your actions and I thank you for that."

I nodded silently.

"However, there is now more that you should know, as you have gained the ability to call upon the power of another."

"I will always listen to the word of the Gods," I announced assuredly.

"That is not always wise..." Mercury stated. "I must tell you, there is more happening than you are unaware of in the mortal realm. There are people that wish you and your gladiators harm *because* of your link to my power. The Dimachaerus who fought your man Marcus on the sands this day was not a battle of chance: He had been imbued with the power of Mars and sent as a Champion of my brother to cut you down," he spoke the last words directly to Marcus, who still seemed in awe of Mercury. "A mortal being, another Sigilarius who is skilled in utilising the divine power of my brother, believes that his should be the only choices that affect the course of glory in the arena. I know that he petitioned Mars for his aid to cut your man out of the mortal realm, and this is where the Dimachaerus arrived from. You have interrupted his plans now, and so I fear for your safety."

Mercury's words made my mouth go dry. I knew that he was telling me that I was in mortal peril, all because someone knew about the sigils and Marcus, but what I was thinking about first and foremost was the way in which my parents had been killed. This was all too much of a coincidence and I understood for the first time, without a doubt, the reason for their deaths.

"Can you protect us from harm?" I asked quietly, trying to shake away my morbid train of thought.

"I cannot. The Gods cannot directly manipulate the mortal realm in such ways, as you may have recognised when my brother attempted to *eat* your Doctore, Vettius here. We rely on the actions of mortals to carry out our will, and that is why we open the channel to our divine powers through our sigils of power."

I thought for a moment before I spoke again. I needed more information if I couldn't get any direct aid, so I asked: "Can you tell me who it was that petitioned Mars for a champion?"

"That, Titus, is the correct question. Where it is not particularly amenable to name the mortals who bear our sigils, we have no problem in discussing the work of Sigilarii. It was the arena master, Galerius, who sent for the gladiator, and I am sure that he will continue to hold onto this grudge until you and your gladiators have been dealt with."

XXI – Dors Incit Omnia.

"Death conquers all."

It had been a day and a night since the visit of the Gods to my small party, and by all accounts nothing much had changed. Marcus had healed from his wounds, we had been paid by the arena and had returned to the ludus without any further distractions.

The roof of the gladiator prep area had not been demolished as Mars had tried to convince us through his divine magic; rather, the scenes that Marcus, Vettius, Dinari and I had been witness to had been manufactured specifically for our viewing. I wondered how many Sigilarii had been tricked by that particular God, and also how many had managed to petition him successfully to allow them the use of his divine power. These were things that I may never discover though.

It was dark outside and my gladiator and his Doctore had been training hard upon the sands of the ludus. I had watched them for a short period of time, though it was much more of the same. I was happy to note, though, that Marcus had made it a point not to get drunk in celebration of his victory in the arena; he must've learnt his lesson from the last time that had happened. I don't blame him one bit.

I was sitting in my office with Dinari upon my lap. I knew that although we spent *all* of our time together, we seldom actually simply enjoyed each other's company any more. We were always present with each other, though I knew that he wanted more attention from me, and this was certainly a good time to rectify that so I stroked his fur and gave him the attention he deserved.

Dinari and I began to play a game from my childhood called 'under over', where I would place a hand on the top of his head and he would then move his head back and around to rest his chin on my hand. This sequence would then be repeated over and over until I got bored with it; the dog would never tire of the game and seemed as happy as could be to continue in this manner forever.

As we played, it made me smile. It was sometimes the simplest things in life that brought you the most joy, and looking down at my best friend's smiling face, I knew that this was one of those times; everything was just so care-free in that moment. That was of course until everything had to change for the worse. Didn't it always?

I hadn't heard anything, but Dinari had. He pricked up his ears and jumped from my lap, stalking low to the ground as he approached the open door into the hallway.

"What is it?" I asked, though I immediately realised that being quieter was probably the better response. Dinari was never like this and certainly not without cause.

Dinari reached the doorway and stopped. Then he barked loudly over and over and I stood up just in time to see a shadow pass by the doorway so quickly that I had almost missed it.

My office was on the first floor of the house, so I had never been too worried about anything getting in through the window, but if someone was *inside* my house without invitation – and it seemed as if that was very much the case – it could only mean something bad.

I wondered if Marcus and Vettius were asleep yet, and moving to the open window I called their names into the darkness, but heard no response. Then I heard Dinari's scampering footfall as he ran away from my office, and a dark robed figure walked in to take his place.

"What is this?" I heard myself repeat my father's last words and I cringed. I had never imagined that I would ever have to feel the way he did when he knew that his end had found him, but I felt very much like this was how it had been.

"I come bearing a message," the robed man said. I couldn't see his face as it was shadowed and shrouded in darkness. His voice was deeply accented and he spoke as though he had a permanent sneer etched onto his face.

"You were warned about what you were doing in the arena, yet you chose to ignore this polite instruction. My master has therefore decided that you must be reminded of your place," the man said.

"My place is right here and if you do not leave…" I started, though I realised half way through my statement that I had nothing to threaten him with.

"You will what? Call on the power of the Gods? Do not take me for a fool, lanista, I know what is required of you to do so and you would be dead on the floor before you could even pick up stylus and ink."

Well, he had me there – even if I had a single sigil that I could draw to help me escape this situation, I doubted I would ever have had the time to draw it. My remaining options were either to try to fight or try to run. The man, though, was standing directly in the path of my exit.

My eyes flickered to the doorway and as they did the robed man revealed a shining blade from beneath his robes.

I knew that my one chance was to take advantage of the element of surprise and gritting my teeth, I launched myself at the man. I was no brute, no gladiator nor trained fighter, but I had seen gladiators train and knew what they did. I was also slightly larger than the man with the blade, so I hoped that would afford me some small advantage.

As I stepped into the man's range though, he whipped his blade out before him and I knew in that short moment that there would be no passing him by; there would be no escape.

The blade shimmered in the torchlight as it rose almost imperceptibly quickly and slashed into my leading arm. The pain was like a searing line of fire along my arm and I howled as I came to a halt before my attacker.

The man rounded me in an instant and took a hold of both my good arm and covered my mouth, stifling any noise that I was sure to have made. I tried to bite his hand, but he wore a thick leather glove which made the act impossible.

"Do not think you are getting away from me that easily; this is not my first time," the man whispered into my ear and his words sent a shiver down my spine. He was indeed well trained, and there was nothing I could do to stop him doing whatever it was that he had come to do.

"I would like you to sit down in that chair for a moment, and if you call out I will cut your throat in a moment. Do you understand?"

I nodded and tried to answer in the affirmative, though my voice was quiet and muffled beneath his hand. My arm was burning too, and I wondered just how serious the wound actually was.

The robed man shuffled me to behind my desk, and forced me to sit in the wooden chair that I'd previously vacated, it was still warm and it welcomed me.

"We are going to see what your God thinks of you, OK?" The man said as he tied my hands to the back of the chair, and then my legs. I hadn't seen where he had retrieved the binding from, though assumed that he had them underneath his robes for just this very reason.

Then he did something that I really wasn't expecting. The man dipped the tip of his dagger into the blood pooling on my arm, and began to draw with it upon the desk before me. It took me a few moments to follow, then I quickly recognised the image as the sigil of Mars that I had just learnt.

"I think that the Gods are drawn to these symbols, no? I wish to learn of their power before I leave you in their hands," the man said.

Then, he finished the sigil and immediately slid the dagger into my stomach as though it was the most normal thing in the world to do. It went in with ease, all the way to the hilt.

My body went cold and sweat covered me from head to toe. I experienced shock that I never thought possible, and then pain. Red hot, searing pain. Once the dagger was removed, it turned ice cold.

"Now we shall wait and see if your God arrives then…" the man said quietly and stood back and away from me.

It occurred to me in that moment that this man was not a Sigilarius. He had simply learned the sigil from watching it being drawn on another, and had made the assumption that it was the only one. Knowing this fact, I was not surprised to note that the sigil did not glow; it did not beckon Mars to my home as it may have done if it had been drawn correctly.

I managed to grin at my realisation. I laughed a little and then coughed, although that was a mistake as pain radiated from my stomach followed by the telltale warmth of trickling blood.

"You… cannot do it…" I managed to wheeze. "The Gods will not… answer you…"

The robed man looked as though he was angered by my words and he stepped closer to me again and placed a hand on my stomach. I exhaled in pain and internally begged for the mercy of the Gods.

"Titus!" Marcus' voice came from the doorway behind the man and I had never been happier to hear my gladiator speak. The robed man moved quickly away from me and I could see both Marcus and Vettius entering the room wearing gladiator armour and holding short steel gladii. I also happily noted that Dinari was sitting behind them, grinning at me although not entering the room.

Marcus leapt at the would-be assassin, who stepped out of the way of the attack and leapt from the window without hesitation. I had the feeling that the fall wouldn't be fatal to him, though hoped he had an uncomfortable landing.

"This is the work of that shit-eating arena master," Vettius growled as he cut the bindings that held me to the chair. I saw Marcus move to the window to follow the man's trail, though he didn't announce what he saw, if he could see anything through the darkness.

With my bindings removed I attempted to stand, but all that happened was that my eyes rolled into the back of my head and I felt the hard stone floor hit my cheek as my wound carried me into unconsciousness.

~

"It is a good thing that your dog is such a clever animal," I heard Marcus say behind my closed eyes. "You know that without him coming to find us, we never would have known that you were in trouble in there."

I tried to open my eyes, though the action was sluggish and my head was hurting badly. When I did manage to force them open, I was lying on my bed with a thick bandage around my stomach and the sight of it seemed to remind my brain that my stomach hurt too... and then my arm. Everything hurt and I willed for the pain to stop, but it was apparently something I did not have any control over.

"So you are finally awake then?" Marcus asked as he noticed my open eyes. He must've been talking to me when I was unconscious and I felt a great amount of gratitude for that fact.

I noticed that the sun was shining outside the window and I realised that I must've been unconscious for the entire night, although I didn't know what part of that was actual sleep, and what was due to my body shutting down from my dire wound.

"Is... Vettius... Dinari...?" I managed to croak out.

"We are fine, Titus," Vettius announced as he entered the room with a wet sponge. As he placed it on my head, Dinari jumped onto the bed and curled up next to me. He had been much more gentle in his act than usual, and I was grateful for it.

"You, however, have a severe fever and I am not skilled enough to know how to cure it. I fear that your very life hangs in the balance... perhaps this is the time to call upon the power of the Gods?" Vettius said quietly.

"No... no Gods..." I moaned and I felt the sweat pooling all around me. "No Gods!" I managed again, though more forcefully.

In my fevered state, I knew what I wanted to say, though those were the only words that I could form. I had made a promise to Mercury that I would never draw a sigil upon myself, else my blood would've been tainted. Walking the tightrope between life and death, the last thing that I wanted to do was to anger the guide of lost souls to the underworld.

"I understand…" Vettius said and moved away from the bed.

"The fuck do you understand! Draw the caduceus on his body and heal him for fuck sake!" Marcus practically shouted at Vettius in confused outrage.

"I will not, if he does not want me to," Vettius said quietly. "Let him rest and fight these demons alone… his life is in the hands of the Gods now."

Over the next indeterminate amount of time my consciousness was scattered and difficult to keep a firm grasp of. When I was partially awake and aware though, I knew that I was burning hot and covered in sweat. I saw things that weren't there with me in the room - my parents, their killer, my attacker, the arena master Galerius, the townspeople of Liternum - they all came and went in my mind, either to see if I was going to cling onto life or simply perish and leave the mortal plane forever.

Eventually, though I did not know if it was through some divine intervention or pure dumb luck, my fever abated and I was able to rest without interruption. After a few days had passed and I was sure that I wouldn't hurt myself by moving around too much, I rolled out of bed and stood up under my own power.

The movement was difficult and my muscles and bones ached from the unwelcome effort and although my stomach ached dully and my arm felt as though it was in a larger man's vice-grip, I knew I had made it through the worst of my predicament.

Dinari was still upon my bed as I stood and I knew that he hadn't left my side for even a moment through all of my pain and suffering. I scratched him behind his ear and noticed that his caduceus sigil was glowing softly beneath his fur. The dog woke up, smiled at me and then realising what was happening, sat up to his full height, expecting more fuss. I dutifully obliged.

"What does a man have to do around here to get a sip of water?" I asked slowly and very, very carefully with a smile as I walked out onto the training sands where my two friends were sparring. Vettius, with his one arm, was having a much harder time defending himself against Marcus now, and the gladiator in training's skill increased with each passing day.

Both Marcus and Vettius immediately dropped their wooden swords and shields and turned to look at me in shocked delight.

"Titus!" Marcus practically cried and Vettius simply smiled and grasped my forearm tightly as we reached each other.

"By the Gods you are alive!, Marcus exclaimed. "When did you rise?"

"Just now…" I said carefully. "I am still not well, but I feel that the worst has passed and I will soon be normal again."

"Well met, Titus," Vettius said levelly. "I knew that the Gods would not let you perish without objection."

"How long has it been?" I managed to ask.

"Since the night of your attack, three weeks have passed and your furry friend here has not once left your side. We have trained and eaten, but we did not think it wise to approach the arena without proper discussion first." Vettius explained.

"That sounds like it was the correct thing to do," I replied, knowing that letting everyone know I was still living and the ludus still standing might have brought its own repercussions.

"There is one more thing that you should know…" Vettius said slowly as he looked behind him and to the cells beside the training sands. "Titus, this is Priscus…"

The boy who emerged to stand before me must have been eighteen at the most, and he looked distinctly nervous to be in my presence.

"G… good day to you, Lanista… of the ludus Brutus," he said without making proper eye contact with me. I could tell immediately from his gait that he had been raised as a slave, and my heart felt for the boy. His heritage was clearly that of Gaul, his skin was slightly lighter than my own, he was taller than I was already, had burning red hair and piercing green eyes. If he was older and not so well washed, I might have thought him to have been a savage beast.

"We found this one skulking around the ludus yesterday; he said that he would only talk to you," Marcus said with a chuckle. "He seemed harmless so we fed him and let him wash in the ludus."

Dinari barked once, then went to sit next to the young Gaul, who petted my friend on top of his head. Dinari closed his eyes and smiled as though it was the best thing in the world.

"So… who are you?" I asked, my voice returning through renewed usage.

"My name is Priscus, and I am a slave. Well… I was a slave. My master brought me and a few of the others here from Neapolis to watch the latest fight in the arena… it is getting kind of popular for the wealthy to travel to smaller towns to watch such events. When I was in the stands, I saw your man Marcus here, and I finally understood what I was supposed to do. I want to be a gladiator of note, and I know that your ludus can help me. I have heard of the feats of gladiators, and the house name of Brutus is not unknown to the people of Neapolis."

That information shocked me somewhat. The people of Neapolis *knew* of my ludus? And after such few fights? Before I could think on it though, I saw that Marcus was practically beaming over the information. This was his doing after all.

Priscus spoke again before I could reply. "I can help you become more noteworthy in time, and in turn repay you the kindness you will show me through training. I do not need you to pay me, I can get my own food and water, all I ask is that in the winter I might be afforded a roof if things get particularly cold…"

That was a very strange statement to make, but the words had mimicked my own in a time long past; I had made this very plea to Ovidius the day that he had allowed me to work with him and live beside the arena. There was no way that this was a coincidence, this was the work of the Gods and I knew that I could not deny them.

"Tell me Priscus, do you think that you have what it takes to become a mighty gladiator? Have you ever fought on the sands, or even held a sword and shield?" I asked.

"Have you ever had to kill a man, to take up a life borne of hard work and training? It could even be a friend, though on the sands you stand as equals," Vettius said, though he smiled at me and winked when the boy wasn't watching.

"I would offer them to the Gods in glorious victory!" Priscus announced forcefully and I could tell that he believed his own words. Though still, he did look slight and certainly not suited for the arena. Well not yet, anyway.

"If you send me away… I fear that I will not find suitable housing in this place…" he added quietly.

"Do not worry, little Priscus, you can stay here in the ludus with us, though I make you no promises on fulfilling your destiny as a gladiator of note, though you will be trained if you so wish…" I announced with a smile.

"One more request," Dominus, Priscus said before I could finish. I nodded for him to speak. "Please may I be allowed to live out here, as a proper gladiator. I do not wish to grow comfortable and forget my purpose."

I agreed to Priscus' request, though when I told him to make one of the three cells his own, I was surprised to see that he had nothing of his own to add to his small room. I didn't know why that was surprising, the ex-slave would have had nothing to his name, but now at least he would have a safe home and no need for forced servitude to simply survive.

I left the three men to their training. Vettius and Marcus returned to striking out at each other with wooden swords and little Priscus was shown how to lift heavy logs and stones so that he could begin to build up his body, ready for the arena sands someday.

As I walked slowly back inside the ludus with Dinari in tow, it struck me that all of this had been extremely convenient for me. I had gained a possible future gladiator, though in the short term, little Priscus could help around the ludus and it would make everything just so much easier – and the best part was that I hadn't had to part with a single coin to bring the boy to service.

I knew that I needed to drink, eat and rest – and that is exactly what I did. I picked up a flask of fresh water, a small half-loaf of bread and took them back to my bed. I would clean my wounds tomorrow when I had a little more energy. For now, I needed sleep, and it looked as though Dinari thought that that was an excellent idea too.

XXII – Acta Deos Numquam Mortalia Fallunt.

"Mortal actions never deceive the Gods."

I had given myself the rest of the day and the following night to rest after standing for the first time in a few days, and by all accounts it made me feel a lot better. The fact that I was able to get some proper rest without the tossing and turning of the fever that I had dealt with did wonders for my fatigue, and I wondered how injured gladiators battled through such injuries (and worse) to return to the arena sands once again.

It made me think of Ovidius, and the way that he always petitioned for a quick death over a prolonged suffering. It was funny too, it made me ponder on the choice that Marcus had made to keep his hand, but lose his freedom, and now he was trained by Vettius, who himself had suffered a similar injury. I wondered if Marcus would have made the same choice if he had been presented with it again.

I had a lot of time to think whilst I was alone. I thought about my past, the people who now relied upon me, the Gods and their powers. But most importantly I thought about the man who had almost killed me in the pursuit of what he thought that the sigils could do for him.

I knew that I was ultimately responsible for the people who called my ludus home, and that led me to the conclusion that if people were out there who would cause me harm for the knowledge that I possessed, they needed to be dealt with as quickly and as quietly as possible. The thought of hurting another human being though… it was daunting. I had never *wanted* to hurt anybody – I was a healer, a helper… but if the dilemma was to hurt one person to save three, who was I to make that call?

I called Vettius, Marcus and Priscus to join me at the dinner table that evening. I needed to know how they felt about the man who had entered my house and see if they had any ideas on how we should proceed. Although Priscus hadn't been there, he too would surely have a voice now. "Not a soul in Liternum knows if you are alive or dead," Vettius announced once I had asked about the almost-killer. "So if the man was working on behalf of another, they will be making assumptions only."

"Do not speak in riddles, Doctore," Marcus said to Vettius, "the man was sent by the arena master, Galerius and we all know that, right?"

I stroked my chin, although I had no beard, before I spoke thoughtfully. "It is likely that you are correct. Galerius does seem to be the most likely suspect, but if we are wrong and we act upon this suspicion it will mean the end of this ludus and your chance of becoming a gladiator of note forever. That goes for you too, little Priscus," I said. "Mercury told me himself that Galerius had sent for your opponent in your last battle, though this seems an extreme step to take."

"Listen, we all *know* it was Galerius who sent the man, right? And this is just further proof – even the God Mercury *himself* told you to mistrust the man..." Marcus said, leaving his sentence open for a response. Vettius nodded slightly and Dinari barked, the dog having snuck up onto a chair to sit at the table as though he was a part of the discussion. Priscus and I said nothing. "Then all we have to do is prove it," he concluded.

"And then what?" I asked. "Who could we tell? And who would believe us? Or care? The man is of high note and we are a small ludus without the might of the citizens behind us."

"Ahh, we can cross that bridge when it arrives," Marcus said dismissively. "First, we need a foolproof way to confirm that Galerius was behind all of this..."

"I think that I may be able to help," Priscus said quietly.

The three of us all turned to him with eyebrows raised and waited for him to continue.

"Well..." Priscus said slowly as though he was forming the plan in his mind. "This arena master does not know who I am, or that I am a member of this ludus... so all that it would really take, is for me to be close by when he hears of, or speaks of the ludus Brutus, and listen to what he says."

"The man would never be so stupid... would he?" I asked the other men.

Vettius looked thoughtful and then he smiled. "Galerius is well known to drink at the games... and you know that drink loosens the lips as they say..."

Marcus pounded his fist on the table and it made me start. "That is it! He will tell little Priscus here what he did, and then we will deal with him once we are sure! The drunken shit will not know what hit him first - my sword or Vettius' sharp wit!"

I looked at Vettius to see if the almost insult had offended him, though it looked as though he didn't care either way.

"Is this OK with you, Priscus?" I asked. "As I have said to any who call this ludus home, I will not order you, nor force you to do anything that you do not wish to."

"No… I shall do it, no problem…" Priscus replied. "I want to help, and this way I think that maybe I can do us all some good."

We spoke about some of the finer details of the plan, and the conversations then moved on to lighter subjects. They were mostly about how Marcus had managed to hit Vettius a number of times during training, or Vettius recounting all of the times that Marcus had been hit by other gladiators. It was light-hearted and I could tell that nobody was offended by anything. On occasion, I even chimed in with gentle insults of my own, though I refrained from laughing too much so that I didn't open my new stomach wound. I noticed too, that little Priscus did not say another word, though he looked determined to prove himself to me. I just hoped that he wouldn't do something stupid that would put his life in danger; if these people were who I thought they were, any repercussions would be both swift and serious.

I had been told by Vettius that the arena games had been scheduled for the next day, so without any delay, Priscus set off and into Liternum to where we knew that the arena master would be. He had set off early so that he could get as close to Galerius' private and covered seating area as possible, armed with a description and instructions on how to get close to the man.

As soon as our latest friend had left though, all three of us remaining at the ludus were clearly anxious, and training was doing nothing to take either Marcus, or Vettius' mind off either the situation or the dire consequences for the boy if his motives were discovered.

I could think of nothing more to do, than to pray to Mercury for Priscus' safety. There was nothing else I could do; if I was seen out by anyone who had thought me dead, it would meant that they would be alerted to my presence, and could possibly have come looking for me again.

The day passed too slowly, much slower than any that I could remember. I took the time to remove my bandages, clean my stomach wound that looked as though it was already beginning to heal nicely, and replace the bandages with new and clean ones. I wondered what shape I would've been in now If I hadn't spent all that time with Ovidius in the healing room and I thanked him as I worked so that if he could have seen me now, he knew that I appreciated everything he had done for me.

There was no sign of Priscus as the sun began to set and it made me worried. I wondered if I should've sent Vettius, as the least recognisable member of the ludus, to Liternum to go in search of the boy, but before I could ask him to do so, Priscus entered the front door and I let out a sigh of relief.

"I come with news!" Priscus announced excitedly as his eyes fell upon me, slowly approaching him. The boy looked as though he was in good spirits, and his robes were still clean, which was a good sign.

"I found Galerius. I brought him flasks of wine over and over – not the kind that had been thinned with water but the strong drink! He just kept drinking it and eventually he was so drunk that he could barely keep his eyes open."

I smiled knowingly and let the boy continue.

"Then I said to him: 'why is Marcus of the ludus Brutus not fighting upon the sands today?' And do you know what he said? In his drunken state he managed to grumble that the ludus Brutus is no more... and that the lanista there had been 'dealt with'!"

I wasn't sure why this information made us both smile, though at least it was confirmation of what we both had thought.

"That is amazing work, Priscus. Have you eaten?" My mind switched from concern for Priscus' safety, to concern for his wellbeing and he nodded happily.

"Then we shall need a plan to 'deal with' Galerius now, will we not?" I said rhetorically. It wasn't something I wanted to think about in a particularly detailed way, though the worst plans were the ones formed in the moment, rather than with the benefit of forethought.

I pondered on the idea of what we needed to do to bring Galerius to justice whilst Priscus and I ate. We had been running low on supplies as we lay low, so porridge and water were all we had, but Priscus seemed grateful and I knew the benefits of eating this simple meal over nothing at all.

I was unsure how Galerius would take to being warned away, or if it would make things a whole lot worse. Inside, I knew that he would probably have never listened to anyone other than himself. He seemed to me like the kind of person that thought he knew best all of the time, and that meant only one thing: he needed to be dealt with permanently. After all, the people who I cared about, and had offered shelter to, were at risk, and that was something that I could simply not abide.

I had decided in my mind what needed to happen, but I needed the others to agree with me. It wasn't because I was unsure of what needed to be done, rather, the plan that eventually Priscus and I had concocted relied on involvement from everybody here.

"So it is agreed then? If we bring Galerius to the ludus, we will take him as captive and discover his motives, and work to dissuade him from further action against us," I said, though I knew that what I truly meant was that we would most likely kill him once he had told us why he had sent a man to kill me.

"It is," Vettius said calmly, "though how will we bring the man to the ludus again without raising suspicions? Surely he will know that some trap has been set, or he will send a proxy in his place?"

"Actually, Priscus has an idea of how to accomplish that feat," I said, nodding to the boy.

"Well… Galerius thinks that his man has killed Titus, so really we would like him to continue to think that, so that he does not simply try again. But if he thinks that there is a chance that it has been discovered that it was his hand behind the deed, then perhaps he will wish to cover up that fact himself, rather than let another individual know his secret – that is how these things work, right? The less people who know, the better?"

"Shit, Little Priscus has a devious mind!" Marcus said through a mouthful of porridge. I couldn't help but agree with him.

"And if the arena master simply goes missing? What happens then?" I asked.

"The people will adjust, and another will take his place," Vettius explained, "though there is one detail that stands to send these well-made plans to ruin: the killer will have told Galerius that we gladiators remain, and bore witness to the attempt on your life. Successful or not, this fact means that the arena master will suspect that a trap is in place."

I scratched my chin slowly. What Vettius had said was indeed correct; there was no way that the arena master would be so stupid and walk willingly to where gladiators lay in wait – or at least one gladiator and his Doctore.

"I can assure him that the gladiators are locked in their cells at night, just like they are in the other ludi," Priscus said confidently. "Do not worry about a thing. I will make Galerius come here and I am sure that he will come alone…"

The more Priscus spoke, the more I liked the boy. He seemed so genuine and so willing to go the extra mile to make sure things always went to plan, and thinking about it, those were some of the qualities that would eventually make a powerful gladiator.

Then I noticed that Dinari, who was sitting at the table as usual, seemed to be far more interested in our conversation, and far quieter than I would've expected from the dog. I could see too, that just beneath the fur on his neck, behind his ear a dull blue sigil was glowing, as though he was channelling the divine power of the Gods.

I stood up, peering at Dinari and the room fell eerily silent at my action. Then I rounded the table slowly and spoke aloud.

"You are not in there, are you my friend?" I asked the dog. He didn't seem to want to reply to me, though I could tell that he had heard me.

"Are you watching us right now, Mercury?" I asked suspiciously.

The sigil on Dinari's neck then shone brightly and the room illuminated with its blinding glow. It became brighter and brighter until I had to cover my eyes and eventually, as I managed to open them again, I was standing in the very apple orchard where I had first met Mercury after learning my very first sigil.

"You have an astute eye," Mercury's voice entered my head before I saw the God appear to my side. "A part of me believed that my deception would remain undiscovered for much longer than it has."

"You see through the eyes of Dinari, do you not?" I asked, though when I looked around to gesture to the dog, I saw that the two of us were alone.

"That is true," Mercury said. "The Gods are limited to the things that we see, though being present in the mortal realm does help that on occasion. Your dog, Dinari, for example has been a very useful vessel to me over the years."

"You have been in there the whole time?" I asked.

"No, not all of the time. I can come and go as I please... though it is apparent that my mark remains with the animal even when I am not present."

"He is a very intelligent dog," I admitted. "And always seems to know when something bad is going to happen, or if someone means harm to my family or friends."

"He is still your dog, and it will always remain so... even without my interference," Mercury assured me and I had no reason to disbelieve him.

I thought for a moment on that. "So you heard about our plan, and the fact that Galerius had tried to kill me?" I asked.

"I was aware that there was an attempt, though the hand behind it had been shielded from my view," Mercury said slowly. "It would appear that my brother has meddled in the affairs of mortals a little more than I had expected, though now with this proof, dealing with this situation may become a little easier."

"And you are OK with the fact that we mortals wish to kill another?" I asked, not really wanting to hear the answer to my question.

"Sometimes these things need to happen, and this is one of those cases where the action is justified. I do not wish for you to put young Priscus in danger though; I have a feeling that in the fullness of time, his life will be valued greatly. In lieu of sending him on this task, I will offer you an alternative solution."

"Thank you," I said genuinely. "It was never my intention to put the boy in danger, but I fear that he has the foolhardiness and arrogance to do whatever it takes to do right upon my family."

Mercury smiled. "Priscus has a good soul, and a fire in his heart that will not easily be extinguished. Nurture the boy and he will show himself to be great."

I nodded silently.

"In place of Priscus, I will ensure that Galerius comes alone to visit your ludus this night. Ensure you are ready, and try to remember that sometimes, removing the head does not mean that the body will fall."

XXIII – Audemus Jura Nostra Defendere.

"We dare to defend our rights."

Mercury had disappeared. As had the apple orchard and all I was left with were his final words: Galerius would be coming to visit us tonight, and alone.

I found it incredibly strange that Mercury would interfere with the dealings of mere mortals on this occasion, where in other times the Gods had seemed so reluctant to do so, but whatever the reason behind wanting to help me was, I wasn't going to argue. I could use all the help that any of the Gods wished to give me.

I was also pretty shocked at the revelation that Dinari had been a kind of spy in our midst, though if I thought upon it, I knew that it would've been borne from a place of care and consideration, rather than anything more nefarious. I'd always thought my best friend had been something a little *more* anyway.

I quickly relayed all of what had just happened to the other three at the table and noted that Dinari had stopped glowing altogether and I assumed that meant that Mercury was no longer with him. As Marcus peered into his eyes as though he would be able to see something, the dog sat there calmly in front of the curious gladiator, then licked his nose, covering him in his wet, doggy saliva. That told me that I was probably correct in thinking that Mercury was there no longer.

"Our preparations then, must begin," Vettius said simply, bringing us all back to our morbid task.

I knew exactly what preparations we needed to make; we would plunge the ludus into darkness and await the arrival of our target in silence as though the house was empty when Galerius arrived. With the four of us – though admittedly I was in no fit state to do anything, and Priscus was yet to be trained or proven in any sort of battle – we should be able to get the best of the man.

Our trap had been set.

When Galerius arrived at the ludus several hours later, I didn't know initially what Mercury had done to ensure that he visited us. When the large man arrived though, I could smell the wine in the air before I could have even seen his figure entering the threshold to the ludus through the open front door. All that Galerius would see though, was a still figure, sitting on a wooden chair in the darkness, facing away from him.

It was almost poetic. I had been sure that this very chair had been set up in the exact spot where my father had been killed so many years ago now. It hadn't been an accident either.

Galerius, being the ever defiant, self assured narcissistic individual that he was, slowly approached the figure in the chair, and making far more noise than he had ever meant to, he unsheathed a long knife. When he was in reach of his target, he unceremoniously slit the man's throat.

~ One Hour Earlier ~

"There is a man approaching in the darkness," Priscus announced as he returned to the dining room where we all sat to concoct our plan. "He is almost invisible in the darkness and he moves erratically. I think that he is coming here - there is nowhere else of interest, is there?"

I nodded. "It sounds as though our divine intervention has paid dividends, Priscus. It seems that our plan is to come into existence and be tested. The will of the Gods be with us."

It was the most difficult thing in the world, to look as though you didn't know something was happening, whilst still attempting to keep your eye on it. The approaching figure needed to think that all of the members of my ludus were unaware and possibly even sleeping, without any sort of alert. Thankfully, we had one thing that I had never thought would be so useful to my family: little Priscus.

Priscus was able to move about in the shadows of the ludus that the few torches and the moonlight cast in order to watch where the man was at almost all times, and when he entered through a window with not so much as a single sound, Priscus knew the importance of his next task.

As a group, we all knew that if the man had come to kill us, he would want to take us out one target at a time. What this meant was that we knew that once inside the ludus, Galerius would first lay in waiting, close enough to wherever we were (or thought we were), but not in clear light so as to telegraph his own position and intent should we come wandering about the house. I proposed that he was going to wait in the shadows behind the doorway that led into the dining room as it was the darkest part of the house and was at an intersection of both floors and most of the rooms. This being the thought process, my gladiators and I sat in the shallow darkness in the dining room.

The time eventually arrived for Vettius to stand up from the table and walk towards the doorway. He did so with a loud yawn as though he had just awoken and stumbled a little so that the noise he was making didn't seem concealed in any way. The problem was though, we had expected an older, possibly drunk and out of shape gentleman that either of the two men could beat easily, so our plans were somewhat loosened since the arrival of Galerius.

We had decided upon Vettius leaving first as I was in no fit state to be putting myself in the way of any harm at all, and with Vettius going alone, it left Marcus free to defend both Vettius and myself should the need to do so present itself. Either way, we all thought that Vettius could take the man alone.

As though it had been designed perfectly, once Vettius reached the doorway and passed through, he arrived a moment later back in the dining room, though now with a blade to his throat and a dark-robed figure behind him. I could see in Vettius' face that he wasn't worried about this new situation and it made me feel much calmer than I would have otherwise.

"I wouldn't do anything stupid else I take this man's head clean off," the voice came back heavily accented and it shocked me for just a moment. Mercury had promised to send Galerius to us alone, but this voice clearly belonged to the assassin that had been sent to end my life previously. A million thoughts ran through my mind at once, though before I could vocalise a single one of them, Priscus silently appeared behind the pair and sank his own blade into the back of our unwanted guest. From where they were standing, the light of the moon outside the house illuminated the pair and I was thankful for the lack of darkness so that we could all see what was happening.

The assassin yelled, but managed to remain present enough to spin on the spot and push Priscus back and away from himself. As he did so, his own dagger bit deeply into Vettius' cheek, though I was glad it hadn't been his throat.

The blade had shocked the assassin, but I could tell that it was doing far less damage than it should have. The assassin then looked about at all of us and I could see his grin through his dark, hooded robe. He rolled up one of his sleeves purposefully and I saw the red glow before I saw the sigil: a bright red shield, the unmistakable Ancile of Mars.

We all saw it, and we knew what it meant: anything we did to try to hurt the man would be far less effective than it should've been if the sigil hadn't been there, though we had all learned the lesson from Marcus' fight – if we used the man's own weapon against him, he could be defeated as though he bore no such mark.

Vettius pulled a short gladius from beneath his robe and the noise of the unsheathing of steel upon leather prompted Marcus to follow suit. Priscus wielded his own weapon behind the man and I simply remained in my chair; if I moved too quickly I knew that I ran the risk of opening my wound and bleeding out. For now, all I could do was watch. I wasn't happy about it, but it was the sensible move.

The assassin lowered his centre of gravity and took a wide stance. He raised his dagger to eye-level and I was sure that I heard him hiss as though he was a snake as he took up the serpentine stance that I'd only seen once before.

Vettius moved in, though with just the one arm and no way to defend himself properly I was worried. Thankfully, Priscus moved at the same time. As Vettius' attack was parried, the assassin's rear leg whipped out and pushed Priscus back before his weapon could make contact with its intended target. Both of my protectors looked worried and very unsure of this man's style of attack and defence.

Marcus then finally joined the fight. His sword shone in the blue moonlight and he moved with the practised ease of a heroic gladiator.

The assassin weaved through the attacks that came in his direction, dodging them with ease whilst all the time peppering back attacks of his own. Small nicks and cuts were showing on the skin and robes of my men, though thankfully nothing looked dire to me. The assassin didn't look like he had yet been touched by steel.

The assassin then kicked out Vettius' leg from beneath him and followed with a strike to Priscus square in the nose with his rear elbow. With the pair out of the way for a short moment, he lunged at Marcus with his entire body weight.

My breath caught.

Marcus, though, *caught* the man in mid air, his strength training having clearly been very effective, then twisted, and slammed him into the hard stone ground. It must've been a crippling blow, though the assassin simply rolled and leapt back to his feet as though nothing had happened.

Marcus, shocked by his opponent's resilience, lunged forth with his gladius and the tip pierced the man's forearm mid-strike. The assassin, did not yelp or cry out this time, he simply smiled and dropped his dagger to the ground with a loud clang.

Marcus pulled his sword back just in time for his opponent to draw a second dagger and swipe it out at the gladiator. It cut deeply into Marcus' torso, though I know that it would've been far worse if my man hadn't have moved.

Marcus dropped to a single knee momentarily, though his intervention had given Vettius time to regroup and my Doctore appeared behind the assassin to plunge his gladius deep between the man's shoulder blades. To both my own and Vettius' horror though, the man's body held onto the blade with a grip afforded by the Gods, and Vettius had no choice but to surrender his gladius to the assassin. The blade remained protruding from the assassin's back.

The assassin then spun on the spot, unaffected by Vettius attack and the sword stuck into his back, then flicked his blade out and it struck Vettius in the side of his throat. My Doctore fell to the ground clutching his neck as blood began to pour onto the ground from the wound. I knew that his fight was over as his red blood coated the plain stone wall behind him and he let out a loud choking sound.

All that was left between me and the assassin was Marcus, and his best efforts had already been thwarted. What I hadn't known though, was that as the assassin had been dealing with Vettius, Marcus had collected his opponent's weapon from the ground and swiftly raked it across the assassin's shins.

The blade cut through bone as though it was butter and the assassin fell to the ground with a scream that made my ears ring. His feet remained in place as the rest of his body parted from them and quickly a pool of red blood began to form at the severed ends of his legs.

Marcus leapt up from the ground and quickly drew his blade along the assassin's throat to end the fight for sure, though he didn't move away from the man in case there were any more divine surprises to be met. Thankfully, there were none.

I slowly brought myself to my feet whilst holding onto the bandage around my stomach. It still hurt a lot, though I knew that if I was careful I'd be OK. I walked over to Vettius who was still on the ground. I pulled him towards me to see how bad his wound was. When I saw his face though, I could see that he was laughing. It was quiet at first, and then he laughed loudly, with Marcus joining in shortly after.

Vettius then shifted his sleeve up and held out his arm to show his three blue sigils shining brightly upon his skin.

"It has been a long while since I have felt the sting of a real blade upon my flesh!" he announced still smiling.

"And you have finally managed to fight alongside a real gladiator again!" Marcus called out with humour in his voice. The scene made me smile, but then it dawned on me; Priscus was still nowhere to be seen.

"Priscus!" I called out. "Are you there?"

No reply came from the hallway beyond the dining room.

"Little Priscus! If I have to come and find you, I will show you what a real strike feels like!" Marcus called jovially. I knew he didn't mean it, though I made a mental note to keep an eye on his light-hearted ribbing.

I walked slowly out of the dining room to where I knew Priscus had fallen, but as I rounded the corner there was no sign of him. I walked along the hallway with Dinari by my side and my two friends behind me all the way to the entrance foyer and at that moment, Priscus ran in through the door.

"He is coming! Galerius approaches on the hill!"

The boy had apparently taken his task very seriously and I honestly couldn't have been more thankful for that fact. After being taken out of the fight he had retaken his watch outside the Ludus and into the darkness in case there were any more surprises this night. He had been correct to do so.

"Quickly now, back to the dining room," I instructed and as one we moved back to where the previous fight had occurred. "How long do we have, Priscus?" I asked as we moved.

"No more than five minutes, I would say," Priscus announced. "Though he does move slowly and he is indeed alone."

"OK, then all three of you need to pick up the assassin and take him into the entrance foyer. We shall sit the man in a chair there to await the arrival of his master.

XXIV – Ad Victorium.

"To victory."

"What is this trickery?" Galerius announced loudly as he discovered that the man whose throat he had just slit was not who he had been expecting. The assassin had already been killed and his throat cut from ear to ear.

Before Galerius could make any more noise though, a sack was placed over his head and drawn tightly so that he couldn't see anything at all. As a group, we then carried the arena master into my dining room and tied him to a chair there. He complained as much as any human that I had ever heard once he was sitting down and I could smell wine on his breath, though the sound stopped once Vettius planted a skilful yet very solid fist into his abdomen.

Once we were sure that Galerius was tightly bound to the chair and would pose none of us any harm, I removed the sack from his head. He spat in my face.

"You are a fool to attempt to move against me," Galerius announced. "You are but a minnow within a sea of sharks and you have no idea of the trouble you stir with your actions."

I had thought that this was the kind of response we were going to receive from the man, though it didn't make me feel any better about his words; I was already worried for the futures of my friends, so the words were not welcome to my ears.

"I think you have this all backwards," Marcus stated with a smile. "It is you who are in trouble, arena master."

Galerius didn't seem to acknowledge the fact that Marcus had spoken and looked directly at me instead.

"I do not converse with gladiators or slaves and if you wish to have a civilised conversation with me, it would do you well to remove this beast from my presence," he said with a sneer.

Marcus, apparently offended by the insult, simply punched the man in the stomach, causing him to cough and splutter in pain. I did not feel bad for the arena master.

"What you have done to me and to my friends," I said, "is nothing short of treachery and a bloody, unprovoked attempt at murder."

"Unprovoked?!" Galerius guffawed. "You think that you are innocent in all of this, do you? You call upon the Gods to sway the fortunes of the fighters in the arena in your favour and you think that you are just? Perhaps it would do you well to think about the friends, the families and the lanistas of the gladiators that your own have cut down in the pursuit of fame and glory!"

I hated to admit it, but Galerius had actually made some sense. I was indeed yet to think about those people, although surely they knew what they were getting themselves into, that there was a good chance that they would die out there upon the sands, didn't they?

"I am the arena master here and I alone prescribe what happens upon my sands, not some upstart lanista who thinks that he is better than the rest of them. To me you are all the same, as pawns to be directed so that the real people may manoeuvre themselves into positions of note and consequence."

"There will be no talking to this man," Vettius said calmly and to me alone. "His mind and will are strong, even if his ideals are weak. We should take his life now and be done with this situation."

"I remember you," Galerius sneered as Vettius spoke. "I remember your treachery upon my sands those years ago and I remember the way in which I ordered the death of your master and the reduction of this very house to ash. That is real power, not a simple one-on-one fight out in the arena where the odds are even."

My breath caught in my chest. I knew that what the man was saying was the truth, though I had never thought that I would hear such an admission from his own tongue.

"You think that you can kill my parents and get away with it!?" I almost shouted. The words hurt as I said them in more ways than one, but I couldn't stop myself. "You think that you can do as you wish and forget any consequence? You old, fat, drunken man who thinks himself better than anyone else?

I felt the rage build up inside me, though something was holding me back from striking the man. I knew that it would've been costly to do so for my own health, but I knew that it would also be so satisfying to have my revenge.

Before I could do anything though, Marcus punched Galerius hard in the face, causing him to fall quickly into unconsciousness.

I looked at Marcus with my mouth slightly open, unable to say a word.

"It is in my experience," he explained, "that doing things you may later regret when in a heightened state of emotion is not always the best way. Take a moment to think things through, and you may see things a little differently."

His statement sounded so alien coming from his mouth that I looked at Vettius who had a single eyebrow raised at Marcus.

"Those are my words you damn fool!" he exclaimed and Marcus laughed. "Apologies, I simply could not help myself!"

Regardless of where the words had come from, they made a lot of sense to me now. I did not need to release any anger or assault the man for he was already as good as dead. What I needed to do, in fact, was keep my wits about me and not let Galerius goad me into doing anything stupid.

"Too... weak to do your own dirty work?" Galerius said as his head lolled around and back to the centre. "You are weak, just like your father was... he could never win without some sort of... trickery."

It was too late to be goaded by words now; whatever the arena master said to me wouldn't have mattered as I had soundly regained my footing in the conversation.

"You will die here tonight," I announced calmly. "You will die for the things that you have done to my family in the past, and you will die for the things that you are capable of doing in the future."

Galerius simply laughed a hoarse, pained laugh.

"Do you think that this will make a difference, boy? It is already too late for you I fear... do you hear the footsteps? They are here and your time is finally up..."

I stopped for a second and indeed I *could* hear footsteps outside the ludus and before I knew it, a line of legionaries spewed into my house and immediately took a hold of Marcus, Priscus, Vettius and myself. I spared a quick look around for Dinari, though he was nowhere to be seen and I was very thankful for that fact.

"Master Galerius," one of the soldiers announced officially. "Are you unharmed?"

Galerius managed to grunt, overacting it marvellously. "Please, good soldier. Release me from this prison, I am but an ageing, simple man and these bindings are far too tight for one of my stature."

"At once, sir," the soldier replied and he abruptly turned his attention to me.

"You are to be placed under arrest until such a time that you are afforded a trial for your crimes, lanista. Do you have anything to say about what you have done here today?" The soldier both looked and sounded stern, but seemed to take his position seriously so I attempted to speak my piece.

"This man ordered the death of my parents and has tried to have my friends and me killed. There is a man in the entrance foyer who had been sent to end my life," I looked downwards to my stomach wound that I could tell was still in danger of reopening as it was burning with pain.

The leading soldier looked to one of the others without saying a word, and the man spoke as though he had been asked a question.

"We saw the man in question, it was a slave of Master Galerius here," he said.

"I came with the slave to discuss the next arena battle, these three men then killed him and placed me in this position when I wouldn't give them preferential placement within the arena… please, release me from this place so that I may now rest…" Galerius practically whined. It made me mad that he thought that he could simply get away with all of this, but I was also worried that his story and the weight of his reputation could make these people believe him.

"Do not listen to that shithead," Marcus sneered. "Everybody knows he has been using the arena for his own perverse delusions of grandeur. He came here to kill us, and that was his assassin out there as Titus has said."

The soldiers all seemed to look at each other, and then the scene before them. I could tell what their conclusion was going to be though; who in their right mind – especially an older gentleman – would attempt to kill a lanista and his gladiators without so much as a small army at hand? Galerius' words, although false, seemed to carry much more believability and weight than my own, and that meant just one thing.

"There must be a trial and your fate will be decided upon by a jurex, not by myself or anyone else present here today. Until such time, however, you are to be confined to your own cells here within your ludus. Guards will be posted to ensure that you have food and water, though your freedom has of this moment been removed from you. Do you understand?"

I thought for a short moment, though nodded. There was nothing else I could have done and at least this way, I got to stay at home until things went in whichever direction that they were going to fall. I hoped that the Gods were watching, and that they had some plan for us in all of this.

Marcus, Vettius, Priscus and I were marched to the three cells by the sands and although tiny and cramped – with just a single bed in each – we shared them, one between two. I shared my cell with Marcus whilst Vettius and Priscus took the other. I wondered again where Dinari had got to, but I knew the dog and Mercury's interest in him, and I somehow just knew that he would be safe.

Marcus paced from side to side in the cell as I sat on the bed. There was no need for the doors to be guarded as they locked securely from the outside and Marcus' pacing was essentially just two steps back and forth. It made me a little dizzy watching him, so I turned my attention to the ground.

I needed more information, and assurances about my friends' safety, though either Mercury had been horribly mistaken when he had said that he would get Galerius to arrive at my ludus alone, or he had been tricked. I didn't really care what the truth was, I just wanted to hear it so that we could make our next moves accordingly.

I painfully pulled my bandage from my stomach and watched as a small amount of blood trickled down onto my waist. I dabbed the end of my finger into the warm liquid and as I had once done before, I began to draw Mercury's caduceus onto the floor. Marcus stopped his pacing to watch me silently as I worked.

The caduceus took its shape and as I completed it, it shone a bright blue as it had always done. I waited for a moment, and when nothing else happened, I sat back onto the bed and closed my eyes with a loud exhale. Of course this would be the day that Mercury would not answer my call.

"No meeting with the Gods today then?" Marcus asked when nothing seemed to happen.

I shook my head.

"They are probably busy, Dominus," he said levelly, "concocting new ways in which to force us to eat shit and smile whilst we do it."

I could tell that Marcus was still angry and that he lacked an outlet for that anger, but I stopped myself before speaking ill of any of the Gods who may or may not have been listening.

I kept my eyes closed for a long while and thought about all of the possibilities and the options that I now had before me. It took a short while, but the only other thing that I could think of was to see if Mars himself could shed any light onto our new incarceration and the events that had led up to it.

I paused for a moment, and then shrugged my shoulders and I drew the sigil for Mars' shield onto the ground. I held my breath as it glowed a bright red. I braced myself for the impact of the roof being ripped from overhead or the door being blown off its hinges by some divine force, but again nothing happened and I exhaled sharply.

Then I felt the rumbling.

"Here we go again!" Marcus called out over the noise that was becoming more and more deafening and for the second time in my life, the very roof from atop my head was removed piece by piece and flowed into a circling mass behind the face of the God of war, Mars.

"Do not think that you are able to summon me as you wish," the God boomed before I could say anything at all.

"I… I tried to call for Mercury…" I said honestly, though I immediately regretted it as I wasn't sure how Mars would've felt about being second in line. "We had a plan... and things do not seem to have gone well…"

Mars then did something that I truly didn't expect: he laughed.

"Mortal being, I do not expect for you to understand the will of the Gods, however I am surprised at your inability to see what is clear before your very eyes. Do you not see the truth?"

I stood silent for a moment and wondered if Marcus had any ideas, though he seemed as stumped as I was.

"Look closer," Mars ordered as his head grew tenfold before us. His single eye that now filled the roof-space above us flickered and turned to a pool of pure glass. Within it, I could see an image of myself.

It was the moment that Mercury had told me that he would ensure Galerius would arrive at my ludus alone, though viewed as though from above. Then, the image switched to Galerius drawing the sigil for Mars on his assassin. I watched as the sigil glowed red and Galerius seemed to be conversing, I assumed with Mars himself, though I could not see the God anywhere – nor did he arrive with such ceremony as he had done to me on two separate occasions.

More images flickered across the God's eye and as I watched, I followed the assassin and then Galerius to my house. I watched as we fought and bested the assassin by the narrowest of margins and then watched as the soldiers arrived to save the bound arena master.

Mars' head shrunk back down to its previous huge size and I could see that he was smiling. I thought for a long moment on what I had just seen.

"You had warned Galerius *after* Mercury had arranged for him to arrive alone?" I asked.

"Congratulations, mortal. You have become a master in the art of the obvious," Mars teased. "But why do you think that I wanted all of this to happen?"

I let my mouth begin to move without thinking this time. "You love war, conflict and bloodshed... so you wanted to watch us fight the assassin or Galerius? To kill them or otherwise be killed so that you are honoured through battle?" I asked.

Marcus placed a hand on my shoulder to stop me in my train of thought.

"It is more than that. He wanted to have us arrested so that we may fight in the arena - all of us. He was not satisfied that you have been able to stand by without raising a sword against your fellow man. He believes that you will be called into the arena and tested as are the rest of us... is this correct?" Marcus asked the God.

"Your gladiator's wit is as sharp as his sword," Mars announced. "Though I come to you now to offer some aid in your battle to come. I will allow the use of my sigils by any of your friends... though I will not permit them to be used by any whose blood has been tainted by the power of my brother..."

"So I can use your sigil... but the only person that can receive your power is Priscus?" I asked slowly.

"Or yourself," Mars answered with a devious grin.

"Titus is not a gladiator," Marcus objected. "And little Priscus is but a boy and you would have them shed blood or have their own spilled just so that you may have a show? What sort of God are you?"

"I am the GOD OF WAR AND I WILL HAVE IT SO!" Mars boomed as his face moved away from the broken roof of our cell. He reached up into the dark clouds above him and retrieved a long spear and very heavy looking round shield and held them to the ready. Then he thrust his spear directly at us and as the steel tip impacted our cell, we immediately returned to the real world around us in complete peace and quiet. Once again the roof was still there above our heads, and nothing else seemed out of place.

"What do you think?" Marcus said quietly after a moment of pondering. "What will you do if you have to fight upon the sands of the arena?"

"I think... I will die," I said calmly though with a smile that I hoped conveyed acceptance over fear. "I have watched gladiators train, live, fight and die for almost my entire life. I was brought up in a ludus and worked within the healing rooms of the arena, though one fact that I have learnt in all of my years, is that gladiators die... and I am a poor facsimile of a gladiator in the kindest of terms."

"You never know, they may let us fight together out there, then I may be able to defend you, Dominus," Marcus said.

"You never know, they may make us fight *against* each other out there," I replied solemnly. Marcus had no reply for that particular statement.

XXV – Alea Iacta Est.

"The die has been thrown."

It was a bizarre scenario for me to be locked up inside the cells of my own ludus. Not simply because it was my own house, rather because I had never expected in my life to have been thrown into prison at all. I had always thought that I'd done right by people wherever I could, walked the line of public decency and so on… and all that it had done was left me with a sense of disappointment. Marcus, though, I could tell he was positively mad.

When the gladiator wasn't walking back and forth in the tiny room, he was muttering under his breath about how the Gods have shafted him once more. He spoke about honouring the Gods on the sands, how he had always fought with honour, created a growing name for himself… and all they had done was shit on him in return. I couldn't say that I blamed him.

"Fucking Mars and that bullshit of wanting to see us fight. And then telling us that we may call upon his power? Who the fuck does he think he is?" Marcus ranted for the fifth time during this particular morning.

"Unfortunately for us," I placated, "Mars is a very real God and I do not think that insulting him continuously will do us much good."

"Ah fuck that, he cannot strike me down in the mortal realm anyway. Besides, where is Mercury in all of this? Right when we need him most he simply fucks off and we are left to deal with the fallout alone! This was his idea after all, was it not?"

I scratched my chin. It was worrying that it seemed as though Mercury had left us to fend for ourselves and I wondered if I had done anything to offend the God, or given him cause to leave us entirely. Whatever the reason, the feeling of being without the God on my side was rather unnerving.

I was also incredibly worried about what had happened to Dinari and the more time passed, the more I worried. I knew that he was intelligent and resourceful and would most likely be OK on his own, but I didn't understand why he had not returned to me. Since the very day that he had arrived in my parents' ludus, I had never been without Dinari by my side; we were best friends, inseparable. Now though … I felt lost and alone without his furry little body by my side, or his smiling face looking up at me.

"Prisoners!" a loud and commanding voice came from outside of our cells and I peered through the cracks in the wooden door to try to see who was addressing us. It was light out and I could see that a Centurion was reading from an unravelled scroll without looking up from it as though this was the most official setting in the world.

"You have been accused of the following crimes: Murder, Attempted Murder, Subterfuge. You have been held here in this ludus for your own safety, and for the safety of others. I am here to collect you to bring you to trial. If you are not willing to respond to this summons, it is within the rights of the Arena Master, Galerius, to seize all of your property or properties as dictated by the governing citizens of Liternum."

I heard no reply and made none myself, but then through the silence I realised that the soldier was awaiting a response.

"We will stand trial," I said clearly. It was the only answer that I could give actually because if I didn't agree to it, it was likely that we were going to be found guilty as it was.

I knew the legal process though. I had taken the time to learn about it in the past and my father had also been sure that I knew about the world that we lived in. There would be a preliminary hearing to appoint a judge, a statement of claims and then the full trial. The trial itself would be undertaken within Liternum and in public so that it would be seen to be fair on all accounts, and there was one thing that I knew would tilt the scales of justice to our favour: the burden of proof was always with the plaintiff.

It appeared that Vettius had been listening too. I heard his voice come in reply from his adjoining cell, and the sound of it, just knowing that he was OK made me smile.

"Can we be assured of a fair trial?" I heard him ask. It was an odd question to ask of an official and it made me think that perhaps I was less informed in the 'ways of the world' than I had previously thought.

The soldier, though, seemed to ignore Vettius' question and through the cracks in the door I could actually see the man smirk. My heart sank.

Once the soldier had finished his statement, he ordered us to move away from the doors and place our hands on the back wall. Dutifully, Marcus and I obliged, and I assumed that both Vettius and Priscus had done so too, as I did not hear any commotion from their adjoining cell. I felt the forceful and rough hands of one of the men behind me as my wrists were bound with rough rope. Then I felt hot breath by my ear as whoever it was that had bound me, whispered at a level inaudible to everyone else present.

"I have a message for you from master Galerius, criminal. He says he cannot wait to see you die before him on his arena sands like the dog that you are."

I closed my eyes. It was all I could do to stop myself from screaming at the man and my thoughts turned to Dinari and his whereabouts again. Thinking about my best friend always calmed me and I imagined his little face as he found a butterfly or a lizard to chase and make best friends with.

As a group, Marcus, Vettius, Priscus and I were then marched from my ludus into Liternum as though we had already been tried and convicted. We walked in silence and as I looked about at my friends, they all looked forlorn to a man and I knew that there was nothing that I could do or say to protect them now… unless… A plan began to form in my mind and as I worked on it, turning the consequences over and over I wondered if it was possible that it could work. With my mind made up, I knew that once the trial began, I needed to take my opportunity to try to help them and I didn't care what happened to me.

We walked thought the streets of Liternum and I couldn't help but remember this very journey all those years ago, my father on one side of me, Vettius on the other and Dinari out ahead, searching for playthings or something to gnaw on. This time though, as we passed the people of the town, they either glared silently, or spewed insults at us. I felt a deep sense of shame, and then I saw Janus.

The labourer approached our line of convicts and walked beside me, matching my pace. The guards didn't seem to care and I wondered if they hoped that the man was there to hit me, or otherwise try to make my day a little worse.

"Titus… What they are saying about you… is it true? Did you kill Galerius' man and make plans to kill the master himself? I know you Titus, what benefit would that bestow upon your house?"

 I turned my head to look the man in his eyes before I spoke. I wanted him to see the honesty there, the lack of malintent and the reasoning that this situation sorely needed.

"Janus, it is true that my house killed this man, though it was in self-defence. The man was sent by Galerius himself, who then came to my ludus to see if the deed had been done. We beat his plan, though the soldiers arrived at the worst of times... It looks bad, though I make you this promise: we have done nothing wrong in this."

Janus simply nodded and took my word as truth. He had always been a simple and straightforward man, and I knew that he knew of my upbringing above most anyone else. Then he filtered away into the slowly amassing crowds on the streets, the people who had come to scorn us for our crimes. I watched him go and wished for him to return. We needed more friends here.

We were taken to the centre of Liternum where a wooden platform had been erected for our trial to be held upon. The four of us were forced to kneel upon the stage and look out upon the people of the town and I couldn't see one smiling face amongst them.

"The people before you today stand trial for crimes against your beloved town," an older gentleman in a white robe spoke clearly to the crowd. "They have killed a man in cold blood, and attempted to kill our own, beloved Arena Master. It was by the luck of the Gods that the soldiers arrived just in time to prevent this heinous act, though I am sorry to say that it was far too late for the first arrival to the Ludus Brutus."

The crowd booed at the mention of the name of my family home and it made my heart hurt.

"These four men alone are to stand to trial to answer for their actions, and we must decide upon their punishment as prescribed by the word of law," the man continued.

"Throw them to the lions!" a woman's voice screeched out with venom in her tone.

"Rip their fucking heads clean off!" a man's voice echoed the sentiment.

Then the crowds descended into overlapping shouts of how we should be dealt with, entwined with more jeering and the odd rotten vegetable thrown in our direction. A few projectiles hit all of us, though they were not enough to cause any real damage.

"Please," the man placated the crowd. "We all desire justice, but this is a trial of law, and it is stated that these men shall be allowed to propose an argument in defence of their actions." The man then turned to face me directly. "Tell me, lanista, did you kill the man who came to your ludus, the man who was once owned by Galerius, our beloved Arena Master?" He did not give me the chance to answer. "And tell me, did you take hostage the Arena Master himself, with the intent to cause fatal harm unto him?"

I opened my mouth to speak when I was sure that the man was finished, though all I could do was tell the truth.

"Yes, but…"

"A clear admission of guilt has been witnessed here today…" the man spoke before I had the chance to finish, though I interrupted him.

"They were trying to kill us… it was self-defence!" I pleaded.

The crowd as one booed again and more projectiles were launched.

"You expect us to believe that an ageing Arena Master and his indentured man thought it wise to approach a lanista and his gladiators with the intent to cause them harm? Do you take us for fools?" the man asked rather sarcastically.

It did make sense. Why would they have done what I proposed? And with nothing else to do, I carried out my one and only remaining plan.

"It was me. I did everything," I said clearly for everyone to hear. "These three men are innocent; they had no hand in any of this. I worked alone."

As I begged for the people to take me in place of my men, I wondered why none of my friends seemed to be pleading, or otherwise agreeing that what was happening was not right. To a man, all three of them were uncharacteristically silent with their heads hanging down and their gaze upon the ground.

"An admission of guilt!" the elderly man announced and it did sound as though he was particularly happy about that. "And as such, I have no choice but to pass judgement now and therefore sentence, upon you and your property," he gestured towards Marcus, Vettius and Priscus as he spoke his last words.

"What? No!" I cried.

"I hereby sentence you to Damnatus ad Arenam. We will let your fate fall into the hands of the Gods."

Then I made a mistake. I attempted to stand up and approach the man and I immediately felt the hard wooden hilt of a soldier's gladius crack the back of my head. The last thing that I would see of the trial, was a sideways glance of a hate-filled crowd throwing rotten vegetables and small stones at me, as the hard wooden floor impacted my cheek.

~

I knew instinctively that I had been carried in the most brutal of ways from the very quick and very unfair trial because my shoulder joints and hip flexors burned with pain as I struggled to regain consciousness. I had been carried face-down by my arms and legs and as I bounced, I tried my best to grit my teeth and endure the pain.

I was about to try to right myself as the pain overwhelmed me, I could feel my stomach was beginning to bleed once more, when we entered into a dark room and I was dropped to the ground with no sense of care whatsoever. I howled with pain, but made no move to try to right myself immediately.

I waited for any further noises that betrayed the actions of the soldiers, but when none came, I gingerly raised myself to my knees and regarded my new surroundings.

Vettius, Marcus, Priscus and I were in the gladiator holding area adjoining the arena. It did not feel like home as it once had, though it put me at ease to be somewhere familiar, somewhere my mind thought of as safe.

My friends still sat with their heads hung in shame, and I could not help but ask why they had not argued for their innocence.

"We have all lived the lives of slaves," Vettius explained solemnly. "We know of the ways of the world and of the shit-headed people within. People like us do not have voices. We are to be toyed with, then discarded. You have unfortunately landed within the same roll of the die as the rest of us. Accept your fate, Titus. It will be easier on you in the long term."

I could tell that Marcus and Priscus agreed with the statement, but I simply couldn't accept that this was reality. The world was *fairer* than that, wasn't it?

"Every man has a voice!" I eventually decided. "Every child and woman; this is the Empire and it is not the way that life works."

"For fuck's sake, Titus, shut up," Marcus announced in a hushed tone. "You are going to get us all lashings if you do not fall in line, OK?"

This was one of the very few times that Marcus had been so blunt with me and I didn't begrudge him that fact. I understood how he was feeling; I was feeling the same way, I was just dealing with it in a very different manner.

I was about to press my point of view, when I heard a loud barking coming from outside of the holding area. My heart leapt as I peered out through the open doorway and past the backs of the two guards that stood there... and sitting before them, barking loudly, was my best friend in the whole world, Dinari.

The sight of him made me smile, though that feeling immediately turned to worry as I realised that he could have been very much in danger right now. I wanted to tell him to run and hide, but at the same time I didn't want these guards to realise that he was here for me either.

Before I could make my mind up on what to do though, the arena doctor appeared from the healing room behind us and walked towards Dinari. I recognised the man as the same arena hand that had been promoted to doctor once I had left, and as he passed by he gave me a fleeting, almost unnoticeable nod.

"Come, Dinari," he said loudly for the guards to hear and the dog dutifully obliged.

The guards didn't even turn to watch, as Dinari scampered in through the doorway and immediately leapt up and onto my lap. The act hurt, but nothing hurt too much when it would mean that I could look into the smiling, happy face of Dinari once more. I was sure, at that very moment, that I knew exactly where home was; it was wherever Dinari was.

Dinari then opened his mouth and dropped a small object into the palm of my hand. I raised it to my eye-line and turned it over and over, searching for an idea of what it was. It was small, comfortably fitting in the palm of my hand and at its centre was a teardrop-shaped glass vessel. On the outside of the glass, encircling the vessel, were two metallic sheaths that turned with the application of a little effort. It was clear from the broken lightning bolt that would be completed when the sheaths were positioned correctly, that this was the intent of the broken symbol.

I moved to turn the container though as soon as I did so, Dinari barked loudly and I stopped what I was doing. When I looked back up and away from the vessel, the world around me had turned to a swirling black mist and standing before me once again was the unmistakable form of Mercury.

I ensured that my expression didn't change from one of defeat as I spoke, knowing that Mercury was the guide of fallen men to the afterworld.

"You can now sense my impending death then, or are you here to take me to the afterlife early to save me from the pain and humiliation?" I asked quietly. I was way past the point of begging for my life or blaming anyone else – I knew that this was the end, and I was going to be damn sure I was as a man in accepting that fact.

Mercury smiled at me. It was a warm and caring smile and it immediately lifted my spirits somewhat. This must've been it – the way in which he collected souls to lead them onto the forevermore. It was actually quite nice, kind of peaceful in a way.

"No Titus, I am not here to take you onward just yet," Mercury said softly.

I decided not to focus on the God's usage of the word 'yet', more importantly I needed to know what he was actually here with me for if it wasn't to guide me on into the afterlife.

"You may have noticed that I have been rather lacking in my presence of late," Mercury said. "I apologise for leaving you the way that I did, but please know that I had reasons to do so."

"You assured me that Galerius would arrive at the ludus alone. You told me that he was behind the attacks on myself and my friends… did you lie to manufacture this situation?" I asked, trying to properly assemble the events of the past few days.

Mercury frowned. I could tell that he was upset at my questions, though I was sure that he could see my reasoning.

"I did not manufacture this situation, and had things remained as they were supposed to be, Titus, our plans would have come to fruition. My brother, however, had decided to take a larger interest in our relationship than I had expected…"

"So Mars did all of this?"

"Mars did *some* of this," Mercury corrected me. "You see, my brother loves war, bloodshed and sacrifice. He is consumed by these things and we gave him an opportunity by concocting a plan so brashly and without subterfuge. My brother knew that if caught, you would likely be placed in the arena, so he warned Galerius to take a man with him, and to alert the guards. He took the opportunity to throw my champions into the arena to see if they could be dealt with through contest and bloodshed…"

"OK… that sounds believable," I admitted, "though where have you been all of this time, and why have you not done anything to help us? We are innocent in all of this and my friends sit there as though they have their tails between their legs."

"Well, there is but one place that I am able to conceal my actions from my brother…" Mercury trailed off and glanced at Dinari who still sat in my lap, looking up at me and panting lovingly.

"In… Dinari?" I asked, catching his meaning.

"Exactly." Mercury replied.

"So what?" I asked.

"So the very object that I sought out over the past few days, the thing that I travelled a great distance to retrieve for you, is my gift to help you. This container is a powerful artefact that you are yet to understand, so please do not assume that I have done nothing to help you."

I could hear the scorn in the God's tone and decided that it was probably best not to press the matter further else I could lose all of his favour entirely.

"I have a few things that I will need to explain to you in order for you to understand the power of this single object, and how it can aid you in the battle to come." Mercury said.

"Please, anything that will help my friends will be greatly appreciated,"

I encouraged, now wondering if there was yet again a glint of hope.

"The vessel that you are currently holding contains the divine power of Jupiter, my father." Mercury said matter of factly. "My father's power has never been offered to a mortal, though within this vessel lies a dormant sliver of his divine will. If a mortal were to call upon his power directly, they would find themselves at the receiving end of his wrath, however this object was created to call upon his power in such a way that no mortal man can be blamed for his summoning. Beware though Titus, I do not know what will happen when this sigil is aligned, all that I know is that the power that will flow into the vessel will be extreme and I do not know what my father will do to those in the vicinity of the power within."

I turned the small container over in my hands looking at it in a new light and wondered just how this tiny object could possibly hold so much power. It did seem a little moot though; if Mercury himself did not know exactly what was going to happen when this sigil was aligned, then what use was it to be for me? What if it just made everything so, so much worse?

"What do you want me to do with it?" I asked the only thing that I could at that very moment. "And if I die, who will care for Dinari?" The dog wagged his entire body at the mention of his name and tried to lurch upwards to lick my face. His breath smelt of fish again and it made me grimace, though it reminded me of just how much I had missed Dinari whilst he had been apart from me.

Mercury smiled early again and stroked Dinari atop his head gently.

"Dinari and I have a bond and I will promise you this: no matter what happens to either of you and when, Dinari will always have a place waiting for him by my side."

Mercury's words made me feel at ease. Of course I would've preferred him to reassure me that this was not going to be the end of my life, but this was second best. It made me feel calm and peaceful to know that Dinari would always be cared for, regardless of whether I was around or not.

"As for what you need to do with the object, I cannot tell you outright. In this form it has been made clear that my actions and plans can be witnessed by others and therefore rendered ineffective. I suspect, however, that you will know what to do with this item once the appropriate time arrives," Mercury said cryptically.

I didn't want to outright ask again for help, and I was grateful for any that I could get. In the end, I knew that I would have to settle for what I had been given, and being given an item from an actual God was probably much more than anyone else could ever hope for.

"I have done one more thing for you Titus," Mercury said as he began to move away and the world started to fade back to reality. "I know that you cannot heal yourself with my caduceus sigil, though I have seen to your wound so that you may fight in this battle with honour."

"Thank you," I managed to reply slowly as I looked down and noticed that my bandages had completely disappeared. "I will do my best."

XXVI – Veni, Vidi Vici.

"I came, I saw, I conquered."

I walked out onto the sands before my friends. I had always felt protective over them, though in this particular instance I also felt responsible for their current situation.

It had come as a surprise to all of us that we would be fighting as a group rather than one on one with another gladiator and I felt as though it was kind of poetic – the captain always went down with his ship. At least my friends would be beside me as we were all taken from this world – all except for Dinari of course, who had remained with the arena doctor in the healing room. I knew that I would be seeing him again soon at least.

We had been given a small amount of additional protection, arms or armour, though I knew that we were surely expected to die this day. As it was, I clutched my spear tightly and gritted my teeth. All that I could do was pray to any of the Gods willing to listen, for myself and for my friends. I had little hope that all of us would escape from this situation unharmed though, let alone alive.

As I came to a halt in the centre of the arena, Marcus and Vettius stopped at either side of me and Marcus placed a single hand on my shoulder, Vettius did not have the free hand to do so. I had never stood on the sands before a crowd in my life and I could see immediately why gladiators were drawn to return after a victorious fight; the spectacle of the crowd all around us and the tornado of roars made my heart skip a beat. Then I realised that most of the crowd were jeering us, and I was brought back to the severity of our situation when a rotting cabbage impacted my chest. The smell was so offensive that it caused me to scrunch my nose and I almost moved a hand to my face though managed to remain stalwart. I didn't need these people to know that they had affected me.

Each of us held a spear in our hands but had been given nothing else to carry. We were condemned men; we were not supposed to be able to survive this. I felt for Priscus, hiding behind our line – this was so alien to him that I could almost feel his fear.

"These men who you see before you," the announcer's voice sounded as though it was being artificially amplified directly into my ears again and I spared another moment for the ingenuity of the designers of such amphitheatres, "stand accused by our very own, respected, beloved arena master, the ever present: Galerius!" The announcer gestured to where Galerius sat, drinking his wine and waving errantly. I had never wanted to punch someone as badly as I did right now.

The crowds erupted into cheers and whoops as though this man was the best thing to have ever happened to them. It made me feel sick to think that these people had been so deceived, though I wasn't sure if they cared or not as they played along with the pantomime of the arena.

When I saw Galerius rise to stand in his private section of the crowds, I noticed that his armed guard had been doubled. It made me smile to think that he was worried to the point of paranoia; at least the man had cause to think upon his own safety, even if there was no chance of any of us reaching him now. He did have a drink in his hand as usual though and I hoped that he would choke on it.

"To bring the accused to trial, a spectacle the likes of which have never been seen before has been arranged by our beloved arena master: a true test that even the Gods themselves could not argue with in all of their divine glory!"

This did not sound as though it was going to end well for me and my friends, but before I had the chance to ponder what was about to happen, the main wooden gates to the arena sands opened, and in trooped two distinct contubernium. The sound of the sixteen pairs of sandals on the ground and the clang of metal against wood as they pounded sword against shield sent a shiver down my spine as they marched in perfect unison. The noise echoed around the arena as they moved. My heart reached out to Priscus but I made no moves to visibly comfort him.

Eventually, the legionaries came to a halt with a loud 'huh' as they stopped and the arena fell silent for a long moment.

Each of the legionaries wore full army attire: a shining silver helmet that hung down on either side to protect their cheeks, overlapping iron stripped plates formed their shoulder and chest protection and at their waists they wore perfect red cloth skirts. We paled in comparison standing across the sands from this perfect company.

Behind the soldiers, once they had stood perfectly still for just a moment, appeared Callistus, the ranks parting to allow him passage.

The man who had once blackmailed me, the man who I'd watched kill one of my parents' murderers out here on these very sands.

Callistus did not wear the same attire as the rest of his soldiers and I regarded him with awe as he came to a halt before his men. He wore a red-plumed helmet, and beneath that across his torso were two simple leather straps crossed in the centre. His body was perfectly sculpted and practically bulging at every single muscle. His eyes though were what haunted me the most; not only were they absent the look of life and compassion, but they also now shone with a piercing green glow.

My blood went cold and my legs began to shake with both fear and anxiety. What was this power that the soldier had been imbued with?

"And sent directly from the arenas of Rome: I present to you for the first time on the sands of Liternum in over a decade, Callistus!" The noise from the crowd was deafening now as they chanted for Callistus. Then the announcer continued and the rabble fell silent once more.

"Callistus has travelled the empire in search of justice. Fighting in arenas across the land against foes who speak of their innocence yet there have been none to find salvation when facing this mighty legionary! I give to you for your excitement and pleasure, the Bringer of Justice!"

This was certainly not good. I had been worried upon seeing the sixteen soldiers before us as it was, my group being ill equipped and at a severe disadvantage against the pair of contubernium, but combined with what I already knew to be imbued with some divine might, our chances of survival had been reduced to none. The arena master had made certain that this was a battle in which we were to be soundly beaten and there was absolutely nothing that I could do about that now.

I wondered exactly how our opponents were going to line up, being so numerous, though I guessed that they were going to act as soldiers would: as a unit without taking any risks. I knew that Callistus had some experience at least in dealing with an almost embarrassing situation and I guessed that it was probably something that he looked to avoid in all of the battles that followed. What happened next though, surprised me.

The soldiers all moved to form a single line around us and held their shields together to form an impenetrable barrier. Thankfully, Vettius was by our side to let us know what to do.

Mercury had told me not to use the object that was imbued with the divine power of Jupiter until I was absolutely sure that it was the right time. If I was honest with myself though, there was no way that I could be sure if this was indeed the right time or not, so I figured that if I was doubting that fact, then it probably wasn't the right time.

"Vettius, Marcus… what do we do here?" I nervously called to my men, though I knew that whatever advice they could give me right now about actually participating in a fight was never going to be enough to outweigh our opponents and their lengthy training.

"We go back to back, all of us," Vettius announced with a confidence that I certainly didn't have. "They have encircled us, and we need to be sure that we are not surprised by attacks from the rear," he explained.

"And if they attack?" I asked rather nervously.

"Then you hit them with the sharp, pointy end of your spear," Marcus interrupted and I could hear the morbid grin in his words. I didn't berate his sarcasm though, I definitely deserved that.

I felt three backs pressed against mine as the four of us formed into a tight square facing outwards. My friends and I would now stand together and die as one, as per the will of the Arena Master Galerius, who I was sure would have been smiling widely at our current positioning. We had nowhere to run, nowhere to hide and I personally had no skills to call upon.

Then Callistus, with his glowing green eyes, leapt high up into the air and landed before us in a whirlwind of motion. In both of his hands he held small hand-axes and they looked both sharp and deadly to my eye.

Vettius was the first to take a step forward and as he did so, Callistus' attention fell squarely upon him.

Callistus immediately threw a single axe at Vettius and it caught my man completely off-guard. A gladiator never threw his weapon at the start of the fight and the move had completely wrong footed the hugely experienced ex-gladiator.

The axe buried itself into Vettius' shoulder and although he howled in pain, I thought that at least it had hit the side of his missing arm, so he had nothing to drop or otherwise be unable to use through injury.

Callistus was behind his thrown weapon in an instant and it meant that the range that Vettius' spear would have afforded him was all but gone.

Vettius brought his weapon up and across his body to prevent the one remaining deadly hand axe from ending his life, though it certainly looked a difficult task.

What I should've been doing though, was paying more attention to my own problems and the soldiers standing before me; one had broken formation and had made a beeline directly for me. I managed to raise my spear just in time to give him cause to step back, though any confidence that I had managed to feign in the effort immediately dissipated and the soldier moved back into range with a smirk.

I heard Vettius yelp from behind me and at the same time felt our formation begin to fail. I knew my friends were there somewhere, but I did not know if they were fighting gallantly, or being systematically removed from the battle.

As the soldiers teased my small party, overhead, dark grey clouds began to roll in and within a moment they had all but blotted out the bright sunlight. They had arrived from seemingly nowhere within the bright skies and something inside me screamed that this was it - now was the time to call upon the might of Jupiter before it was too late. Things were already going from bad to worse.

Lightning crackled in the sky above and the rumble of thunder betrayed the proximity of the storm that had seemingly come from nowhere. Rain began to pour down from the skies in volumes that I had never thought possible. Then I heard the loud clang of metal spear on wooden shield as the world around us flashed again with bright lightning. I could hear people in the crowds scream in terror at the unexpected change in atmosphere.

I felt a tingle throughout my entire body as I listened to the sounds of battle beginning to resume all around me. The soldier who was engaged in my own assault had paused for a single moment to look up at the sky, but had since refocused his attention and I knew that I had but a moment. I pulled the glass vessel from my loincloth and twisted it without delay to reform the sigil of Jupiter that was etched across its surface. It offered no resistance and fell perfectly into place.

I looked up to the sky as the tingling in my body morphed into a searing hot pain and that was when I saw it: A bright white thunderbolt forked down from the clouds, cutting through the rain and then it hit me.

I felt as though my head was going to burst and I raised my hands to my temples to try to will the pain away but the thunderbolt just seemed to cling onto me, boiling the very blood inside my veins. I opened my mouth to scream but no sound would come out, or if it had then I couldn't hear it over the rain and thunder. My entire being was on fire and I begged for an end to arrive, to release me from this torture.

Then I felt a rising deep inside of me. It started in my stomach and as it grew, the pain of the thunderbolt began to wane. I could still feel the power within me, though I felt like it was more tolerable now, more natural.

The feeling grew, and grew until it enveloped my entire being and then with a deliberate shout of defiance, I released everything that I had within me.

The feeling of releasing such power from my body was unlike anything that I had ever experienced before. My arms flew out to my sides and in an arc all around me and in all directions, the lightning strike that had hit me exploded outwards from my fingers, hands, arms, mouth, ears and everywhere that protruded from my body. It was a bright white and I sensed that it was impacting everyone around me without prejudice. I feared for my friends.

I could suddenly sense though through the lightning that the power seemed to be avoiding whatever it had sensed had divine power coursing through it – and I hadn't been stupid in preparing for this battle. Vettius and Marcus had both received all three of Mercury's sigils, having worn them previously and therefore unable to call upon the divine might of Mars – the only other God with a sigil that I knew how to draw. That left Priscus, and the young boy I saw fit to imbue with the power of Mars.

It didn't matter if my friends were imbued with the power of Mercury or Mars though, I could feel that the power that had left my body was indiscriminate in its ability to avoid damage to those with the sigils. The moment that the sound of a hurricane left my ears and the lightning abated, I searched for my friends.

The rain still poured down upon us and my skin was soaked. I could see too that Marcus, Vettius and Priscus were wiping water from their faces and as we looked at each other standing upon the drenched sands, we began to laugh.

The soldiers all around us lay dead on the ground. I knew that their bodies lay on the ground hot from the divine might of Jupiter as steam rose from their still forms. I felt bad for them – they hadn't asked for any of this, they had just been doing their jobs. Deep down though, I was much happier that my friends and I remained standing upon the arena sands.

The crowd was silent.

XXVII – Et Tu, Brutus?

"And you, Brutus?"

As my friends and I laughed heartily though, I could see that both Marcus and Vettius' eyes were glowing bright blue, and when I looked at Priscus, his were a deep, blood red. The rain was also causing steam to flow from them as they glowed and all of them looked as though they had been possessed by the Gods.

It was this sight though, that telegraphed to me the fact that Callistus had not departed the sands; he rose to his full height, having leapt out of the way of the divine power not knowing what it was, and raised his single hand axe toward me threateningly.

"You will not stand in the way of the will of the Gods!" he shouted for us all to hear.

"Do you not see what has happened here today, Callistus?" I called back to the soldier. "Can you not understand that it is obvious to everyone that our deaths are not the will of the Gods?"

"What do you know of the will of the Gods, murderer? I have been sent by divine will to enact the wrath of justice onto those deserving of Diana's swift and powerful might! I still stand now because of the will of the Gods and you will fall because of that same will. You have been tried, and you will be tested!"

I could see that madness had enveloped Callistus over the past years as he had been carrying out this purge of his, though I couldn't tell whether this was some personal vendetta, or whether the power of apparently Diana had corrupted him in some way. It didn't matter, though he had clearly been training over these years. There were four of us though. Granted we weren't well equipped, Priscus and I were untrained and Vettius had just one arm, but that still afforded us the advantage of numbers.

Callistus leapt at me with a shout and as his axe cut the rain in front of me in half, two spears crossed before my eyes to nullify the blow. To my left and right, Vettius and Marcus had defended me perfectly.

There was a moment then where nothing happened and I wondered if they were waiting for me to attack, or kick Callistus back, though before I could make up my mind to do so, Priscus took a hold of Callistus from behind, his arms snaking around his neck.

Priscus' eyes burned with the deep red anger of Mars and I was shocked that his arms had become noticeably more muscular, and when Callistus attempted to free himself, he was unable to do so.

Marcus and Vettius both knew not to allow such an opening to pass them by and they both stepped back to afford them the space to wield their spears properly. I held my breath and as one, both spear tips penetrated Callistus' torso, who howled in pain. I half expected a loud cheer to come from the crowds or at least a gasp, though over the sound of the unrelenting rain I could hear nothing past our insulated little contest.

Callistus' blood burst from his body as the spears tore into his skin, though somehow he had dropped his own weapon and had taken a hold of Vettius' spear in both his hands. It was to be a contest of might between the two men, though Vettius thought better of it and simply let go of his weapon; after all, Marcus still had a hold of his own spear and Vettius' weapon still protruded from Callistus' body. Priscus still held on tight to the man's neck.

Callistus stepped back and pulled the spear from his body. As he moved, Marcus also pulled his own spear free and blood flowed free from the open wound. Priscus still managed to cling onto his enemy, but could do nothing to stop the muscular, larger man from moving around the arena sands.

Strangely, I felt bad for Callistus. He had come here with a job to do and now he had been left to face us alone. On the other hand though, he did seem hell-bent on killing me and my friends – and had some kind of divine power within him to aid in that endeavour.

Marcus then swiped with his spear at Callistus and a plume of blood streaked from his large chest as the steel bit into flesh. Priscus still held on with all his might, though he seemed unable to choke the large man effectively and simply seemed to be more of an annoyance than anything else.

Priscus then decided that enough was enough and released his opponent, kicking him in the back towards Marcus and Vettius. My two well-trained men then sprang into immediate action. I didn't know if it was the additional perception that was afforded them by Mercury's sigils or not, though I certainly wouldn't have had the ability to swiftly drop my spear in time to catch the man, let alone what Vettius and Marcus did.

Vettius managed to punch Callistus in the jaw with a loud, ear-splitting crunch and as he fell to the side, Marcus spun on the spot and drove his heel into his opponent's face. Somehow – and again, I was not sure how this had happened – Marcus had reclaimed his spear from the ground during the movement and he followed his devastating spinning kick with a thrust of his spear, penetrating Callistus in the centre of his stomach.

My own stomach stung as though it was reminding me of the pain of such an injury, but I could do nothing but simply watch as Callistus fell to his knees.

Priscus then kicked the man in the back again and he fell to the ground in a cloud of agitated sand.

Marcus raised his arms through the rain and slowly rotated to the crowd around us. He roared loudly and the spectators called with whistles and hoots in return, apparently pleased with our victory. I laughed and saw that Vettius and Priscus had joined me. We stood together on the sands in victory, and the feeling was unlike anything that I had ever experienced before.

Then suddenly the cheering crowds went eerily silent once more.

"You do not think that the divine power of Diana, the Goddess of the hunt would be so easy to silence did you?" Callistus frowned from behind us and when I turned to look at the man, he was back on his feet and green light was cascading from each of his bloody wounds.

Within a second, the light had faded and the wounds closed as though they were being *sucked in* by the green power. I looked to my friends and the fact that their own eyes had stopped glowing seemed like a bad sign to me. Also it had stopped raining and the storm had all but dissipated, letting the sun shine brightly in the sky once more.

"You could not possibly understand the power that you see before you; each time this vessel has been injured, it has just been another counter to be placed upon your heads," Callistus said.

"I do not like this," Vettius said with a slight twinge of worry in his voice.

"We took this jester down once already, doing it for a second time should not be any different," Marcus announced as he stepped forward.

"Be careful, Marcus," Vettius warned in a low tone, "I believe from what he is saying that all of the damage that has been caused in this fight may return to aid him… tread carefully as you approach."

Marcus looked back and smiled at us. "I do not need to be careful when I have the power of Mercury on my side, right?"

Then Marcus lurched forward. He moved far quicker than anything I had ever seen before and straight towards Callistus, who simply stood in waiting.

Marcus reached his opponent in but a second with his spear before him as though he was participating in some mountless joust, though when he arrived within range, Callistus simply bore his axe down upon the weapon and *snapped* it clean in half.

Marcus did not stop though; he brought both ends of the spear down against Callistus over and over though the muscular soldier simply blocked each strike as though they hadn't been imbued with divine speed at all. Then the soldier blocked a strike from Marcus with his hand axe and punched him so hard that I *heard* my gladiator's jaw break and he fell to the ground in an unmoving heap.

"Marcus!" I yelled and made to move towards him, though Vettius held me back.

Vettius stepped in front of me just a second before Callistus began to run directly at us.

"Brace yourself," Vettius ordered – though I was not entirely sure what I was meant to do with that instruction.

It didn't matter; Callistus was upon us in a heartbeat and when he was within range of Vettius, it all happened so quickly. A single strike from his hand axe cut deeply into Vettius' neck before he could even make a move and my man fell to the ground as Marcus had, though this time I was sure that Vettius' life had come to an end. I saw that the life in his open, surprised eyes had all but disappeared.

Once again though, before Callistus could end my life, as I was sure that he would have been able to do with ease, Priscus leapt to my rescue. The young addition to my house had managed to collect one of Callistus' hand axes and held it in one hand and his spear in the other. It looked awkward to me; I thought that it would be difficult to wield either effectively whilst holding both.

I could see that Callistus thought the same thing as he bore down on my man menacingly, though Priscus did look very assured of himself as he stood his ground.

The soldier smiled as he regarded the young man and I could tell that he had no issues with ending such a short life. As if to confirm my suspicions,

Callistus spoke calmly to Priscus.

"Your life has been short, though you have managed to associate yourself with a murderer and a liar. It is the will of the Gods that I end your life now, though I promise to make it swift for you."

Priscus, to his credit, did not respond though I was sure that his knuckles had turned a little whiter than before and his eyes which had returned to their normal green had flashed red at his opponent's goading.

Priscus then shot forward before Callistus could make the first move and swung his spear menacingly at the soldier. Callistus, to his credit, managed to block the attack though it had left him off-balance and Priscus moved in with his hand axe. The sharpened end of the weapon bit into the soldier as he half-dodged the attack and I could see that a wound had opened at the top of his thigh.

Priscus swung the spear about again, making Callistus stumble backwards and as he fell, the last expressions that I would ever see on his face, were surprise and fear.

The soldier fell backwards and hit the ground though before he could even attempt to right himself, Priscus had buried Callistus' own hand axe into his chest. The weapon had been thrown with such force, that the man had been killed immediately and when Priscus stood back up to leave the axe buried in his opponent, I could see just how deeply the strike had landed.

The crowd once again fell silent, though this time it was for a combination of our victory, and the shock of the brutal attack that Priscus had managed to deliver.

Then, cutting through the silence as though it was the loudest sound in the world, I heard a man coughing. Then I realised, he wasn't coughing, he was choking.

I looked up into the stands and saw immediately that the man who was choking was Galerius. His hands were at his throat and his face had turned a deep shade of purple.

Galerius' guards looked as though they were unsure of what to do and one of them began hitting the Arena Master on his back as though he had some food stuck in his throat and he looked to dislodge it, though it did not seem to be working. Galerius turned deeper and deeper purple until he eventually slumped forward and unceremoniously died where he sat.

The man's death had been bittersweet. The revenge of my friends had been stolen from us by what seemed like some freak accident, but I knew that this was the best way – there was no way that we could have been blamed for this occurrence now.

"The Gods strike down the enemies of the house of Brutus!" a shout eventually came from the otherwise silent crowd.

Some murmurs of agreement came from all around us and I wondered how this was now going to play out.

"They are clearly innocent! They fought and survived by the will of the Gods, and their accuser has been struck down!"

That made sense. I didn't believe it of course, but it made sense.

The arena announcer then gingerly entered the sands and walked to the centre, not too far from where Priscus and I stood. Marcus had also returned to his feet and was looking decidedly sheepish.

"It would seem that the Gods have... uh... made their opinions of these individuals clear," the man said, though his words were absent conviction. "I therefore have no choice, other than to declare these three men victorious in their plea for innocence and freedom!" He looked about as though waiting for someone to give him the nod, though with Galerius falling so quickly, it seemed that there was nobody left to call the shots. Presumably another would take Galerius' place soon, though I was unfamiliar with that particular process, having lived through the reign of a single arena master only.

Epilogue – Mors Vincit Omnia.

"Death always wins."

Marcus, Priscus and I sat in the dining room of my ludus in silence as we spared a moment to pay our respects to Vettius, who had never risen from the place where he had fallen on the sands this very day. We drank a little wine and had said few words since we had returned home and all of us were torn between the feeling of sadness for Vettius's passing, and the happiness we had for winning our freedom.

Dinari sat in his chair at the table and looked very much as though he was unsure why we seemed so morose. He looked as though he was smiling widely as he panted and looked back and forth across the table at each of us in turn.

"… It is how he would have liked to have gone to the afterward…" Marcus said eventually as he could bare the silence no longer. "Falling gallantly in battle, in glory on the arena sands? I could think of no better way to die."

"How about not dying at all?" I queried sarcastically.

Priscus then chimed in, "such is the life and death of the gladiator. We all wish to live until there is no more glory, and then die whilst we are loved…"

It was a strange statement for the youngster to make, it was as though he was calling himself a gladiator – though technically he had killed another gladiator on the arena sands in front of a crowd, so who was I to judge? I'd never even drawn blood myself so I certainly didn't suit the title.

"Everybody dies," Marcus said almost nonchalantly. "It is how we die that makes the difference."

Dinari barked and I couldn't tell if he was agreeing with the gladiator or not. Either way the dog had said his piece and it made me laugh. It was the first time that I had truly smiled in a while and still a part of me felt guilty for it. The ludus just didn't feel the same without Vettius.

There was a loud knock at the front door that interrupted my overanalysing of our situation and it made Dinari bark again. He didn't make any movements to go towards the door; he just liked to let us all know that he *knew* that someone was there.

"Alright, Dinari," I said as I got up from my seat and walked to the front door. Dinari followed me with his tail wagging so hard that his entire body wriggled as it always did. He made a few gruff barks as we walked under his breath and I smirked at the familiar noise.

When I opened the door, behind it stood a young, darker-skinned girl that could not have been any older than eighteen. She had jet black hair tied atop her head and wore the peach robes that many of the servants around Liternum had to wear to show their position.

"Can I help you?" I asked. Ever since my friends and I had been taken to prison and forced to fight for our lives, I knew that I had to be careful of the intentions of others. It was an appropriate response though, I felt, to be a little mistrusting of those around me and to be a little more protective over what we had, not least of all our freedom.

"I… I have come to beg of you… if you will listen to what I have to say… please… that is to say that…" the girl said, looking very anxious and unsure of the situation herself.

"It is OK, you can speak freely here," I said softly. "Why not start from the beginning again?"

The girl took in a deep breath before she spoke again. "My name is Tullia, and I am a former hand of the house owned by Galerius, the former Arena Master. I have come to ask if you would be willing to give me shelter, and perhaps take me as a hand in your ludus?"

I was very taken aback by the question. I had not expected someone to come to my house to ask for shelter, and say that they wished to work for me – and I had thought even less that it would have been a member of Galerius' own staff.

Tullia spoke again quickly before I managed to cough out a response. "Janus told me to come in search of you, that you would be understanding and sympathetic of my situation. I do not ask for free lodgings or meals, I will work as whatever you require in your ludus; I am multi-skilled and have been raised as a servant in a house of high repute…"

I held up a single hand to stop her talking. If Janus had sent her, then that was all the convincing that I needed.

"Come in and out of the darkness," I commanded. Tullia looked a little nervous but did as she was told. I gestured for her to follow me into the dining room where Marcus and Priscus still waited, and I was very happy to note that as we walked, Dinari jumped into Tullia's arms so that she had to carry him. He licked her face and to me that was an endorsement of a quality character.

"Marcus, Priscus, this is Tullia, formerly a servant of our friend Galerius," I introduced them all to each other. I noticed that Marcus' expression turned to that of a scowl and I spoke again before he could say a single word.

"Tullia has come here to seek shelter, and to work within the ludus after Galerius' death. She says that she is multi-skilled and would be a fine addition to our household. Plus, Dinari seems to like her," I added as an afterthought, "which is always a good sign."

"Is this another trick?" Marcus asked. "A spy sent into our household, or another assassin?"

"I think we should let her tell us her own story," Priscus said slowly. It was strange that the boy had spoken up in defence of the girl, though deep down I knew what the most likely reason was: he was a boy, she was a girl, they were around the same age…

Tullia apparently didn't need to be asked twice.

"My mother… my mother was a servant in the house that I was born into. She was not treated well by Galerius and she had kept it a secret from me for a very long time… but Galerius… he was my father."

Marcus stood up abruptly, ready to fight. He had moved so quickly that his wooden chair had made a loud screeching noise against the stone floor.

"WHAT THE FU…" Marcus started.

"I hated him," Tullia said quickly, cutting Marcus off. "He attacked my mother and that is where I came from… my mother died a few years ago but not before she told me that I needed to do whatever I could to get out of there… I never had the opportunity until your battle in the arena."

"What do you mean by opportunity?" Priscus asked in a very soft tone and my eyebrows raised just a little.

"My mother taught me how to make a poison that could be inserted into wine, that would cause no change in smell nor taste – not that that fat oaf would have noticed the difference anyway – and I had planned to use it to kill Galerius for the things that he had done to my mother, and had planned for me too… but it would always have been so obvious, and I could not risk the lives of everyone in the household for the simple act of revenge. When I heard that Galerius had called for a trial by arena battle, I knew that if he was to die, then people would call it retribution of the Gods, and the household would have been spared."

"But how did you know that we would win our freedom?" I asked, turning the girl's words over and over in my head.

"I did not," she admitted. "I thought that you would die as most did, but it did not matter. If you had died, and Galerius' death had followed shortly afterward, the people would argue that fault lay on both sides and that the Gods had seen fit to end the lives of all involved. The fact that you earned your freedom made everything seem so much more believable… not to mention the thunder and lightning thing… I do not know what you did or how you did it, but the favour of the Gods clearly shines upon your family and your ludus."

I nodded slowly as Tullia spoke. I could not believe that this young girl had managed to do what four men - two of which were trained gladiators - had failed to do.

"I am sorry for what you have had to live through, Tullia," I said softly. I will welcome you into our household with open arms. But tell me, what did Janus have to do with all of this?"

Tullia smiled back at me having received the response that she had clearly come for.

"I knew Janus from the times when he had carried out work in the household, and had seen him in the town on a few occasions. He is a good man and I trust his judgement. He had told me of your household and your need for staff previously and it was always my intention to beg of you to afford me shelter in return for work. Janus told me to come to you if I ever found myself in need of a safe and welcoming place. It must have been the fate of the Gods that forced our paths to intertwine as they have done on this day."

Dinari barked loudly at the mention of the Gods and I realised that Tullia was yet to put him back down on the ground.

"I guess that Dinari has the final word in this situation," I said with a chuckle. "Welcome to the Ludus Brutus."

~ Six months later ~

I watched as Priscus attacked Marcus with terrible form out on the training sands. His feet were barely moving, being dragged along the floor as though forced to do so against their will, and the boy's movements seemed so clunky, slow and predictable.

"Come now little Priscus, have you learnt nothing over the past weeks and months?" Marcus goaded as he easily slipped past a slow attack from the boy.

Priscus, though, was now anything but little. He had grown taller and wider and his muscles had begun to form to an almost bulging degree. From what I could put together, I could tell that it had something to do with the power that Mars had afforded him when he was out on the battlefield.

He was yet to fight in the arena since our trial though. I was cautious that he didn't enter the sands too soon, though in the past six months, Marcus had fought and won six battles. He had been fighting as a Retiarius, where Priscus had been training to take up the mantle of a Dimachaeri and I knew that he was going to be a deadly opponent for anyone who stood against him… eventually

"I would fight properly if you had not tricked me into drinking my own body weight in wine last night…" Priscus panted back at Marcus.

Marcus tripped Priscus, who fell flat on his face and I winced slightly.

"Little Priscus, if you fought in one hundred arena battles in your lifetime, do you think that you will be in perfect condition in each and every one of them? It is the gladiator who wins on his worst day who shall become glorious on the arena sands."

I smiled at Marcus' recitation of Vettius' lesson. Marcus was quickly becoming as useful as a trainer as he was a gladiator, and there was nothing I wanted more than for the gladiators of my house to be well trained and thoughtful. After all, battles in the arena were half of the body and half of the mind.

"I have brought you all some water," Tullia announced as she arrived at my side. She had appeared along with Dinari who had taken to spending his entire day following the young woman about as though she was giving him secret food – she probably was, but I didn't mind. If Dinari was happy, then I was happy.

It was very nice to have some real help around the ludus. Tullia had been raised in a large household and had learnt the instincts of a housekeeper. She knew when things needed to be done and simply did them, and when we were thirsty or hungry she always just seemed to appear with food or water right at the opportune moment. She had become close to Priscus too and by all accounts my ludus was much more of a family than the gladiator training school that the people of Liternum had grown to respect as a place of quality, with gladiators who were both caring citizens of the town but would also put on a show worth taking the time to watch.

Marcus took a large swig of his water from the cup, though he held onto Priscus' cup as he did so. I could see Priscus wishing that he could take the cup for a drink to wet his obviously dry throat, but he respected Marcus and would never question his training regimen.

Then Marcus smiled and handed Priscus his cup.

"Drink, little Priscus. Wet your tongue and recover. Our ever illustrious lanista told me this very morning that your first real arena fight approaches. You will need all of the strength you can muster."

Priscus turned to look at me as he drank with a questioning expression upon his face.

I nodded. "In a week's time, Master Augustus has said that the people of Liternum are looking forward to watching another gladiator from the house of Brutus grace their sands."

The End

~

Poem of Priscus:

Martial, liber de spectaculis 29:

"As Priscus and Verus each drew out the contest and the struggle between the pair long stood equal, shouts loud and often sought discharge for the combatants.
But Titus obeyed his own law
(the law was that the bout go on without shield until a finger be raised).
What he could do, he did, often giving dishes and presents.
But an end to the even strife was found:
equal they fought, equal they yielded.
To both, Titus sent wooden swords and to both palms.
Thus valour and skill had their reward.
This has happened under no prince but you, Titus:
two fought and both won.

A Thankyou

Again, your investment of your own time and money is always well appreciated and again, I ask that you **rate** and **review** everything that you read – and not just this book, so that lesser-known authors can grow their audience and gain the credibility that they deserve for their hard work.

Also, check out my website, it's usually kept up to date with current works, reviews and a few extra little bits. You'll find it at:

www.davidlingard.com

Thank you

www.ingramcontent.com/pod-product-compliance
Lightning Source LLC
Chambersburg PA
CBHW071435080526
44587CB00014B/1863